THE THEORY AND PRACTICE OF
METALWORK

Third Edition

GEORGE LOVE

Formerly head of the Crafts and Technology Department
Purley High School for Boys

Longman

LONGMAN GROUP LIMITED
*Longman House, Burnt Mill, Harlow, Essex CM20 2JE, England
and Associated Companies throughout the World.*

First published 1967
Second edition published 1974
Third edition published 1983
ISBN 0 582 33137 4

*Printed and bound in Great Britain
by Collins, Glasgow*

By the same author
The Theory and Practice of Woodwork

Contents

Acknowledgements

My sincere thanks to the firms and organisations listed below, both for their courteous treatment and for their help, always readily forthcoming, in the form of information and illustrations. Without such active cooperation, a production on the lines of this book would have been an overwhelming task and I am most grateful for the help received. It is to their credit that I found many firms willing to produce new photographs and drawings specially to suit the needs of a textbook rather than a toolmaker's catalogue. For these things I am greatly obliged.

To the Colchester Lathe Company, my thanks for the almost complete illustrations in the chapters on *The lathe* and *Lathework*, recently updated. This was a very considerable task which is much appreciated.

To my one-time colleagues, P. A. Bosanquet, M.B.E., B.Sc., and A. Buckley, A.M.I.Prod.E., my thanks for the unenviable task of manuscript reading. To M. A. Johns, C.Eng., M.I.Mech.E., my thanks for the illustration, Figure 11 in Chapter 1.

Acknowledgements are made to the following companies and organisations:

Abrasive Tools Ltd., William Allday and Co. Ltd., Aluminium Federation, Aurora P.L.C., Benson Verniers Ltd., British Steel Corporation, W. Canning and Co. Ltd., Clarkson International Tools Ltd., The Colchester Lathe Co. Ltd., Copper Development Association, Easterbrook Allcard and Co. Ltd., Thomas Ellin (Footprint) Ltd., Firth Brown Tools Ltd., Gate Machinery Co. Ltd., C. and J. Hampton Ltd., Hydro Machine Tools Ltd., Jones and Shipman P.L.C., Johnson Matthey Metals Ltd., Kerry's (Great Britain) Ltd., Thomas Mercer Ltd., Miracle Mills Ltd., Moore and Wright (Sheffield) Ltd., H. D. Murray Ltd., Neill Tools Ltd., F. Pratt Engineering Corporation P.L.C., Rabone Chesterman Ltd., Stanley Tools, Peter Stubs Ltd., Charles Taylor (Birmingham) Ltd., Tucker Fasteners Ltd., William Whitehouse and Co. (Atlas Forge) Ltd., Zinc Development Association.

Extracts from British Standards are reproduced by permission of the British Standards Institution, 2 Park Street, London W1A 2BS, from whom complete copies can be obtained.

Introduction

The three slim books making up the original production of this work were metricated and merged into one volume in 1973, since when minor changes have been made at reprints.

In addition to a few amendments and some updating of illustrations in this new edition, two important changes will be found.

The first of these is in Chapter 1, *The manufacture of iron and steel*, which has been completely rewritten in line with modern practice in the use of basic oxygen converters in steel making and methods of continuous casting of steel. Several new illustrations are included, one of them being a large flow diagram of the industry which it is felt will be of more interest than the original 'family tree' diagram. The Bessemer converter and the open hearth furnace are mentioned briefly.

The second change is in Chapter 8 where tables and references to the silver brazing alloys have been amended to conform with data and nomenclature found in the current publications of Johnson Matthey Metals Ltd.

Some consideration was given to the deletion of Tables 7 and 12 (pp. 100 and 152), there being many excellent proprietary brands of cutting fluids now available. These tables have been retained however, as it is felt they may still be of some use. Cutting fluids are dealt with more fully on pp. 151–2.

A few isolated references to Imperial measure will be found, and Chapter 16, *Standard tables and other data*, is retained almost in its entirety since conversion tables and such like may be of occasional use in the UK, and will almost certainly be needed by readers overseas.

G.H.L. 1982

1

The manufacture of iron and steel

The iron and steel industry is today so vast and complex that it would be impossible to give more than an outline description here and, indeed, this is all that is needed for our purposes.

Something of the order of the processes in turning iron ore into finished iron and steel products is illustrated in Fig. 1 and this flow diagram can be used for reference as the various processes are discussed.

Iron making – raw materials

Iron ore

Iron ore could be described as any mineral substance which contains enough iron to make its smelting a viable proposition, i.e. with an iron content of not less than about 20 per cent. Ores vary considerably in form and composition from one source to another, some being found as very hard rock, some as granular masses and some as loose earthy materials and with colour variations from black to brick red.

Iron is found as a chemical compound (usually an oxide) within the ore and those ores most generally smelted contain the iron oxide materials *magnetite*, *hematite* and *limonite*. Magnetite ores are the richest known, with around 65 per cent of iron. Magnetite is ferrosoferric oxide (Fe_3O_4); it is black, dense and strongly magnetic and is found in Sweden, the USSR, the USA and Canada. Hematite is ferric oxide (Fe_2O_3) and these ores contain around 60 to 63 per cent of iron, are red–brown in colour and give iron that is low in sulphur and phosphorus. Hematite is found in many parts of the world, with large deposits in Australia, India and Brazil. Small deposits in the UK are now almost exhausted. Limonite is a 'lean' (low yield) ore giving only around 20 per cent of iron. It is a hydrated iron oxide and is found in Europe and the UK.

Coke

Coke plays a triple role in the blast furnace: (1) as a fuel to provide the heat for smelting, (2) as a rich source of carbon monoxide gas (CO), which is the main reducing agent in converting iron oxides into iron, and (3) as a non-clogging support for the burden (the charge) in the blast furnace, its porosity aiding the free passage of gases through the furnace. It is made by the roasting of specially selected coking coal in large sealed ovens. Volatile substances released from the coal provide a number of valuable chemical by-products whilst the gases released are cleaned and used as fuel in other parts of the plant.

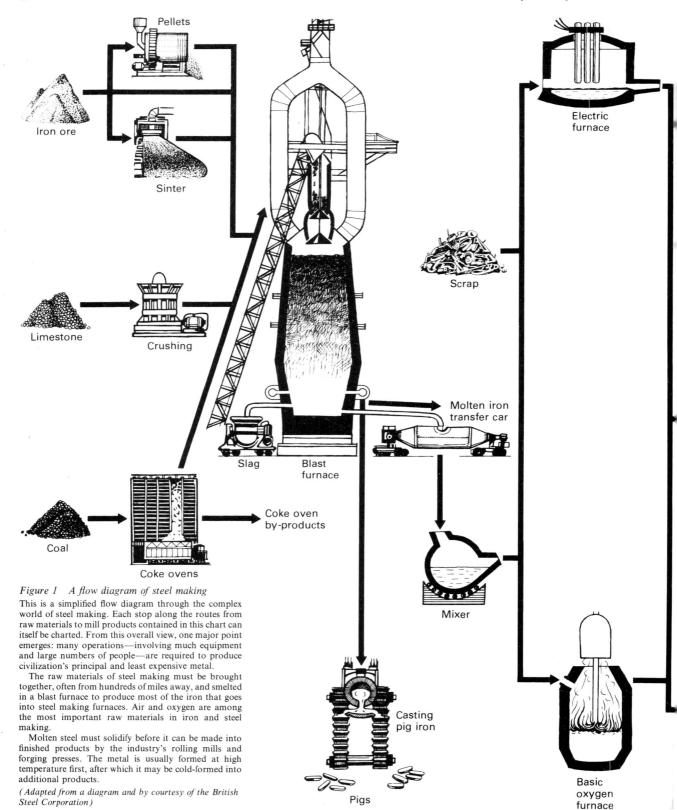

Figure 1   A flow diagram of steel making

This is a simplified flow diagram through the complex world of steel making. Each stop along the routes from raw materials to mill products contained in this chart can itself be charted. From this overall view, one major point emerges: many operations—involving much equipment and large numbers of people—are required to produce civilization's principal and least expensive metal.

The raw materials of steel making must be brought together, often from hundreds of miles away, and smelted in a blast furnace to produce most of the iron that goes into steel making furnaces. Air and oxygen are among the most important raw materials in iron and steel making.

Molten steel must solidify before it can be made into finished products by the industry's rolling mills and forging presses. The metal is usually formed at high temperature first, after which it may be cold-formed into additional products.

(Adapted from a diagram and by courtesy of the British Steel Corporation)

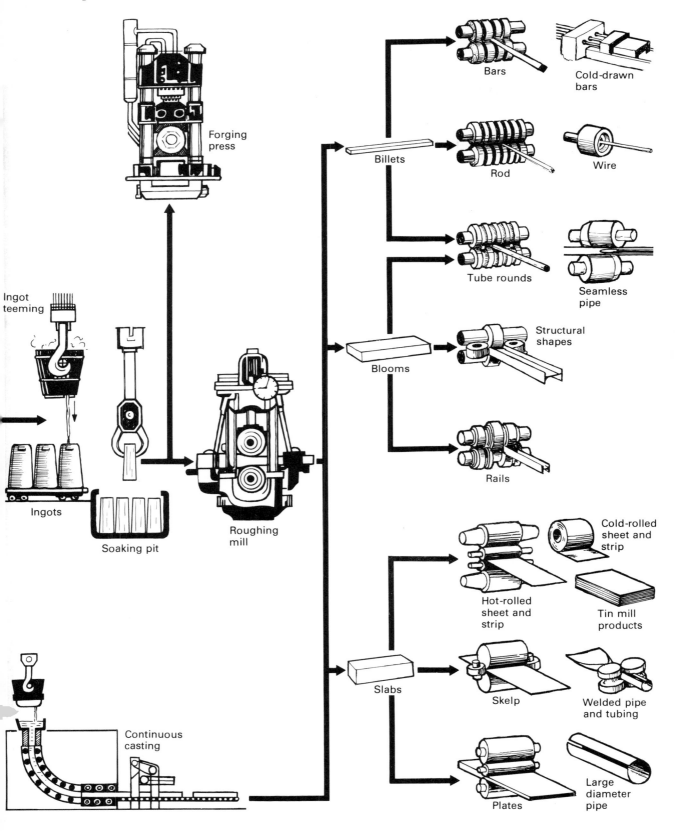

Forging press

Ingot teeming

Ingots

Soaking pit

Roughing mill

Continuous casting

Billets

Bars

Cold-drawn bars

Rod

Wire

Tube rounds

Seamless pipe

Blooms

Structural shapes

Rails

Slabs

Hot-rolled sheet and strip

Cold-rolled sheet and strip

Tin mill products

Skelp

Welded pipe and tubing

Plates

Large diameter pipe

Limestone

Limestone is included in the charge to serve as a fluxing agent with the extraneous materials ('gangue') associated with the ore. It combines with these materials (clay etc.) and makes them more readily fusible, forming a liquid slag which separates from the iron.

Preparation of iron ore for smelting

All ores require some preparation before they can be smelted, so that furnaces can work efficiently and economically. They need regular and uniform 'diets' from which as much as possible of the unwanted material has been removed. Either the richness or the size and density of the lumps needs to be improved and this can be done in a number of ways: (1) by the concentration (up-grading) of low quality ores with the removal of unwanted materials by washing and/or

Figure 2   Diagram of blast furnace, hot blast stoves and part of gas cleansing plant

For clarity, only the relevant pipelines are shown, diagrammatically.
(Adapted from a diagram and by courtesy of the British Steel Corporation)

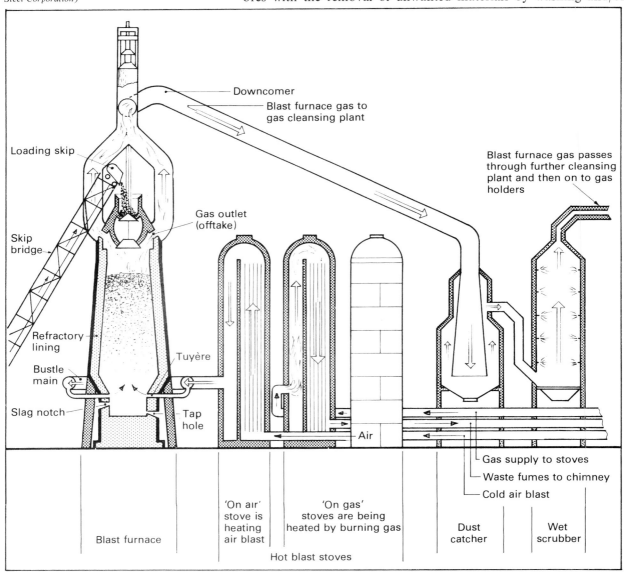

Downcomer
Blast furnace gas to gas cleansing plant

Blast furnace gas passes through further cleansing plant and then on to gas holders

Loading skip

Gas outlet (offtake)

Skip bridge

Refractory lining

Tuyère

Bustle main

Slag notch

Tap hole

Air

Gas supply to stoves
Waste fumes to chimney
Cold air blast

Blast furnace

'On air' stove is heating air blast

'On gas' stoves are being heated by burning gas

Dust catcher

Wet scrubber

Hot blast stoves

Figure 3   The operation of charging mechanism on a blast furnace

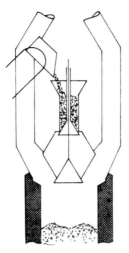

Both bells closed.
Charge tipped into
hopper

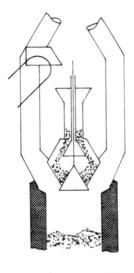

Small bell opens.
Charge falls on to
large bell

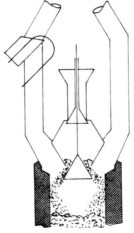

Small bell closes.
Large bell opens.
Charge falls into
furnace

gravity separation or, in the case of magnetite ores, by magnetic separation; (2) by crushing and screening (sieving) to a suitable size. The powdery residue from the screening, known as 'fines' is mixed with coal dust or coke breeze and a sintering (controlled burning) process follows, resulting in the fusion of the fines into hard lumps that can be included in the furnace charge. Sinter is being used more and more nowadays and in some plants it forms 100 per cent of the charge; (3) by the blending of different ores to obtain a consistency in quality, or (4) by forming powdery ores into pellets.

The blast furnace

The blast furnace (see Fig. 2) is typically about 30 m high and 10 m in diameter at the widest part, although some modern furnaces are even larger than this. The furnace casing is of heavy steel plates with a very thick lining of refractory brickwork which is water-cooled around the melting zone (or bosh) to avoid damage from the extremely high temperatures inside. A slight increase in diameter towards the base allows for some expansion of the stock as it descends, and at the bosh there is a reduction in diameter where melting begins and stock volume decreases.

Encircling the bosh is the bustle pipe which distributes the hot air blast to ten or more nozzles or tuyeres (pronounced 'tweers') spaced evenly around the furnace. The tuyeres, water-jacketed for cooling are each about 125–175 mm in diameter and they deliver the powerful and very hot air blast right to the middle of the furnace, causing the coke to burn fiercely. This forced draught carries the hot furnace gas up the stack, through the offtake and into the downcomer. It passes through the gas cleansing plant and then on to the gas holders and is ready for use in the hot blast stoves to heat air for the furnaces.

The stock level must be maintained in the furnace and at regular intervals, weighed charges of ore, coke and limestone (and sometimes some scrap metal) are added. The raw materials are carried up in skips which discharge into a rotating hopper. This spreads the charge evenly around and it then enters the furnace through a double bell mechanism (Fig. 3). This is necessary to provide a gas seal since the blast cannot be shut off at any time during the lengthy periods of operation.

The hot blast stoves
Each blast furnace is usually equipped with three stoves which burn furnace gas to heat the air blast. Each is almost as high as the furnace and up to 7 or 8 m in diameter. Inside is a honeycomb of fire-brickwork and a combustion chamber in which gas is ignited, the flames sweeping through the honeycomb and heating it on the way to the chimney. When the brickwork is fully heated, the gas is cut off, the chimney damper is closed and the stove is put 'on air', i.e. the air blast driven by powerful turbo blowers, passes through and absorbs the stored heat. The air temperature reaches from 650 to 800°C.

Usually two stoves are 'on gas' (heating up) whilst the third is on air. When this one cools down, it is put back on gas and another stove is put on air, all three being used in rotation.

Smelting

Iron smelting involves two main processes in the blast furnace: (1) the reduction of iron from its compounds and (2) its separation from its physical mixture with the gangue materials.

In the furnace, the charge is constantly moving slowly downwards against the forced flow of very hot gases which bring about the evaporation of moisture from the charge at the top. A little further down, the limestone decomposes into lime and liberates carbon dioxide. The main reaction is the reduction of the iron oxides, carbon monoxide (from the combustion of coke) combining readily with oxygen in the iron oxides, forming carbon dioxide and leaving the iron free.

Reduction begins quite high in the stack and is progressive as the charge descends and, at the melting zone, both iron and slag trickle down into the hearth. The slag, being lighter, floats on the iron.

At regular intervals as the hearth fills, slag is tapped off, followed by the iron, which goes into huge storage vessels called 'mixers', for holding in the molten state until required in the steel making plant, usually quite near the furnace. In addition to holding a reserve of hot metal, mixers serve a useful purpose in that they will compensate for variations in composition between successive additions of hot metal, giving a more uniform product.

An *inactive* mixer does no more than to hold a stock of metal but in an *active* mixer, some refining takes place with the making of a slag therein.

The term 'pig iron' derives from the old manner of dealing with molten iron. It was run off direct from the furnaces into long, open channels which fed into numerous short channels on either side, bearing a faint semblance to a sow suckling her piglets. Pigs were broken off from the sow when solid. A small amount of cold iron is still made today, but in pig-casting machines. Crude iron is still known as 'pig' iron today. The term 'hot metal' is used to denote molten iron.

Composition of pig iron

Pig iron contains about 90 to 95 per cent of elemental iron together with a number of other elements—mainly carbon, silicon, phosphorus, manganese and sulphur—in varying proportions depending on the compositions of the raw materials and the mode of operation of the blast furnace.

Pig iron may hold from 3.0–4.5% of carbon, 0.5–4.0% silicon, 0.025–2.5% phosphorus, 0.15–2.15% manganese and up to 0.2% sulphur. The composition required for steel making differs from that required for use in iron foundries to make iron castings.

Cast iron

Cast iron is a form of iron of high carbon content (2.5–4.5%), alloyed with small percentages of other elements. It is used in a wide range of items such as pipes, sanitary ware and especially in the engineering industry because it can be made into quite intricate castings of considerable strength and hardness. Cast iron is not ductile and cannot be bent without fracturing. Many kinds of cast iron are used, including chilled, malleable and alloyed iron castings.

Iron for casting can be made in several ways, viz: by the mixture of various selected grades of pig iron or of pig iron and steel scrap, or of foundry scrap and steel scrap with additions of special ferro-alloys and other metals. By these selections, by control of cooling rates and by heat treatments, a vast range of irons becomes available. Some are very hard and brittle, some quite soft and tough and some of great strength and durability and with resistance to corrosion.

Foundry iron is usually melted in the cupola which is like a miniature blast furnace but generally operated on a day-to-day basis. See Fig. 36A. It is charged through a side door at the top with alternate layers of coke, metal and limestone and is then fired.

Other elements in cast iron

Carbon has a great influence on the properties of cast iron and is found mainly in one of two forms depending on the cooling rates and on the proportions of other elements present. It can appear either combined with iron, forming cementite (iron carbide, Fe_3C) which is very hard, or as free carbon (graphite) in flake form. These conditions can be modified by certain heat treatments.

Silicon also has a marked effect on the properties of iron, chiefly through its effect on the form of any carbon present. It tends to throw carbon out of solution and so produces 'soft' grey iron. It plays an important part in malleabalising.

Phosphorus In addition to causing a brittleness in castings, a high phosphorus content tends to increase contraction on solidifying and this sets up stresses in corners and where thicknesses of adjacent parts vary considerably. A high phosphorus content tends to produce a porosity in large masses and for all of these reasons, this impurity is kept at a low level in high quality castings. However, phosphorus does give a fluidity to the molten metal and this effect can be used to advantage in making slender castings for light duties.

Sulphur from the coke is taken up by iron melted in the cupola. It forms iron sulphide which has a low melting point and is soluble in molten metal but tends to segregate as the iron solidifies, making faulty castings. The presence of sulphur accounts for a brittleness in certain kinds of chilled castings and it also causes increased contraction on cooling. Therefore, inaccurate castings with a tendency to cracking can result when the sulphur content is too high.

Manganese is always present in iron. Its most important function is probably in helping to neutralise the effects of sulphur. It forms manganese sulphide which has a high melting point and is only sparingly soluble in iron, going instead, into the slag.

Chilled castings

Rapid cooling in castings leaves the iron with a high proportion of cementite compared to graphite and makes the metal very hard. The hardness resulting from rapid cooling can be exploited to advantage when castings are required with some surfaces hardened, for example, the slideways on machine parts. This is done by the use of 'chills'—usually pieces of heavy plate incorporated in the mould—at appropriate places to conduct heat away, thus cooling the required hard surfaces rapidly. Chilled castings are made from ordinary low-silicon iron or iron alloyed with small amounts of nickel or chromium.

Thin sections and small castings with always cool rapidly and if it is desired that they should be 'soft', then iron with a higher silicon content is used. This causes more carbon to appear as graphite flakes, giving the iron a darker colour. This iron is more easily machined, but its tensile strength is reduced. This weakness can be overcome with the addition of a small amount of magnesium alloy in the molten iron, causing the carbon to form into nodules with some increase in strength.

Malleable cast iron

The problem of low tensile strength in cast iron due to the presence of flake graphite is avoided in castings made in 'white iron', which is low in silicon and manganese. The carbon present is almost entirely in the form of cementite and the iron is so hard that it is almost unmachinable. This extreme hardness can be rectified by one of two treatments which render the iron much softer.

If the white iron has a high carbon content, the process used is the 'Whiteheart' process in which some of the carbon is removed. The castings are closely packed with hematite ore in sealed containers and are heated to 900–1000°C for two to three days, followed by slow cooling. Surface carbon is oxidised by contact with the ore, combining with oxygen and escaping as carbon dioxide gas. Much of the combined carbon at the centre diffuses outwards and is also oxidised, and in heavy sections, any remaining carbon will form into nodules. The iron is very white after this process—hence the name 'Whiteheart'.

In the 'Blackheart' process, applied to iron of lower carbon content, no attempt is made to remove the carbon. The castings are packed in containers with non-reactive materials such as crushed slag or gravel and annealing takes place at 850–900°C for a period of up to five days. The cementite is decomposed into iron and fine graphite, which is precipitated in the form of nodules within the iron. The dull black appearance of the metal gives it the name 'Blackheart'. Malleable castings are commonly used in car components, for machinery and agricultural equipment.

Alloy cast iron

The addition of one or more alloying elements to iron makes a wide range of alloy cast irons available and these have many specialised applications in engineering. Amongst the alloying elements are nickel, chromium, molybdenum, titanium, vanadium and copper, as well as high levels of silicon or manganese.

The alloy irons are used where high tensile strength, rigidity and resistance to wear and to corrosion are required. Nickel–chromium iron, for example, is notable for its extreme toughness and hardness and its ability to withstand repeated elevations to high temperatures without any deterioration. Many of the compositions are patented and sold under trade names.

Steel making

Steel

'Steel' is a general term of wide reference which includes some comparatively 'soft' steels, some which are very hard and some very tough, whilst others are specially suitable for making cutting tools. There are spring and high-tensile steels, free-cutting steels for ease of machining, various kinds of stainless steels, deep-drawing steels for press work (e.g. car bodies) and a host of 'special' steels, all of which are needed to meet the demands of modern technology and all of which begin as crude iron.

Although steel can be defined as an alloy of carbon and iron, it should be understood that no steel contains only these two elements. As a result of manufacturing and from the very nature of the raw materials used, all steels contain small and varying amounts of the impurities, phosphorus, sulphur, manganese and silicon, together with other trace elements. It would be virtually impossible to remove these impurities completely from the metal.

When one or more other elements such as nickel, chromium, tungsten, etc., are added, the steel is known as 'alloy steel', the carbon–iron alloys being commonly referred to as 'straight (or plain) carbon steels'.

Pig iron into steel

The conversion of pig iron into steel is brought about by refining processes in which all five elements, carbon, phosphorus, sulphur, manganese and silicon, are either lowered to particular levels or almost entirely removed. Of these elements, it is carbon which plays the key role in determining the grade of steel produced, from low to medium and high carbon steels. The level of carbon is adjusted to specifications ranging from approximately 0.1 to 1.3 per cent and sometimes higher.

It is in the refining that we find steel-making falling into two chemical divisions, viz: *acid* processes and *basic* processes. The division comes about because of the differing compositions of pig irons, some containing high levels of phosphorus and sulphur whilst others are higher in silicon and lower in phosphorus and sulphur.

The removal of carbon, manganese and silicon presents no great problem and can be dealt with equally well in basic or acid processes. The removal of phosphorus and sulphur, however, calls for conditions found only in the basic process in which lime is

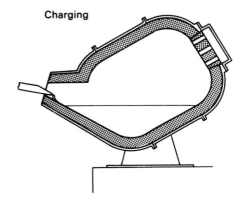

Charging

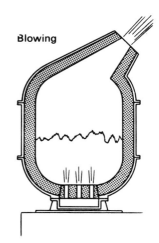

Blowing

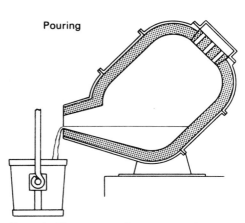

Pouring

Figure 4   The sequence of operations in the Bessemer converter

Figure 5   Open hearth furnace shown in part section
(Adapted from a diagram and by courtesy of the British Steel Corporation)

included in the charge to form compounds with both of these elements, removing them in a basic slag, the making of which is an important part of the process.

Because of the chemical natures of the slags in both processes, it is important that the refining furnaces are lined with refractory materials which will not react chemically and become eroded through contact with the slags. It must be remembered that acids and bases will combine readily and especially so at high temperatures. For this reason, basic furnaces are lined with magnesite and dolomite–magnesite bricks, and acid furnaces with silica bricks.

The terms acid and basic may be taken as referring to the furnace linings and to the natures of the slags formed in each of the processes. The bulk of steel production today is in basic processes.

Refining of the molten metal is by oxidation, brought about by passing oxygen into the metal, the gas combining with unwanted materials, forming oxides which are either absorbed in the slag or passed out as gases. Some of the iron itself is oxidised and dispersed in this way but can be reclaimed. The removal of sulphur will depend on the basicity of the slag and the temperatures reached during refining.

The Bessemer converter

Sir Henry Bessemer's discovery in 1856, that impurities could be removed from molten iron by their oxidation with an air blast through the hot metal was a major step forward for nineteenth-century industry. The operation of the converter, which is not used today, is illustrated in Fig. 4. The converter linings were silica or ganister bricks and this was the beginning of acid steel making. The chemistry of iron and steel making was not fully understood at this time and attempts to refine phosphorus- and sulphur-bearing irons resulted in disappointment until basic linings were introduced to deal with such metals.

The open hearth process

For many years the open hearth was one of the main sources of high

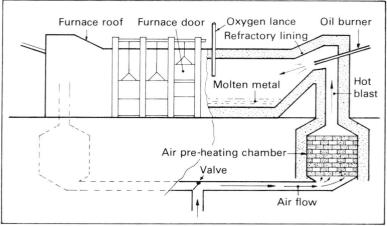

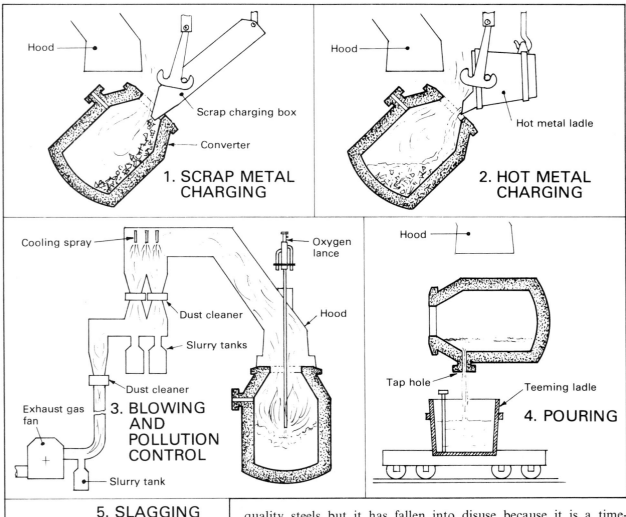

quality steels but it has fallen into disuse because it is a time-consuming process.

The furnace (Fig. 5) consisted of a shallow bath with roof and walls lined with refractory brickwork and with charging doors arranged along one side. Firing was operated from alternate ends with oil burners and a hot air blast passing through regenerative stoves and absorbing waste heat from the furnace. The furnace accepted steel scrap together with hot metal and in more recent times, oxygen lances were used to speed refining.

Modern processes

The main methods of steel production today are the basic oxygen process and the electric arc furnace.

The basic oxygen process

This is readily seen as a development from the air blown converter, but whereas air was blown into the metal through the base of the

Figure 6   Diagrams showing the operation of the basic oxygen process in steel making

Bessemer converter, in this process pure oxygen is blown in from the top. Widespread use of the oxygen processes became possible with the advent of pure oxygen in bulk. Although air was effective in burning out impurities, nitrogen was absorbed from the blast and this caused a brittleness in the metal. This cannot happen with oxygen gas.

A big advantage of the basic oxygen process is its flexibility in handling irons of differing compositions. It will operate with hot metals containing 0.2–2.0% of silicon, from 0.4–2.5% manganese and up to 0.3 or 0.4% of phosphorus with one slag. If a second basic slag is made, the process will deal with hot metal containing up to 2.0% of phosphorus.

The furnaces are of large capacity, up to 350 tonnes being refined in one operation lasting from 40 to 45 minutes in all. As shown in Fig. 6, the vessel, pre-heated, is tilted to receive the scrap metal charge of 25 to 30% of its capacity. Hot metal, brought from the mixer in torpedo-shaped containers running on tracks, is transferred into large charging ladles. These are hoisted for pouring into the furnace which is then returned to the upright position.

With the hood for fume collection in place over the neck, the oxygen lance is passed through to a pre-determined level above the metal and the blow begins as oxygen is forced through the bore of the water-cooled lance. Slag-forming fluxes (lime, fluorspar and mill scale) are added through a chute immediately after the blow is started. The blow causes great turbulence in the metal and as the impurities are burnt out, there is a temperature rise and any remaining scrap is melted. Fumes are sucked up into the hood and passed through a cooling and cleansing plant which eliminates atmospheric pollution.

The blow lasts for about 15 minutes only and at the end, the furnace is tilted for metal sampling and immediate analysis. The metal temperature is checked and, if too high, is adjusted by adding scrap and limestone; if too low, the lance is lowered again with the vessel upright, and oxygen is blown for a short period.

Figure 7   The use of oxygen in converters

With analysis and temperature correct, the lance and hood are

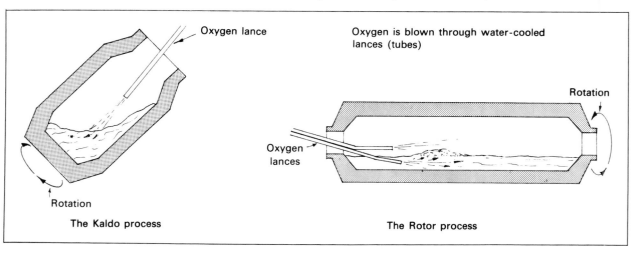

raised and the furnace is tilted for tapping the steel from beneath the slag into a teeming (pouring) ladle. Specified alloying elements are added to the ladle during tapping. Finally, the furnace is tilted the opposite way for 'slagging'. The steel is then either teemed into ingot moulds or taken to the continuous casting machine for processing.

Two other converters in which the oxygen lance is used are shown diagrammatically in Fig. 7.

The electric arc furnace

In this process, the heat for melting the charge is generated by electric arcs struck between several graphite electrodes and the cold metal charge. The arc furnaces most generally used in steel making are of the direct arc type such as the tilting furnace shown in Fig. 8. At one time, they were used mainly in making high quality carbon and alloy steels but they are now also used quite extensively in making ordinary carbon steels.

The electric arc is a very 'clean' heat source for melting and, because it has no influence on the furnace atmosphere, it is possible to make oxidising or reducing slags at will. This facility permits close control over final composition and the taking of sulphur to a very low level. Acid lined furnaces are used mostly in the steel foundries and basic furnaces are in general use in steel making. The metal part of the charge is usually of selected steel scrap.

In starting the process, the electrodes are first raised clear of the roof which is then swung aside for charging the furnace from a container lowered from a travelling crane. The charge consists of

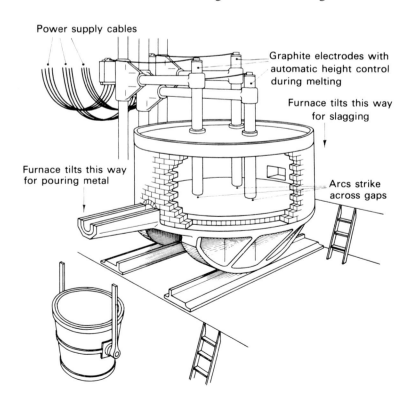

Figure 8   The electric arc furnace
The mechanism for tilting is beneath the furnace

scrap together with lime, fluorspar and mill scale (iron oxide) to make a basic oxidising slag. With the roof back in place, the electrodes are lowered and adjusted above the charge so that when the current is switched on, arcs flash across the gap, generating a fierce heat which melts the charge. The gap is adjusted automatically as melting proceeds so that the arcs are maintained.

Samples of slag and metal are taken for analysis and the slag is raked out. If further refining is needed, a second basic slag is made to remove more phosphorus and if excess carbon is to be removed, this can be done quite rapidly with the oxygen lance.

A double slagging method is used to make low sulphur steel, the oxidising slag being followed by another made with lime, a little fluorspar and coke or graphite dust. This makes a reducing slag which takes the sulphur to a very low level.

With refining complete and the metal analysis satisfactory, the slag is removed and the pouring temperature adjusted. Any alloying elements required are often added at this stage and then the furnace is tilted for tapping the steel into ladles.

The induction furnace

The high frequency induction furnace is operated as a melting furnace only, no refining being done. It is used in the making of highest quality alloy steels of all kinds in small quantities.

The all-scrap charge is melted in a cylindrical crucible inside a coil of copper tubing, through the walls of which the current is passed. Tubing is used because it is better suited to conducting a high frequency current than a solid conductor. The powerful magnetic field which surrounds the coil has the effect of inducing eddy currents in the pieces of metal in the crucible and the resistance they offer to the passage of these currents generates sufficient heat to melt them. One special feature of induction heating is that the eddy currents cause the molten metal to circulate in the crucible, ensuring a complete and even distribution of any alloying elements added.

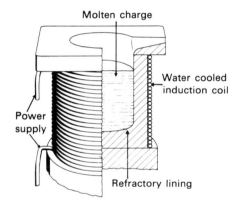

Figure 9   High-frequency induction furnace

The processing of molten steel

Molten steel must, of course, be solidified before anything can be made with it, and the metal can be dealt with in three ways: (1) it can be cast into ingots, (2) it can be teemed into the continuous casting machine, or (3) it can be used in making steel castings.

Ingots

Heavy cast iron moulds are used in casting ingots in weights and dimensions arranged to suit the particular subsequent processing. Weights vary from 4 to 20 tonnes for the rolling mills, up to 200 or more tonnes for forging (by pressing or hammering) in the making of things like boilers, pressure vessels and other highly stressed components.

In the casting of ingots, steel is teemed from the bottom of the ladle in several different ways as shown in Fig. 10: (1) straight into

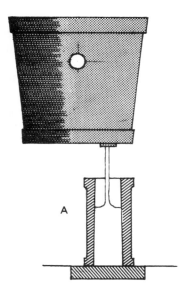
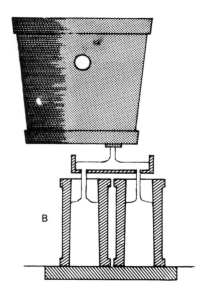
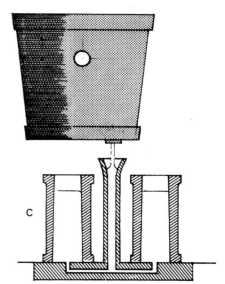

Figure 10   Teeming steel ingots
A. Direct   B. Tundish   C. Trumpet teeming

the mould without any splashing, which would make a faulty ingot, (2) into a tundish (a smaller form of ladle) which allows the metal to flow quietly through one or more outlets into the moulds, or (3) into a trumpet from which ducts lead into several moulds for certain kinds of ingots.

Segregation is a fault caused by small amounts of impurities in the steel which always tend to remain in the molten metal. This tendency causes them to migrate to the heart as the ingot cools from the outside.

Pipe or 'piping' is a defect caused by contraction as the ingots solidify (see Fig. 11). Its effect can be minimised by providing a feeder head which serves as a reservoir on top of the mould. The reserve of metal feeds down into the ingot as it contracts and the cavity is largely confined to the feeder head.

Blow holes can be avoided by 'killing' the steel with small amounts of ferro-manganese or aluminium and silicon. The ingots are then known as *killed ingots*. Blow holes are not always regarded as undesirable since their presence inside an ingot tends to reduce piping and their formation is often permitted by only partial killing of the steel. The resulting ingots are known as *balanced ingots* since the blow holes tend to 'balance' the effect of contraction. Provided that blow holes are within the ingot, they remain unoxidised and weld up when the ingot is rolled.

A special, low carbon steel which is partially killed, is cast in the form of *rimming ingots* for rolling into sheets for tinplate. Blow holes weld up on rolling and a thick outer layer of almost pure iron gives the sheets a superior finish.

Processing of ingots

Ingots are processed at almost white heat by: (1) passing through the roughing mill (a heavy-duty rolling mill) to produce large sections, viz: slabs and blooms, or (2) forging under hydraulic presses or

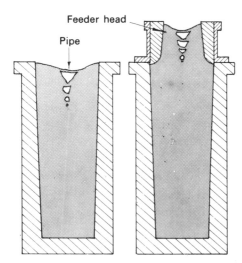

Figure 11   Showing how the effect of pipe (or 'piping') is confined within a feeder head

power hammers. Forging is used to make large items which will have to withstand severe stresses in service.

The hot working of steel in these ways is important because of its beneficial effect on the crystalline structure which, after casting, is coarse. Hot rolling brings about re-crystallisation, the structure becoming fine, of uniform character and slightly fibrous in the direction of rolling. In forging also, the crystalline structure is improved. Of equal importance is the fact that grain flow will follow the shape of the forging, giving an overall soundness and maximum strength.

Very heavy items such as large boiler drums are forged under the hydraulic press, which can exert pressures of 12,000 tonnes or more, while smaller ingots are worked under the power hammer. The drop-stamp is used in making medium and small sized items, often of intricate shapes, such as in crankshafts.

In rolling, major changes of section are always made at almost white heat, but many sheet and strip products are cold rolled in the final stages.

Continuous casting

This is a fairly recent development in which molten steel is teemed directly into a casting machine to make slabs, blooms or billets or in one continuous operation. This dispenses with the need for ingot casting, with big savings in plant, time and energy. Although the concept of continuous casting might be regarded as simple, the design and application of this method of handling a continuous flow

Figure 12   Diagram showing continuous casting using a curved mould
(Adapted from a diagram and by courtesy of the British Steel Corporation)

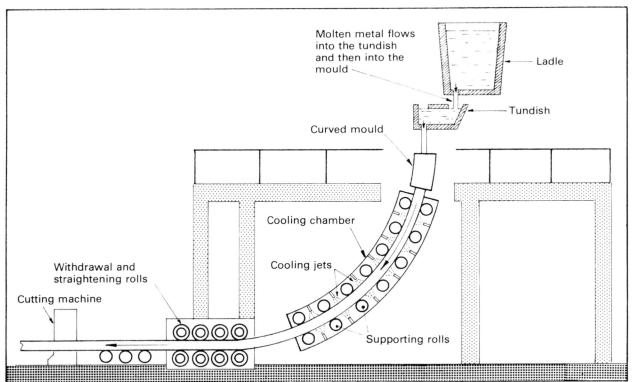

of molten steel is a remarkable achievement, representing a major advance in steel production. The process is illustrated in Fig. 12.

Molten metal flows from a tundish into a water-cooled copper mould and as teeming begins, steel solidifies and attaches to the shaped end of a dummy bar entered in readiness at the bottom of the mould. As the mould fills, metal freezes (solidifies) at the outside, forming a solid skin, whilst the core remains molten. The mould is oscillated up and down to avoid adhesion between mould and metal and as the metal solidifies sufficiently, withdrawal of the dummy bar begins, pulling the partly solidified steel section with it.

Obviously, the rate of teeming, cooling and withdrawal are quite critical if a perfect product is to be obtained. Water jets bring about further cooling as the steel is guided through a secondary cooling chamber and withdrawal of the product is controlled as it passes between a set of rolls which grip on both sides, pulling it without distorting its shape. The dummy bar is detached as it reaches the run-out table and from then on, the metal is flame-cut into lengths as it emerges in one continuous length.

Several forms of casting machines are used but all work the same sequence of operations. The diagram in Fig. 12 shows a machine with a curved mould and cooling chamber, the finished product being extruded horizontally. In two other machines, the mould, cooling chambers and withdrawal rolls are set in a vertical plane. In one of them the steel extrusion is formed into an easy bend so that it makes a horizontal exit from the machine and in the other, it is cut into lengths as it makes a vertical descent, each length being lowered sideways on to the run-out table.

Continuous casting is used extensively today to produce mild steel sections, but ingot casting is still needed in the making and shaping of steel for forging and for special purposes.

Finishing processes

Hot rolling

From Fig. 1 it will be seen that the large sections from continuous casting or from the roughing mill are hot rolled to produce marketable products in the form of plates, sheet, wide and narrow strip, rails, rods, bars, wire, skelp and rounds for tube making, and various sections for structural work.

Cold rolling

A small proportion of the production of hot rolled strip can be used without further treatment, but the bulk of it is passed on for finishing by cold rolling. This gives metal with clean, bright surfaces and with precisely controlled thickness. Sheet for tinplate is prepared in this way.

Before rolling, scale is removed from the strip by passing it through a pickling bath of hot, dilute sulphuric acid. It is then washed and dried before going to the rolling mill. Cold rolling results in considerable work hardening, which is rectified by annealing the coils of strip in furnaces containing inert gases so that no oxidation takes place. An interesting feature of cold rolling is that the coiler into which the strip passes is used to supply much of the power for *pulling* the strip through the mill. This could not be done in hot rolling.

Cold drawing

Hot rolled steel bars are often finished accurately to size and section by cold drawing, which gives the metal a bright, smooth finish with work-hardened surfaces. The finished product is known as 'bright drawn'.

The bars are pickled and cleaned before drawing is carried out on the 'draw bench'. The tapered (or tagged) end of the slightly over-size bar is passed through the tapered hole in a die, made from very hard alloy steel. The end of the bar is gripped by steel 'dogs' attached to an endless chain and the lubricated bar is pulled through the die which squeezes the metal, making it bright, smooth and true to shape and size. No metal is removed and the bar finishes considerably longer and with improved tensile strength.

Rods (15 mm or less in diameter) are often continuous drawn from one coil to another, passing through the die en route.

Large diameter bars are often finished by turning in a lathe or by 'centreless turning'. In centreless turning, the bar is passed through a revolving head fitted with cutters. Where greater accuracy is required, the turned bar is left a little over size and is then finished by grinding on centres or by passing it through a centreless grinder to bring it within very close limits of size.

Steel scrap

With upwards of ten million tonnes of steel scrap being absorbed in UK steel plants every year, this is obviously an important raw material and a brief look at its collection will be of interest. There is much more to it than the mere gathering of anything made of iron or steel.

Steel scrap has always played a part in steel making and is perhaps even more important today than previously. It is included in the initial charge in oxygen-blown converters, and is also used as a means of lowering the temperature of melts to a level suitable for tapping. Electric arc furnaces operate on charges of up to 100 per cent of scrap steel and account for the bulk of demand for this material, which is obtained from within the steel plants, from industrial waste and from general salvage work.

The final selection and grading of scrap is no haphazard affair, several points being considered in assessing its market value and suitability for making specified steels: (1) its chemical composition (carbon, alloy or stainless steel), (2) its condition as regards contamination with non-ferrous metals, non-metals (plastics etc.), dirt, grease, oil, rubber, paint, etc., (3) its size and shape (large masses or irregular shapes cause difficulties in charging furnaces), and (4) its density (machine swarf is voluminous and lightweight, and makes transport and melting unprofitable, so it is usually compressed or baled).

Scrap arising within the steel plants will be of known composition and can be recycled with confidence in making steel to specifications. Scrap from the dismantling of ships, locomotives, railway lines, constructional beams and so forth is also likely to be of known and consistent composition, and processing will present no problems beyond the need to reduce the size for convenience in handling.

It is important that the compositions of scrap alloy and stainless steels are known and that the various steels are segregated properly, otherwise there would be confusion and doubt about the composition of recycled steel and its scrap value would fall. In the making of carbon steels, strict control of the scrap charge is essential to keep out elements such as chromium, nickel and silicon which have adverse effects on carbon steels.

Contamination with non-ferrous metals and other materials is dealt with by their physical removal during preparation of the scrap. Oil, grease and rubber are undesirable contaminants because they all tend to increase sulphur levels. The steel used in tinplate and in tin cans is of good quality and is well worth recovery, but unless the tinplating is removed by electrolytic or chemical processing, the metal is unsuitable for recycling.

2

Steel

Crystals

All metals are of a crystalline structure and when a piece of metal is deformed by cold working, movement takes place within each crystal, in most cases along slip planes which lie parallel to each other, movement taking place more readily in the direction of these planes than in any other way. As slip occurs, the crystals become elongated and then show more and more resistance to further deformation and the metal becomes 'work hardened'. Because the crystals are found in haphazard arrangements, the weakness in each is supported by neighbouring crystals whose slip planes will lie in various other directions. If the crystals are very large, the movement in each will be more pronounced, not only because of the crystal size but because the support from surrounding crystals will be less effective. The resultant movement will be more damaging to the structure than if the crystals are small. Crystal size is of importance where strength and toughness are required.

Re-crystallisation

As a result of slow crystal growth on cooling, metals generally solidify with a coarse and uneven grain, but they can be re-crystallised, some metals more easily than others. Lead, for example, can be re-crystallised by cold working alone and it can be distorted severely without any work hardening occurring, but in most cases, some form of heat treatment is necessary.

Grain refinement by re-crystallisation is very desirable in steel, but with this and many other metals, cold rolling or working causes crystal deformation as seen in Fig. 13, the metal becoming harder and more resistant to further deforming.

Re-crystallisation can be brought about by annealing and this heat treatment restores the metal to its original softness and ductility, removing the effects of work hardening. However, the two processes, *working* and *re-crystallisation* can often be combined in one operation by hot working and this is always done with steel, the finishing processes in the steel mill (rolling or forging) producing the required shape and at the same time, refining the grain.

Carbon in steel

The complicated relationship between carbon and iron depends largely on two main facts: (1) that although carbon combines chemically with iron, making *cementite,* it exists as a separate substance within the structure and is known as a *phase,* it is quite distinct from the iron (ferrite) phase, and (2) that iron is an allotropic element, i.e. it can exist in more than one crystalline form.

(1) On the question of phases, although carbon is in solution in molten steel, it comes out of solution in solid steel, being precipitated within the crystalline structure, not as carbon but as the intensely hard chemical compound *cementite* (Fe_3C) and its presence can be detected microscopically. This is the second phase in steel.

Cementite can appear in two forms in steel, either as: (1) an intimate mixture with ferrite forming *pearlite* which contains approximately 13 per cent cementite and 87 per cent ferrite, or (2) as itself (cementite). The presence of free cementite will depend on the amount of carbon in the steel and we can now see how the carbon level affects the constituents, looking first at a low carbon steel; for example, mild steel at about 0·3 per cent C. At this level there will be insufficient carbon to change all of the ferrite to pearlite and so the steel will contain both ferrite and pearlite. Pearlite is very hard because of its cementite constituent, but the presence of ferrite in the steel will give the metal ductility, depending on the ratio of ferrite to pearlite, i.e. the less pearlite there is present, the softer the steel. Conversely, as the carbon content increases, we find more pearlite, until at approximately 0·85 per cent C, the steel consists entirely of pearlite. As the carbon content approaches this level, the hardness of the metal increases and this is accompanied by a decrease in ductility and toughness (resistance to shock loads). When the carbon is higher than 0·85 per cent and up to a maximum in practice of about 1·3 per cent, the steel will contain pearlite and free cementite which will impart extreme hardness and brittleness. (2) Many elements are allotropic, i.e. they can exist in more than one form, e.g. carbon, which can exist as diamonds or as graphite. The allotropy of iron is connected with its temperature and whilst not so spectacular as that of carbon, is nevertheless of great import in the structure of steel. At normal temperatures, pure iron (ferrite) is soft, ductile and magnetic and when in this condition is known by the Greek symbol α (alpha) as a means of easy reference. When heated to above 910°C, a re-arrangement of the crystalline structure takes place, it loses its magnetism and there is a slight increase in volume. The iron is then known as γ (gamma) iron. There are two important points about this change from the α form to the γ form, one being that whilst γ iron *can* hold cementite in solid solution, α iron *cannot* and on cooling, cementite is precipitated as the γ iron changes back to α iron. The other point is that as the carbon content is increased, the 'critical point' (the change from γ to α iron) becomes depressed and is at its lowest temperature with a carbon content of 0·85 per cent, above which the critical point occurs at higher temperatures. All of this is shown in the equilibrium diagram in Fig. 14, the top line of the graph showing the *upper critical point,* whilst the horizontal line drawn through the lowest point indicates the *lower critical point.*

Whatever the carbon content may be, it is all held in solid solution in γ iron (as cementite) at temperatures above the upper critical point and the form of the alloy is then known as *austenite.* When the carbon stands at 0·85 per cent, the change from γ to α

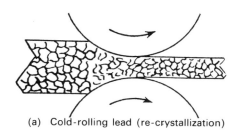

(a) Cold-rolling lead (re-crystallization)

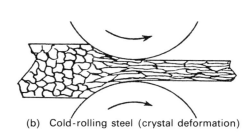

(b) Cold-rolling steel (crystal deformation)

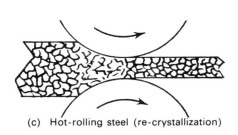

(c) Hot-rolling steel (re-crystallization)

Figure 13   The effects of cold and hot rolling

iron causes all of the cementite to be thrown out of solution at once, to form pearlite and at all other carbon contents, the change from γ to α iron takes place over a temperature range indicated by the vertical distance between the upper and lower critical points seen in the diagram.

With carbon contents of less than 0·85 per cent, the ferrite appears first, on cooling and when the remaining γ iron is *enriched* to 0·85 per cent carbon, it changes to pearlite. With carbon contents of more than 0·85 per cent, cementite appears first, on cooling and when the remaining γ iron is *reduced* to 0·85 per cent carbon, it changes to pearlite.

Each of the three constituents of steel reflect their own particular properties in the different grades of the metal. *Ferrite* is soft and ductile and therefore low carbon steels will exhibit similar properties according to the amount of ferrite present. *Pearlite* is very hard and will impart this property to the steel which becomes progressively harder as the proportion of pearlite increases, the metal becoming less ductile and more resistant to deformation. *Cementite* is intensely hard and brittle and steels with free cementite (i.e. containing more than 0·85 per cent carbon) are only used where this extreme hardness is of particular advantage, as in certain tools and items like ball bearings.

Heat treatments

The metallurgy of steel is largely dependent on the fact that iron can exist in two forms. With the temperature above a critical level, it is in the γ form and can hold carbon in solid solution. On cooling below this critical level, it reverts to its original form of α iron and throws out the carbon to form pearlite and cementite. This structure, however, only appears when the metal has been allowed to cool slowly, during which time diffusion of the constituents takes place throughout the whole mass which finally arrives at a state of equilibrium. By varying the rate of cooling it is possible to produce and control a range of different structures in the steel although the carbon content remains unaltered, these structures imparting different physical properties to the steel. By speeding up the rate of cooling it is possible to prevent the structure from reaching a state of equilibrium and to trap or 'freeze' it in a condition which will impart the desired physical properties.

The three principal heat treatments employed with plain carbon steels are: (1) *annealing*, (2) *normalising*, and (3) *hardening and tempering*.

Annealing

One form of annealing—'process annealing'—has already been mentioned (page 20) and this is used to bring about re-crystallisation in steel which has been cold worked. The metal is not heated above the upper critical point. In the other form—'full annealing'—it is heated to just above the upper critical point so that all of the carbon

Figure 14   Equilibrium diagram

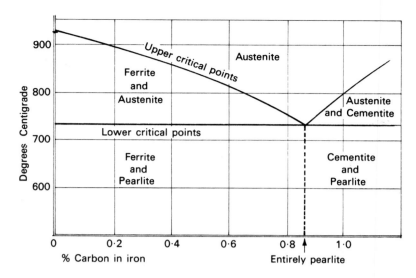

is absorbed in γ iron, forming *austenite*. The steel is then allowed to cool slowly in the furnace. The slow cooling is an essential feature of the process which is carried out to make the steel as soft as possible and to relieve internal stresses. In annealed steel, the grain structure is comparatively coarse and ferrite and pearlite are found divided, forming into separate areas.

Normalising

The normalising process is employed to restore steel to a uniform and stress-free condition after being subjected to forming and working during its manufacture. There is some similarity to annealing, but in normalising the steel is heated to just above its upper critical temperature and is then allowed to cool in still air, which gives a faster cooling rate. This leaves sufficient time for complete separation of pearlite and cementite, and instead of forming into separate areas in a coarse structure, the two are intimately mixed in a much finer structure.

Normalising is carried out on low carbon steels. It is not intended for giving maximum softness and the ease with which the steel can be machined afterwards will depend on its precise composition.

Hardening and tempering

Hardening   When steel is quenched from above the upper critical point, cooling is so rapid that precipitation of carbon is entirely suppressed and the structure is 'frozen' in a solid solution. The steel is intensely hard and brittle and under the microscope, is seen to have a needle-like structure known as martensite. Plain carbon steels, usually quenched in water, are so hard and brittle that not many uses can be found for them in this condition.

The properties resulting from quenching from a full red heat—brittleness and intense hardness—are not usually a good combination (especially in tool making) and this can be improved by a second heating.

Tempering   In this second heating, the steel is heated to below the lower critical point and this allows some of the carbon to be precipitated, not as pearlite, but in a very finely divided form known as *sorbite*. This results in a slight decrease in hardness but the steel becomes tougher. After raising to tempering heat, the steel can be quenched or allowed to cool slowly. The exact temperature for tempering will depend on the purpose for which the steel is to be used and some examples are given in Table 2. The degree of hardening obtained after quench hardening depends on the carbon content of the steel, those with less than 0·3 per cent C showing no noticeable change. Maximum hardness is reached at about 1·2 per cent carbon content.

Heating

Where accurate control is desired over the final condition of the steel, uniform heating and accurate temperature control are essential and these are best achieved through the use of a furnace made for such purposes. Many different kinds are made, often with automatic heat control, for operation on oil, gas or electricity and ranging in size from small, bench-type muffle furnaces to very large structures for treating big forgings, bars, sections, etc. Salt baths, lead and lead-tin baths are also used in the heat treatments of metals. Lead has a wide temperature range when molten, from 327 to about 900°C and is used in the hardening and tempering of steel. Various types of 'indicating' paints and crayons are used for indicating the temperatures of parts being heated, the work being marked before heating with the substance which changes colour or appearance at the desired temperature. Other methods are by the use of indicating cones and pellets. Seger cones are well known and these are made from a mixture of kaolin, felspar, quartz, magnesia, lime, boric acid and iron oxide. The composition is adjusted so that the cone wilts and finally collapses at the desired temperature. Indicating pellets, placed on the part being heated, melt sharply at known temperatures, giving quite accurate indications.

In the absence of the proper equipment for heating and for temperature control, one can only use 'rough and ready' methods at the forge or the brazing hearth, judging temperatures by luminous heats in hardening and by oxide colours when tempering. Despite the uncertainty of these methods, surprisingly good results are obtained with carbon steels in such things as cold chisels, screw-drivers and so on, which as forging exercises and examples for heat treatments, provide good educational material.

In Table 1 are shown various red heat colours with the corresponding temperatures. It must be remembered that these luminous colours will appear different on bright days and heated metal should be viewed away from windows or sunlight. Table 2 lists the tempering colours with the corresponding temperatures together with items for which these tempering heats are suitable. These heats are all within the 'black heat' range, i.e. the metal does not glow, the colours indicating the shade of the oxide film which

Table 1   Red heats

Approximate temperature degrees C.	Heat colour
500 to 600	Very dull red. Just visible in dim light
550 to 600	Blood red
700 to 750	Dark cherry red
800 to 850	Cherry red
850 to 900	Light cherry red
950 to 1 000	Orange
1 000 to 1 100	Yellow
1 300 to 1 400	Yellow-white

The student must bear in mind the effects of tempering, viz., a reduction in hardness with an increase in toughness, these two effects becoming more apparent as higher tempering heats are employed. Those tools subjected to shock, e.g. cold chisels, need to be tougher than those subjected to steady pressure, e.g. lathe tools.

For toughening only, without any marked degree of hardening: 450 to 600°C.

Table 2   Tempering colours

Colour of oxide film	Approximate temperature degrees C.	Articles for which suitable
Pale straw	230	Turning tools for brass. Scrapers
Dark straw	240	Turning tools for mild steel
Brown	250	Shear blades. Wood turning tools
Brownish purple	260	Punches, rivet snaps. Plane irons and other wood working tools
Purple	270	Axes
Deep purple	280	Cold chisels, setts (Cold)
Blue	300	Springs

forms on the bright surface of the metal. The oxide colours can be made to appear in two ways: (1) if a piece of polished steel is heated slowly and uniformly in air, it will first dull over and then a pale, straw coloured oxide film will appear over the whole surface. As the temperature increases, the film will darken, finishing up a dark blue at about 300°C. The metal will begin to glow at about 425°C: (2) if a piece of bright steel is heated at one end, the oxide colours will be seen to travel along the surface in a band or 'rainbow' of colours as the heat is conducted. The more rapid the heating, the narrower will the band of colours be.

Quenching media

The quenching of steel from well above 700°C is a very drastic treatment and this rapid cooling is often responsible for cracking and distortion of the work. Because cooling starts from the outside on immersion, a hard and contracting shell is immediately formed around the core which cannot begin to cool and contract at the same moment. As heat is conducted away, the core begins to cool and as it passes through the upper critical point there is an expansion (associated with the change from γ iron to α iron). The hard shell has already been affected by this change and is then contracting on the core as the slight expansion takes place. These are the causes of cracking.

A number of media are used in quenching to give different rates of cooling. A 5 per cent caustic soda solution gives a very fierce quench and next in order comes brine and then cold water. Warm water gives a slower cooling and next in order come mineral oil, animal oil and lastly vegetable oils which give the slowest rate of all. Oils used in quenching should have a high flash-point otherwise there will be a danger from fire. Where extreme hardness can be forsaken in favour of increased toughness, the less drastic quenching media can be used with less risk of cracking. Distortion can often be avoided by the manner in which the work is introduced into the water, e.g. long slender items should be plunged end on, for if plunged in sideways, one side would cool and contract before the other, causing bending. All articles should be agitated in the water to prevent a jacket of steam forming over the surfaces and slowing the cooling rate.

One effect of the slower cooling of the core, particularly on large sections is that the steel inside is almost certainly not as hard as the outsides. There will have been time for the precipitation of carbon and the steel at the centre will contain some pearlite. This is not necessarily a disadvantage as a slightly softer core will render the article less brittle and tougher.

In making tools such as cold chisels, it is not necessary or desirable to quench the whole tool and only the cutting end need be quenched and tempered. In this way, the shank of the tool is left softer and more able to withstand shock without cracking. When quenching the tip, the work is agitated, for if held quite still, the water line might well be the point at which cracking takes place.

Case hardening

In case hardening, articles made from low carbon steels are given a hard skin by carburising the surfaces, thus enclosing a soft core in a case of high carbon steel. The articles retain the toughness associated with mild steel and so can withstand shock, whilst the hardened surfaces are able to withstand wear. The process is carried out by heating the articles in the presence of: (1) a solid, (2) a liquid, or (3) a gas, rich in carbon. During the heating, carbon is absorbed to a depth which depends on the duration of the heating and on the method employed.

(1) This is the oldest method and is known as 'pack hardening' in which the articles are enclosed in an iron box and closely surrounded with substances such as charcoal and bone dust. Other chemicals, e.g. barium carbonate are often included to act as energisers in the process. With the lid sealed on, the whole thing is heated in a furnace at 850 to 900°C for a number of hours and at this high temperature, carbon diffuses into the low carbon steel, converting the surfaces into high carbon steel to a depth of about 0·8 mm after three to four hours' heating. Any parts of the work not to be case hardened can be protected by copper plating or by coating with clay. The box and its contents are allowed to cool slowly before unpacking. The articles will then require heat treatment because of the coarse grain structure resulting from the prolonged heating. Refining of the core is accomplished by heating to a little above the upper critical temperature (about 900 to 915°C) and then quench-

Table 3   Grades of carbon steels and their uses

Type of steel	Carbon per cent	Uses
Dead mild	0·0 to 0·1	Rolled sheets for cold working and for tinplate. Solid drawn tubes and wire. Good welding properties.
Mild	0·1 to 0·33	Rolled sections for structural work. Plates for ship building, etc. Very good machining properties, bright drawn bars used extensively in general engineering work of all kinds. Good welding properties.
Medium carbon	0·34 to 0·6	Drop forgings, axles, crankshafts and other stressed components. High tensile wires, springs, forging dies, hammers and other tools.
High carbon	0·6 to 0·9	Springs, punches, dies, drills, shears, chisels and cutting tools.
Tool steel	0·9 to 1·1 1·1 to 1·3	Cold chisels, taps and dies, picks, axes. Hand files, razors, wire-drawing dies.

ing, usually in oil. This is followed by hardening of the case which is done by heating to between 750 and 760°C, followed by quenching. This will leave a glass-hard case which can be treated further by tempering at about 200°C.

(2) Mild steels can also be carburised in a salt bath, usually containing molten sodium cyanide which is a compound of sodium, nitrogen and carbon. The cyanide process is used extensively in industry and since there are certain risks entailed from poisonous fumes and from splashing of the molten salt, this is not a process for use in the school workshop. Immersion in a salt bath ensures even heating of the parts, distortion is minimised and the surfaces are left clean and bright. After treatment, parts are washed and then receive heat treatments as applied after pack hardening.

(3) In gas carburising, extra carbon can be introduced into mild steel surfaces by heating the metal in a furnace through which a gas rich in carbon is passing. Methane, butane and propane are used in this process, which is suitable mainly for small components. *Nitriding* is a process employed in surface hardening of alloy steels, the parts being heated in the presence of ammonia gas. Hardening results from the absorption of nitrogen.

Case hardening in the handicraft room   Small items in mild steel can be given a thin case by the use of proprietary hardening compounds. The work is brought to a red heat and the compound, often used in powder form is sprinkled on or the work can be dipped into the powder. After further heating, the part is quenched and the resulting case will probably reach ·03 mm or more in depth.

Flame and induction hardening
The slide surfaces of machines (lathe beds, etc.) are often hardened by flame or induction hardening. In the later stages of manufacture, the surfaces are heated by a flame or by means of a high-frequency induction coil and are immediately sprayed with cold water which quenches the metal, leaving a surface layer of martensite. A similar

treatment is given to rails as they leave the last stand in the rolling mill, a spray of water causing rapid cooling from above the upper critical point on the surfaces, forming a layer of martensite. As the rails cool afterwards, in the air, the main part of the section becomes normalised, and heat travelling back to the martensite layer, tempers it and forms sorbite.

Alloy steels

In addition to carbon, other elements are included to make steels which will meet special conditions of service with silicon, nickel, chromium, manganese, molybdenum, vanadium and tungsten commonly used as alloying elements in varying combinations.

Silicon
Silicon and manganese in small amounts are often used to produce a grade of steel superior to carbon steel for use in leaf springs, etc.

Nickel
Steel of low carbon content (about 0·1 per cent) with 2 to 5 per cent nickel are used in case hardening and with carbon at 0·25 to 0·4 per cent and nickel at 3 to 3·75 per cent, the steel becomes shock resistant and has a high elastic limit. Manganese, silicon and chromium in small amounts are also included and these steels are used in such items as crankshafts, engine components and in armour plating. With a high nickel content of 36 per cent, 0·2 per cent carbon and 0·5 per cent manganese, the coefficient of thermal expansion of the steel is extremely low and this is called 'invar' steel which is used in measuring-instruments and clocks.

Chromium
Whilst nickel steels are tough, ductile and of high strength, chromium steels are noted for their resistance to wear and for their hardness and when nickel and chromium are alloyed together in steel, an extremely useful range of alloys is produced. With 3·5 per cent nickel, 0·7 per cent chromium and 0·3 per cent carbon, a steel is made which can be machined readily when annealed and afterwards, heat treated. This high tensile steel is used in making stressed components such as bolts, shafts and aircraft parts. With 4·5 per cent nickel, 1·25 per cent chromium and 0·35 per cent carbon, the steel becomes 'air hardening', i.e. it can be hardened by simply allowing it to cool in the air.

Stainless steels
The resistance to corrosion in stainless steels is due to the presence of chromium at above 12 per cent. A wide range of steels is made, some containing only chromium in addition to carbon, some containing nickel also and others containing further alloying elements.

The steels may be classified as: (1) *Martensitic stainless steels:* hardenable alloys containing 12 to 14 per cent chromium and with carbon varying from 0·2 to 0·3 per cent, these are quenched and tempered and are used in cutlery and for items working at elevated temperatures such as in steam valves, piston rods, etc. The '18/2' (18 per cent chromium, 2 per cent nickel) alloy has a much higher corrosion resistance and is used in fittings, valves, etc. subjected to high temperatures. (2) *Ferritic stainless steels:* in these alloys, with 16 to 18 per cent chromium, the carbon content is so low (0·1 per cent and less) that the steel cannot effectively be hardened and is often referred to as *stainless iron*. These alloys are soft and readily cold formed. (3) *Austenitic stainless steels:* these are non-magnetic, very susceptible to work hardening and are *softened* by quenching. A number of alloys is included in this group and well known among them is the '18/8' (18 per cent chromium, 8 per cent nickel) stainless which is used for pressing and cold drawing. The '12/12' stainless is easier to cold work and is used in ornamental goods.

Manganese

Manganese is always present in steel and when the content is at 13 per cent, it has the effect of stabilising the austenite at ordinary temperatures so that no change takes place as the metal cools. The steel is austenitic and is non-magnetic. This steel has very pronounced work hardening properties and is able to withstand intense wear in such things as the teeth of dredger buckets, mechanical shovels, crushing machines and railway crossings.

Molybdenum

Molybdenum is added to nickel chromium steels to avoid a defect known as 'temper brittleness' which is induced during cooling after tempering or after prolonged soaking at elevated temperatures such as in boilers and other steam plant. The molybdenum content is around 0·5 per cent.

Vanadium

Usually alloyed with chromium in chromium-vanadium steels which have high tensile strength and are very resistant to repeated stresses, these steels are particularly suitable for spanners, wrenches, springs, motor car axles, engine forgings, etc.

Tungsten—high speed steels

The first high speed cutting steel was Mushet's self-hardening tungsten-vanadium steel, produced in 1860, but its value for high speed cutting was not fully appreciated for a number of years. The main constituents in high speed steels today are 14 to 18 per cent tungsten, 3 to 5 per cent chromium and 0·6 per cent carbon and vanadium and molybdenum are also included. The addition of cobalt in 'super high speed steel' with 20 per cent tungsten gives a steel which is capable of cutting very hard materials. High speed steels are air hardening and will retain their hardness even at red heat.

Mechanical properties

Tensile strength

The strength of a metal is measured in a standard tensile test in which a test piece of a known cross-sectional area is pulled in a tensile testing machine until the piece finally breaks. Much information is gained, not only from the load at which failure takes place, but also from the behaviour of the test piece as the loading is increased up to the breaking point. Gripped in two pairs of jaws, the piece under test is subjected to known and controlled loads and at first it exhibits *elasticity* in its ability to return to its original length when the load is removed. Then a point is reached at which is shows permanent distortion (i.e. slip has occurred) and this is the *elastic limit.* Beyond this, increased stress produces *plastic deformation,* the metal stretching and remaining elongated. Plastic deformation continues until the test piece gives way altogether, 'necking down' rapidly as it reaches this point which is its *ultimate tensile strength.* With certain soft steels, there is a *yield point,* just beyond the elastic limit at which the metal suddenly elongates a little without any further load being applied.

Ductility

This is the ability of a metal to undergo distortion whilst cold without fracture. An indication of ductility is obtained in the tensile test from the elongation and the reduction in cross-sectional area just before breaking point is reached, by comparison with the

Table 4   Workshop tests for iron and steel. Identification

Test applied	Cast iron (grey)	Mild steel	Medium and high carbon steels	High speed steel
Drop piece of metal on concrete floor or anvil	Dull sound on impact	A definite metallic ring	A clear and higher pitch ring than with mild steel	A metallic ring, but not so clear as carbon steel
Hand filing	Files cleanly producing a black powder-like swarf	Files nicely but slight clogging of file	Difficult to file. Worse with higher carbon content	Not quite as difficult as with high carbon steels
Saw or nick part way through bar then grip in vice and snap off	Snaps off very easily. Fractured surface shows large crystalline structure, dark in colour	Bends well before breaking. Ragged fracture	M.C. steel: slight bend before break. H.C. steel: strong resistance then snaps with a ringing sound. Both show fine, silvery structure	Strong resistance then snaps suddenly. Fine, silvery structure
Spark test. (Grind on high speed grindstone)	Dull red sparks, showing an occasional bright bursting spark	Stream of long bright sparks	Very bright spark stream with secondary (branching) bursts becoming more prominent as carbon contents increases	Distinctive dull red sparks, not unlike those from cast iron. Sparks also show a yellowish tinge

original length and cross-section. High ductility enables a metal to be drawn easily into fine wire.

Hardness

An indication of hardness is obtained by measuring a metal's resistance to indentation and this can be done by pressing a hardened steel ball or a diamond pyramid into the surface and measuring the size of the indentation. According to the pressure applied and to the size of the ball or the diamond point, so the area of the indentation gives a comparative hardness number. The steel ball is used in the Brinell hardness test and the diamond point in the Vickers Pyramid hardness test which is better suited for use on the harder metals.

In the Rockwell hardness test system, which is in common use, a diamond cone is used for harder materials and a ball for softer ones. Values are given as R_c or R_b respectively.

Toughness

This is the ability of a metal to withstand shock loads and is measured by impact testing in which a notched test piece is firmly gripped in the testing machine and is then broken by impact from a heavy pendulum. The energy absorbed in breaking the sample reduces the swing of the pendulum after impact and the joules of energy absorbed are indicated on a scale on the machine. As a general rule, harder metals with higher tensile strengths are less ductile and show lower impact values. In other words, they are more brittle.

3

Non-ferrous metals and their alloys

Aluminium

Metallic aluminium was first prepared in 1825, but such small amounts were produced that it was regarded as a precious metal. The difficulty, which was not overcome for a long time, is that aluminium shows a great affinity for certain other elements, especially oxygen and it was impossible to extract the metal in any appreciable quantities. The problem remained unsolved until advances in technology and in electrical engineering enabled an electrolytic reduction process to be used in the extraction of larger amounts of metal from alumina (aluminium oxide) extracted from the ore. The production of aluminium today is closely tied up with the supply of cheap electricity and it is for this reason that Britain's aluminium extraction plants are to be found in the Scottish Highlands, where a number of large hydro-electric schemes have been developed.

The source of aluminium is in the so-called bauxites, which consist of impure aluminium oxide with combined and free water and with silica and iron oxide as the main impurities. Bauxite is found widely distributed over the world and particularly in tropical and sub-tropical areas, most of it being obtained by open-cast working. The Bayer alumina process is commonly used in extracting alumina from crushed bauxite which is first digested with a hot caustic soda solution. This dissolves the alumina as sodium aluminate. Impurities are then separated by filtration and the aluminate liquors are treated to obtain alumina of high purity. In the electrolysis of the oxide, a direct current of high amperage is passed through the melt at about 1 000°C, the alumina being dissolved in a flux consisting mainly of cryolite.

The furnace consists of a refractory-lined steel box with an inner lining of carbon which forms the cathode (the negative electrode). The anode (positive electrode) consists of carbon blocks suspended in the melt and as reduction proceeds, molten aluminium collects in the bottom of the furnace, being removed by suction at intervals into a travelling ladle. The purity of the metal is from 99 to 99·8 per cent and to obtain a metal of super-purity a further refining is given and this results in a purity of 99·99 per cent and above.

The most notable property is its lightness, the specific gravity of aluminium being about one-third that of iron or steel. It is an excellent conductor of heat and electricity, coming next to copper in these respects. It can be forged, cast, machined, soldered, brazed and welded, spun, stamped, deep-drawn and impact-extruded. It is wrought into a great variety of products for further manufacturing from sheet, plate, strip, rods, tubes, wires and sections.

Pure aluminium is soft and ductile, but when alloyed with

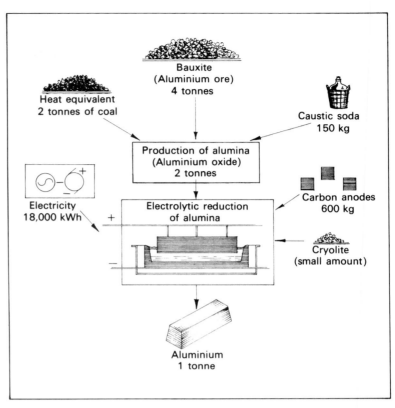

small amounts of other elements, its hardness and strength are increased, some of the alloys having strengths up to and above those of mild steel. These alloys are used in stressed components with highly satisfactory results and some of them are also resistant to corrosion in marine atmospheres.

The applications of aluminium are manifold: it finds its way into our everyday lives in the form of cooking pots and utensils, foil for cookery, milk bottle caps and food and tobacco wrappings. In the super-pure form it is used as a decorative medium, e.g. in wheel and other car 'trims'. It is used in electrical work for bus bars and in cables for the grid system, the necessary strength for the long spans being obtained with a core of high tensile steel wire. In transport by land or sea, the higher intial cost of aluminium is more than offset by the savings in power resulting from weight reduction. Its use in aircraft is known to all and it is now also used in railway rolling stock, motor vehicles and in the super-structures of ocean-going vessels.

The building industry makes good use of the weather resistant properties of aluminium in the form of 'cladding' (coverings in the form of wall panelling), flashings and roof coverings, architectural features and fittings of all kinds. Aluminium powder is used as the base in a very effective priming paint.

Surface finishing
Unprotected aluminium quickly acquires a thin film of oxide

which forms a protective layer against further atmospheric action. Aluminium can be painted, enamelled or lacquered, but a most effective and durable finish is obtained by 'anodising' which is the anodic oxidation of the surfaces in an electrolytic bath. A current, passing through the metal and the electrolyte to a cathode, reinforces the normal oxide film with a near-transparent film whose thickness can be controlled. This film is hard and being slightly porous, lends itself to permanent colouring with organic dyestuffs in a range of very attractive colours. Anodised surfaces are usually sealed and can be finished with lacquers.

Aluminium alloys

A great range of alloys is manufactured and all are standardised and readily identified by British Standard Specification numbers. The alloying elements are added to improve the mechanical properties—hardness, machining qualities, tensile strength, fluidity for casting purposes and to give increased resistance to corrosion. The alloys are used in cast or wrought form ('wrought' means worked in some way; for example, rolling, forging, deep-drawing, etc.) and the properties of some of these alloys can be improved by certain heat treatments, whilst in others, the only changes are those resulting from annealing or from work hardening. The alloys fall into two main groups, viz, those which are *cast* and those which are *wrought*, and in both we find some that are heat treated and some which are not, except, of course, for annealing.

Copper

With its distinctive, warm red colour, copper is easily identified. It is one of the world's most important metals and is employed in the pure state, in the form of alloys and as an added element to influence the properties of other metals. The properties which make it of such great importance are: (1) its high heat and electrical conductivity, (2) its malleability and ductility, (3) the readiness with which it forms alloys, and (4) its resistance to the corrosive effects of the atmosphere through the formation of a protective layer of oxides.

Copper is mined in many countries but mainly in the USA and Zambia, Canada, Chile and the Belgian Congo and in a smaller way in Finland, Jugoslavia, Germany, Scandinavia, Spain, the Urals, Australia, Rhodesia and South Africa. Only a very small quantity is mined in Britain. The ore is found in several forms, the commonest being the *pyrites*, with a copper content of around 34·5 per cent, together with iron and sulphur.

The extraction of copper involves the disposal of much waste rock and the processes differ according to the nature of the ore. Where it contains much sulphur, it is generally ground to a fine powder and the copper-bearing dust is separated by a method of flotation. The resultant concentrate is then smelted in a reverberatory furnace in which a flux is employed to form a slag. The *matte* of copper and iron sulphides obtained is then treated in a process similar to that in the Bessemer converter for the removal of the sulphur and iron by oxidation. The metal is then cast in the form of cakes of 'blister copper'. Although this may contain as little as 1 per cent of impurities, it must be treated further to be of value commercially, and this is done by: (1) fire refining in furnaces of the reverberatory type, or (2) by an electrolytic process carried out in tanks containing dilute sulphuric acid and copper sulphate solution. This liquid mixture is the electrolyte and acts as a conductor for an electric current passing betweeen the anodes (slabs of impure copper suspended in the electrolyte) and the cathodes (thin sheets of pure copper). As the current passes, the anodes slowly dissolve away and pure metal is deposited on the thin cathodes which increase in size as the anodes dissolve.

Copper alloys

Brasses

The term 'brass' covers a wide range of copper-zinc alloys with a corresponding range of properties and applications. (See table 5.) Where the copper content exceeds 80 per cent, the alloy is known as *gilding metal* on account of its rich, golden colour. Apart from their uses in decorative work, the brasses find many applications in engineering, not only because of a marked resistance to corrosive elements, but because of the ease with which they can be rolled,

Table 5   Brasses (Copper-Zinc Alloys) Average Composition

Description	Percentage of copper	Percentage of zinc	Characteristics and uses
Gilding metal	85	15	Architectural metalwork and cheap jewellery on account of the golden colours and its ability to be brazed and enamelled.
Cartridge brass	70	30	A deep drawing brass with maximum ductility of the copper-zinc alloys. Used for cartridge cases, containers, headlamp reflectors, etc.
63/35 brass	65	35	A good cold-working alloy.
Basis brass	63	37	A general purpose brass, suitable for simple forming.
Muntz metal or Yellow metal	60	40	A hot working alloy which can also be cold worked to some extent. Used extensively in hot pressing of water fittings, household and engineering components.
Naval brass	62	37	Used largely in forgings. Tin reduces corrosion, especially from sea water. Lead is added when good machining properties also needed.
Admiralty brass	70	29 plus 1 per cent tin and small amount of arsenic.	A standard alloy for condenser tubes. Has very good corrosion resistance.
Free cutting brass (Leaded brass)	58 to 61	39 to 36 plus 2 to 3 per cent lead.	Suitable for high speed machining. The lead reduces ductility.

pressed, forged, extruded, drawn, cast, machined and joined by hard and soft solders.

The brasses fall broadly into two groups according to their hot or cold working properties, those with more than 63 per cent of copper being readily cold worked, whilst those with 60 per cent or less are suitable for hot working by pressing or forging.

A small percentage of lead in the 60/40 brass imparts free-cutting properties but leaded brasses are less ductile and where a brass is required for machining as well as hot pressing (water taps and other fittings) the lead content is reduced to reach a compromise.

Bronzes

The term 'bronze' covers a range of copper-tin alloys, but the term is used loosely to describe other copper based alloys. With a tin content of up to 10 per cent (and more) other elements are added to make bronzes such as *phosphor bronze* (5 to 6 per cent tin plus small amounts of phosphorus) which is used in making springs. Phosphor bronzes of higher tin contents (6 to 12 per cent) are used extensively in bearings and for engineering castings whilst bronze with a 20 per cent tin content is used in making bells.

Other bronze type alloys are the *gun-metals*, at one time used in gun barrels and these contain zinc and often lead also, to improve machining and anti-friction qualities. These leaded gun metals are used extensively in engineering in the manufacture of valves for steam or water.

Aluminium bronze

A copper aluminium alloy (without tin) is used in marine and general engineering work where resistance to corrosion, good strength and hardness are the conditions of service at high temperatures.

Manganese Bronze

Special 'brasses' of high tensile strength and with good resistance to corrosion contain manganese, tin, iron and aluminium.

Cupro-nickel alloys

A number of cupro-nickel alloys are in common use and with a nickel content of 5 per cent, greatly increased resistance to corrosion is exhibited. Above about 15 per cent nickel, the alloy has a grey-white colour and with a 25 per cent nickel content, the alloy is used in the present British 'silver' coinage. Cupro-nickel alloys are used in condenser tubes where high resistance to salt water corrosion is required. *Monel metal*, with 29 per cent copper, 68 per cent nickel and small quantities of iron and manganese, combines good mechanical properties with very good corrosion resistance and is used in chemical engineering plant and in internal combustion engine components subjected to high temperatures.

Forms and uses of copper

A large proportion of world production of copper is used in wire

Table 6 Bronzes and Gunmetals. Average Compositions

Description	Percentage of copper	Percentage of tin	Percentage of other elements	Remarks
Coinage alloy	95·5	3	1·5 Zn	Used in British 'copper' coinage.
Phosphor bronze	94·5	5·25	0·1 P	(Ordinary quality) Good elastic properties, good resistance to corrosion and corrosion fatigue. Used for springs and instrument parts. Also made with lower and higher phosphorus contents.
Phosphor bronze (Rods)	94	5·5	0·1 P	(Ordinary quality) Used mainly in a slightly work-hardened condition for engineering parts subjected to friction. High tin ph. bronze (8·25 per cent Sn) is an improvement on ordinary quality ph. bronze for manufacture of bearings.
Phosphor bronze (Free machining)	95	5	0·01 per cent P plus lead or other additions.	These alloys have machining qualities comparable with free cutting brass.
Phosphor bronze (for general purposes)	90	9·5	Remainder Zn Pb and P.	An alloy suitable for general sand castings. Other phosphor bronzes are made for the casting of bearings, gears, etc., in sand, die or chill castings.
Admiralty gunmetal	88 (approx.)	10	2 Zn 1·5 Pb 1·0 Ni	Gunmetals are widely used in pumps, valves and other sand castings, including statuary. Other gunmetals include nickel gunmetal and leaded gunmetals, the latter being used when optimum mechanical properties and pressure tightness are required.

drawing, mainly for electrical work, copper of high purity being an excellent conductor. In wire drawing, copper 'wire bars' are first rolled to form rods and these are drawn through tungsten carbide dies of progressively smaller diameters. Very fine wire is drawn through diamond dies.

Copper plates and sheets are rolled from slabs in hot rolling mills for the thicker gauges, but sheet is nearly always cold rolled and is finished very accurately to gauge under polished rollers. Hardening due to the rolling is adjusted to the various requirements of industry by partial or full annealing where necessary.

Copper has been used since the eighteenth century in the sheathing of wooden ships' hulls and this is very necessary in tropical waters to prevent attacks by the 'ship worm' (*teredo navalis*) which attains great sizes in these waters. Copper strip is used in roof coverings, flashings and damp courses and, in recent years, is being used more and more in domestic plumbing work, not only because of its resistance to corrosion and to frost damage, but also because of the ease with which joints and bends can be made up with pressed brass fittings. 'Strip' metal is of thin gauge and 450 mm or less in width and when less than 0·17 mm is known as 'foil'. This finds many uses in such things as the fins on car radiators and in printed circuits. Copper and copper alloy strip are used in many everyday items for domestic use for such things as headlamp reflectors, washers, gaskets, etc., and is used in the spinning of vessels of all shapes by forcing a disc against a former as both rotate in a *spinning lathe*. In the printing industry, copper alloy sheet is used in making printing plates by various processes.

Seamless copper tubes are made from cylindrical 'billets' which are pierced lengthwise to make 'tube shells'. These are pointed at one end and are then drawn through dies to the finished sizes, the bore being controlled by a steel plug held in place by a long rod attached to the draw bench. In modern practice, the plug is left floating (free) and it is then possible to draw some sizes of tube in very great lengths. Among the different sizes made are capillaries and sections of all kinds in copper and alloys, some are precision drawn for making microscopes, telescopes and musical instrument slides or as wave guides whilst another important use is in the form of printing rollers for the textile trades.

Rods, bars and sections are rolled, drawn or extruded. Drawing is done by *pulling* the cold metal through the hole in a die, and in extrusion, the metal is *pushed* through the orifice. Copper and its alloys can be used in sand or die casting of all kinds.

Powdered copper and its alloys are used in many ways, including paint manufacture, and in engineering, metal powders can be compacted in shaped moulds and fixed by sintering (roasting) and this method is used in making small bushes and bearings. Graphite powder, mixed in with the metallic powder, makes such bushes self-lubricating.

Lead

With a specific gravity of 11·3, lead is the heaviest of the common metals. It is very soft and malleable and is easily cut with hand-saw or knife. It has a silvery lustre when first cut but the surface quickly tarnishes in air, forming a protective oxide film. Lead is resistant to many acids, but oddly enough, is attacked by *pure* water.

The chief ore of lead is the 'galena' (lead sulphide) and it is found in many parts of the world. Lead ores are frequently associated with those of zinc and when found together, they are often dealt with by first separating them into concentrates by flotation but in the most modern practice, the two ores can be smelted at the same time.

Lead has a low melting point (330°C) and is an essential component in a number of alloys, for example, *plumber's* and *tinman's solders* in which it is alloyed with tin in varying proportions. *Pewter* is an alloy of one part of lead to four of tin, whilst *type metal* contains 45 to 70 per cent lead, the balance being made up of antimony and tin in varying proportions. A number of alloys of lead, tin, bismuth and cadmium are known as *fusible metals*, melting below 100°C and being used in such things as automatic fire sprinklers, temporary pipe fillings during bending operations, for dental work, etc. Lead is used in *bearing metals* (see opposite) and as an additive for improving the machining qualities of steel and brass.

Tin

Melting at 232°C, tin is a white metal showing a yellowish tinge. It is very malleable and can be rolled into tinfoil, but its main uses are in tin plating, mainly in the canning industry, and as an alloying element in bearing metals. It is, of course, also used in making the soft solders.

The chief ore is tinstone, found in Devon and Cornwall and at many places throughout the world although the main source is in Malaya. The ore is first crushed and the lighter gangue is removed by washing, after which it is roasted to get rid of the sulphur and arsenic. Reduction of the ore takes place readily and is brought about by heating a mixture of the ore, powdered anthracite and lime in a reverberatory furnace, the crude metal being drawn off into moulds. Refining is done by melting the metal and running it off from the dross after which, stirring brings any remaining slag to the surface for skimming.

An interesting characteristic of tin is the peculiar 'crinkling' noise known as 'tin cry' which can be heard if the metal is bent close to one's ear. This noise is due to the manner in which crystal deformation takes place.

Bearing metals

As a general rule, metals used in bearings (for rotating shafts and other engine components) are dissimilar to, and softer than the shaft itself and are mostly alloys containing a hard component in a soft matrix. The idea behind this is that whilst the hard metallic component will withstand wear, the softer matrix (or 'body') will yield under loading. This yielding tendency in the metal will help to prevent any seizure which might result from slight misalignments of the shaft in very hard bearing metals and it will also help to maintain the oil film under load. It is probable also, that the softer matrix, wearing slightly faster than the hard component, leaves minute recesses in which oil is retained.

White bearing metals may be either tin or lead base (according to which metal predominates in the alloy) the former being known as 'Babbitt' metals, after Isaac Babbitt, their original patentee. The tin base white metals are used in high duty bearings to withstand greater pressures and speeds whilst lead base metals are used under less exacting conditions. All of these alloys contain between 3·5 and 15 per cent of antimony which combines with most of the tin forming a compound which is the hard component in the alloy.

Bronze bearing metals are used where bearing loads are high, both phosphor bronze and plain tin bronze satisfying the requirements. *Sintered bronze* bearings and bushes are often used in low duty bearings, i.e. where the motion is intermittent such as in control mechanisms, or where speeds and loads are low. These are made from a mixture of powdered copper, tin and graphite which is heated and moulded under very great pressure to the required shape. The presence of the graphite makes the bearing 'self-lubricating'. *Leaded bronzes* are used in heavy duty bearings such as main bearings (crankshafts) in diesel and petrol engines. The *brasses* are frequently used in small, light-duty bearings for cheapness and also as backings in bronze bearing 'shells'.

Zinc

Zinc is a lustrous, bluish-white metal which shows a good resistance to atmospheric corrosion and this property is used to advantage in the galvanising of sheet iron ware, piping, wire, nails and so on, the coating of zinc being given by dipping in a molten zinc bath.

In addition to its use in the copper-zinc alloys, it is also used in a range of zinc base alloys for die casting. The alloys, containing zinc, copper and aluminium are used in a wide range of items, including carburetters, washing machine parts, model toys, etc.

Zinc ores are widely distributed throughout the world and much of the extraction is from the sulphide ores, often associated with lead, silver and sometimes gold. Lead and zinc concentrates are separated from each other after the finely crushed ore is turned to a pulp by mixing with water. Separation is brought about by flotation processes, the addition of certain chemical reagents and the aeration of the pulp causing, first, the lead to rise as a froth which is raked off, after which the addition of further reagents and continued aeration cause the zinc to rise. This froth also, is raked off.

The zinc concentrate is filtered and is then roasted to form a zinc oxide sinter which is then mixed with anthracite, bituminous coal and clay and pressed to form briquettes. These are pre-heated before charging into retorts from which zinc is obtained by *distillation*, zinc vapour passing from the retorts and cooling to form liquid zinc in the condensers. Refining involves a further distillation for the removal of cadmium, lead, iron and other impurities. In the distillation of zinc, heat is supplied to the retorts from the outside and the process is known as the 'vertical retort process'.

Reference has been made to the most modern method by which lead and zinc can be extracted simultaneouly and this is done in the *zinc blast-furnace*. Heat is supplied from inside the furnace, the charge consisting of coke and sinter. The separation of zinc and lead concentrates is unnecessary and whilst lead can be tapped from the bottom of the furnace, the zinc vapourises, passes from the top of the furnace and is condensed to metallic zinc. A certain amount of lead also vapourises and is condensed with the zinc, but the two are readily separated whilst molten because of their very different densities.

4

Foundry work

Manufacture of castings

This is yet another of the highly specialised branches of the engineering 'world' and embraces many skills, including those of the pattern-maker, the moulder, the core-maker, the furnace men or 'melters' and the metallurgists.

Castings are made in steel, iron, copper, brass, aluminium, bronze and most other alloys, foundries usually specialising in one metal or type of metal. In addition to the making of castings by running molten metal into sand moulds (*gravity casting*), pressure and gravity *die casting* and *centrifugal casting* are also employed. In die casting, metal moulds are used in making repetition, precision castings, whilst centrifugal casting is used in making pipes and similar things, the metal running into a rotating mould. This causes the metal to be thrown outwards and to spread over the profile of the mould.

Patterns

The pattern, usually made in wood, represents the first stage in the production of a casting, being used to form a cavity of the desired shape in sand which is firmly rammed around the pattern within the confines of two, and sometimes more, moulding boxes or 'flasks'. The pattern is removed from the sand mould and after certain preparations (described later) have been completed, molten metal is run into the cavity, forming a casting.

Foundry work involves many complex processes, especially in the making of patterns, cores and moulds for intricate shapes and although the description just given is divested of many important details, it summarises the processes in broad outline. It will also indicate that pattern-making and moulding are very closely tied and it is in fact difficult to talk about one without the other. The pattern-maker must always consider how the moulder will take the impression of the pattern, how it will be removed from the sand and how it will be moulded to produce a good casting, but before these things are discussed further it is necessary to understand a few basic facts about patterns and about moulding processes.

Contraction allowances All metals contract on cooling and solidifying, the amount varying with different metals. This contraction must be allowed for by making the pattern proportionately larger in every dimension and this is done by means of a *contraction rule* which is used in place of the normal standard rule. Since cast iron, for example, contracts approximately 2·5 mm in 300 mm, a length of 300 mm on a pattern would contract to 297·5 mm in the casting. This is a contraction of 1 in 120 and a rule for making

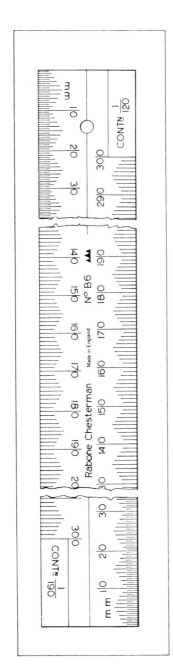

Figure 16   Contraction rule
(Rabone Chesterman Ltd.)

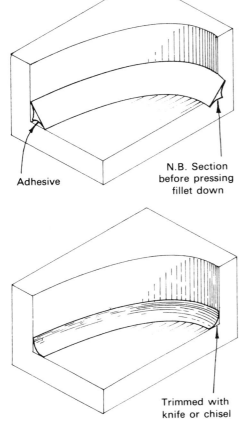

Adhesive

N.B. Section
before pressing
fillet down

Trimmed with
knife or chisel

Figure 17   The use of leather fillets in patterns

patterns for iron castings would be marked 'Contraction 1/120'. On this rule, a length of 302·5 mm would be divided into the sub-divisions found on a normal rule and contraction allowances are then automatic on every measurement.

Where a pattern is to be used repeatedly, it is often cast in metal to withstand wear and tear in the foundry, the metal pattern being made from a master pattern in wood. There will, of course, be two lots of contraction to allow for in making the master pattern and this double contraction is allowed for by using a rule which gives twice the normal allowance, for example, for cast iron, the representative fraction would be 1/60 instead of 1/120.

Taper or 'draft'   In order that patterns may be drawn from the sand without difficulty, they are given a slight taper or 'draft', also referred to sometimes as 'draw'.

Corners   Sharp internal corners are always avoided because they will cause a casting to crack. Internal radii on patterns can be formed by gluing on specially made leather fillets as in Fig. 17, or with plastic wood or plaster. Bees-wax can also be moulded in by melting it with a heated ball-end formed on a short rod.

Changes of section   Sudden changes of section or thickness are best avoided because uneven cooling may cause distortion or cracking. Very thin parts should be avoided because they may not cast cleanly and cooling more rapidly than the rest of a casting, they will become much harder.

Finish of the pattern   All surfaces of patterns should be accurately and finely finished with glass paper and then painted or varnished so that the smooth, hard surfaces give a clean draw from the sand and so that moisture is not absorbed, for this will cause the wood to swell and distort. Colour schemes for identifying parts of the pattern are always used and although some foundries have their own schemes, the colours are the subject of a British Standard Specification. In the iron foundry, black is used for surfaces to be left 'as cast', yellow indicates surfaces to be machined, whilst red is used to indicate core prints. These are explained later.

Machining Allowances   In addition to allowances for contraction, extra metal must be allowed for machining purposes. These allowances are always on the generous side to ensure that the 'as cast' skin can be removed, together with any small blemishes. for general purposes, an allowance of 3 mm for machining is satisfactory.

Manner of casting

Before he can start work, the pattern maker must consider the way in which his pattern is to be moulded and cast. Most times this is done in two flasks and the first decision is on the location of the joint line. Sometimes this is readily located (see Figs. 18 and 19), but there are no hard and fast rules, each case being decided by consideration of the external shape of the object, or by the locations of cavities or because of overhangs and projections.

The position of the pattern in the flask will often be influenced by the fact that the metal at the base of a casting will always be the least affected by impurities or by sand inclusions or by gases which will always rise to the top. Patterns are therefore made in such a way that important surfaces for machining can be moulded face downwards, e.g. lathe beds would almost certainly be moulded and cast upside down.

Moulding

Moulding practice falls into two main divisions, viz: (1) *green sand* and *dry sand* moulding, and (2) *loam* moulding. Within the scope of this book it will suffice to say that loam mouldings, made in a special sand mixture, are used in certain kinds of heavy iron casting and differ greatly from green and dry sand mouldings in that they are built up with the loam often coated over brickwork. The mould is formed or struck to the required shapes with contoured strickles or with sweeps which are rotated on a spindle for producing cylindrical forms.

Green sand moulding is so called because the sand is damp and has nothing to do with its colour. Green sand moulds can be *open* or *covered*, open sand moulds being made with the top surface of the casting exposed. This method is used when it is not necessary for the top of the casting to have a smooth surface. Covered sand moulds are made entirely within the two or more moulding boxes (or 'flasks') or with part of the mould formed in the floor and covered with a moulding box.

Dry sand moulding   Procedure is much the same as for green sand work, but a different sand mixture is used and, when complete, the mould is baked quite dry. This could not be done with green sand which would crumble if dried out. Dry sand moulds produce very clean castings and, because very little gas is generated, this is a safer method, especially with castings in steel at very high temperatures.

Foundry sands

Green foundry sands must fulfil certain conditions: viz: (1) they must have a good green bond, i.e., retain the moulded shape whilst moist, (2) they must be highly refractory, i.e., resistant to heat, and (3) they must not contain impurities which might cause scabbing of the casting surfaces.

Such sand will contain a high proportion of silica and its bonding quality will depend on the presence of some kind of clay material. When moist, the clay acts as the bonding agent for the sand grains. *Natural* moulding sands are those which are suitable as found and *synthetic* sands are sharp sands (clay-free) to which clay materials are added.

The moisture content of a green sand mould is of the utmost importance since an excess of moisture will make the sand impermeable, creating a dangerous situation when the molten metal is run into the mould. The sudden generation of steam which cannot escape through the sand, as it should do, may well cause molten metal to spurt back up the riser or runner. The very least that can happen is a casting ruined by blow holes.

In industrial foundries, moisture content is controlled in a preparation plant, but where one must rely on his judgement, water is sprayed a little at a time on to the sand heap whilst turning it over thoroughly. At intervals, a handful is squeezed firmly until the moisture content is such that the sand does not fall apart and when, on breaking it gently, it shows a clean break. It must be remembered that over-moist sand will pass this test and if there is any doubt, then dry sand must be worked in.

Core sand Specially selected sands are used in making cores of all shapes which are used inside moulds to form holes or recesses in castings. Core sands must possess the following qualities: (1) *green bond*, (2) *dry bond*, the property of holding a shape after drying completely, (3) *permeability*, i.e. it must allow any gases generated to pass away rapidly, and (4) it must collapse readily after casting so that cores can be removed easily.

Silica sands, which have no natural bond, are used in making *oil sands* for cores, dextrin and water being added to give a *green* bond. Linseed oil is also added, and whilst this gives no green bond, it oxidises and gives a *dry* bond when the core is baked, leaving the sand permeable and not so firmly bonded that it will not 'give' a little under pressure as the casting contracts on cooling, or so hard that it is difficult to remove later.

Facing sand A number of different materials are used to protect the faces of moulds against the action of molten metal and to help produce sound and smooth faces on the castings. Moulding sand is, of course, highly refractory but this can often be improved and metal penetration of the mould prevented by: (1) adding small proportions of such things as pitch, coke or coal dust to the facing

Figure 18   Cut-away of moulding boxes with moulding for a bracket casting complete

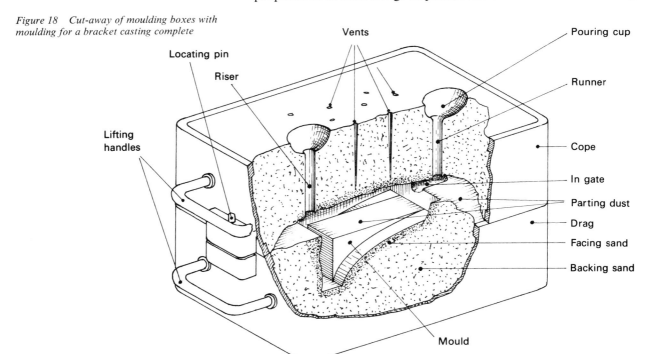

sand which comes into contact with the metal, or (2) by dressing the face of the mould after the pattern is removed, dusting on talc (French chalk) or by spraying or brushing on plumbago or zircon in the form of a liquid suspension. These materials are often inter-mixed for different purposes and one important effect is that gases are generated which prevent direct contact between metal and sand by forming a 'cushion' and leaving cleaner surfaces.

Green sand moulding

In Fig. 18 is shown a cut-away of a mould for a cast iron bracket, with the moulding boxes (cope and drag) assembled ready for pouring. Note the locating pins which ensure accurate registering of the two boxes. This bracket is a simple item which can be moulded in one box (the drag) and it will serve nicely for an explanation of a number of points in moulding practice, the sequence of the actual moulding operations being described later.

The disposal of the sand in the boxes is indicated in the drawing, *facing* sand around the cavity, *parting* sand (also known as parting 'dust' or 'powder') separating the contents of cope and drag, and a *backing* of foundry 'floor' sand filling the remaining space in each box. Metal is poured into the runner cup, and passing down the runner, enters the mould via the 'in-gate', the purpose of which is to ensure that the metal runs 'quietly' (without any turbulence) at a point where its flow will not be checked by the shape of the mould. A riser is not always employed in small castings but in large work it provides a feeder or reservoir to make good the shrinkage or 'drawing' in the casting as it cools. It also serves as a vent for steam and gases generated within the mould when pouring and gives a clear indication when the mould is full. Although the cups on runner and riser are shown formed in the moulding sand, they are often formed on top of the cope in general foundry work, a little sand being shaped with the fingers inside iron rings or 'bushes' placed over the holes. The extra height gives a little more 'head' for feeding into the mould. Additional venting for the escape of gases is provided by piercing the sand with a pointed wire, a number of small holes being made reaching almost to the cavity.

Moulding procedure

A sketch of the pattern for this casting is shown in Fig. 19, with all the tapers exaggerated for clarity. The pattern is placed face down on a moulding board and the lower half of the box is placed over it. upside down. Both pattern and board are dusted with parting sand which is very fine, dry sea sand, burnt sand or bone dust, the essential feature being that it has no bond at all and thus prevents the moulding sand from adhering. This is followed by a layer of facing sand, riddled (sieved) over and around the pattern to form an even layer all over it. The box is then part filled with foundry sand and, taking care not to disturb the facing sand, is rammed evenly with the pegging rammer, shown in Fig. 20. This will leave irregular and broken surfaces which will bond readily with the next lot of sand added. If the sand is rammed flat the layers will

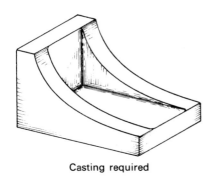

Casting required

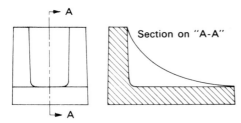

Section on "A-A"

Elevations of pattern showing draft (taper) and rounding of internal corners

Figure 19   Casting and pattern

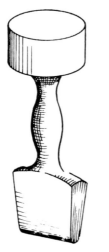

Figure 20   Rammer

The pegging rammer (wedge shape) is used in ramming up the box evenly. The flat rammer is used before strickling off

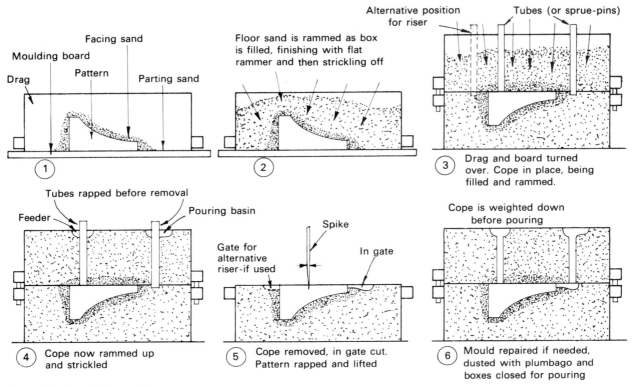

Figure 21 *Stages in the moulding process*
Runner and riser can be cut with thin-walled tubes
after the cope is rammed

not bond and will fall apart when the boxes are turned over.
Finally, with the box a little over full, the sand is rammed quite
firm and the excess is strickled off by drawing a straight-edge over
the box.

Care must be taken not to pack the sand too hard or its
permeability will be reduced and gases will be trapped and cause
blow holes in the casting. Over-firm ramming will also cause
scabbing of the casting surfaces. On the other hand, over-soft
ramming will give poor definition in the mould which may break
when the pattern is drawn or the flow of metal may scour away the
mould shape. Experience is undoubtedly the best teacher in the art
of packing the sand to the right density.

The next step in the moulding process is to turn both the board

Figure 22   A. *Un-fettled casting*
          B. *Sprue pins*

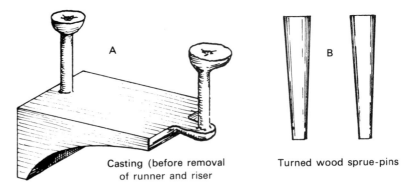

Figure 23   A. Rapping plate
B. Pair of dowel plates

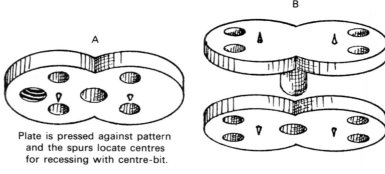

Plate is pressed against pattern
and the spurs locate centres
for recessing with centre-bit.

Plates are turned to show
the centre spurs

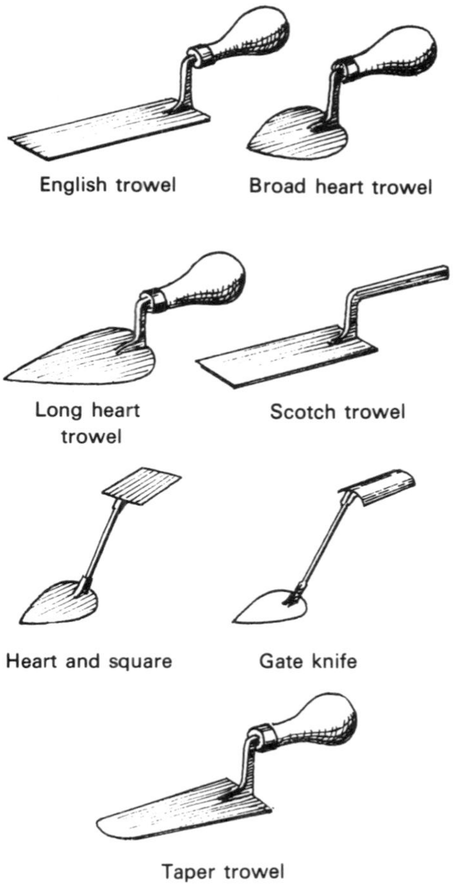

and box over together and on removing the board, the pattern will be seen lying flush with the sand face. Loose sand is blown away with the hand bellows, the cope is placed in position and the joint face is dusted with parting sand. This is followed by a layer of facing sand, riddled over the pattern. A piece of tube (or a sprue pin, seen in Fig. 22) is then positioned to form a runner, being pressed a short way into the drag sand and a short distance away from the pattern. Another tube or sprue pin to form a riser, is rested on top of the pattern as the backing sand is shovelled in and rammed. The box is rammed up as before and is finally strickled off and then, using a spoon tool, a pouring cup or basin is formed around the runner tube whilst a feeder of similar shape is made around the riser. The tubes (or sprue pins) are then withdrawn carefully, rapping them lightly to loosen them. Any sharp edges in the pouring cup are smoothed out so that there is no chance of loose sand being washed in with the metal. The cope is then lifted off and placed upside down, very gently on the bench.

The riser tube will have left an impression in the sand in the drag and from this point, the in-gate is cut with the gate knife. The pattern is now ready for removal, but first it must be eased a little in the mould to ensure that it is quite free and can be lifted cleanly. This easing is done by rapping, and for light patterns, a sharpened steel rod can be pressed into the top surface and as this is rapped lightly all round, the pattern will be seen to move slightly and it can then be lifted out. For handling heavier work, brass rapping plates are sunk in flush with the pattern face and in addition to having plain holes for rapping, they are also provided with tapped holes into which lifting hooks can be screwed. It would be far too risky to try lifting large patterns with spikes. The mould can then be repaired where required, using the tools shown in Fig. 24 and any loose sand can be removed with the bellows, taking care not to damage the mould with the nozzle or violent 'blasting'. The mould is then sprayed or brushed with the appropriate coating, the two parts of the box are reassembled on the foundry floor to await pouring, until which time both runner and riser are covered over. Where no securing devices are provided on the boxes, the cope is heavily weighted down to prevent any lift which comes from the head of metal inside.

Figure 24   Moulders' tools

English trowel

Broad heart trowel

Long heart
trowel

Scotch trowel

Heart and square

Gate knife

Taper trowel

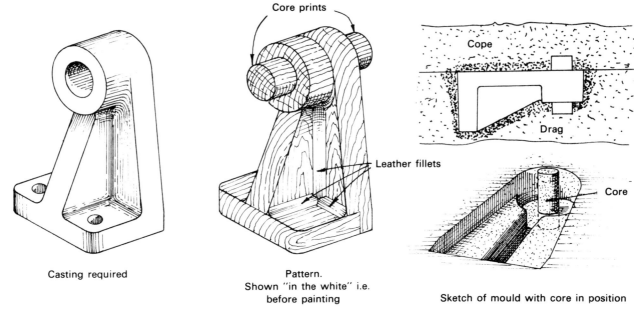

Core prints

Cope

Drag

Leather fillets

Core

Casting required

Pattern.
Shown "in the white" i.e.
before painting

Sketch of mould with core in position

Figure 25   Examples of casting requiring a core

The casting shown in Fig. 25 resembles the one just dealt with in that it is a 'flat back' pattern and can be moulded in one box. There is, however, a boss through which a hole is required as a journal for a shaft, the hole being cast under-size and then machined out. Now the sketch of the pattern does not show a hole, but instead there are *core-prints* standing out on each side. These prints form recesses in the sand in both top and bottom boxes and these recesses are used to position a *core* which forms a hole in the casting. The core can be seen in position, in the sketch. A core such as this would be cut from a stick, these being supplied ready made in standard diameters from 12 to 150 mm or so. Other non-standard cores require forming for each job and the way in which this is done is described later.

Split patterns
The moulding of patterns in one box is limited to items such as the angle bracket already dealt with, i.e. with one large flat face which can conveniently be arranged to coincide with the joint faces of the boxes. Where the shape is more involved, the pattern is moulded in two (and sometimes more) boxes, with the joint coming at some convenient sectional plane. The pattern is generally divided ('split') along this plane, the parts being accurately located one on the other by means of metal dowel pins.

An example which requires a split pattern is shown in Fig. 26, in which is shown the required casting together with the split pattern, and in Fig. 27 is shown the split core box for this job, together with the core which it will produce. Note the vent which is formed right through the core so that gases formed therein can escape freely.

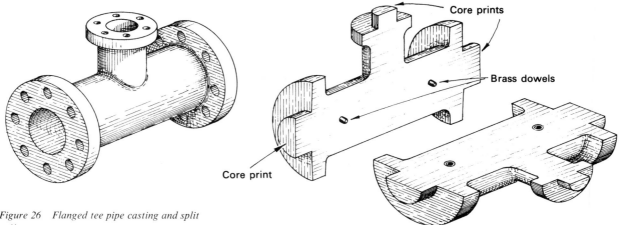

Figure 26   Flanged tee pipe casting and split pattern

The moulding process is straight-forward. The pattern section without pins is first inverted on the board and the drag half of the box, also inverted, is filled and rammed up in the manner already described. Both box and board are turned over together and the board is removed. The other section of the pattern is put in position, the cope is added and filled and rammed up, with tubes or sprue pins to form runner and riser. After separating cope and drag, the in-gate is cut and the pattern sections rapped and lifted. Any repairs necessary are made to the mould and the core is placed in position, checking that it does in fact enter fully half-way. Loose sand grains are blown clear with the bellows. A continuation of the core vent is made by scoring small channels along the joint face at each end so that gases can escape freely. This method of scoring shallow channels in the joint face is also used to provide vents for castings and is sometimes done by trapping pieces of twine between the two boxes when they are finally closed. The pieces of twine are drawn out before weighting or locking the boxes and each piece forms a clear vent.

Figure 27   Split core box and core for casting in Fig. 26

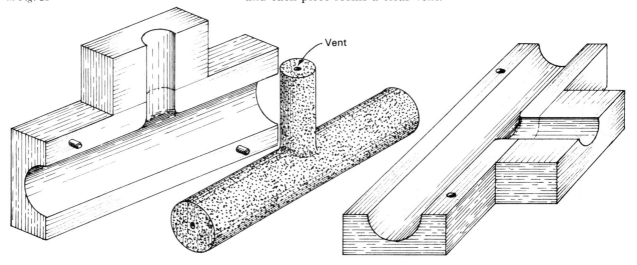

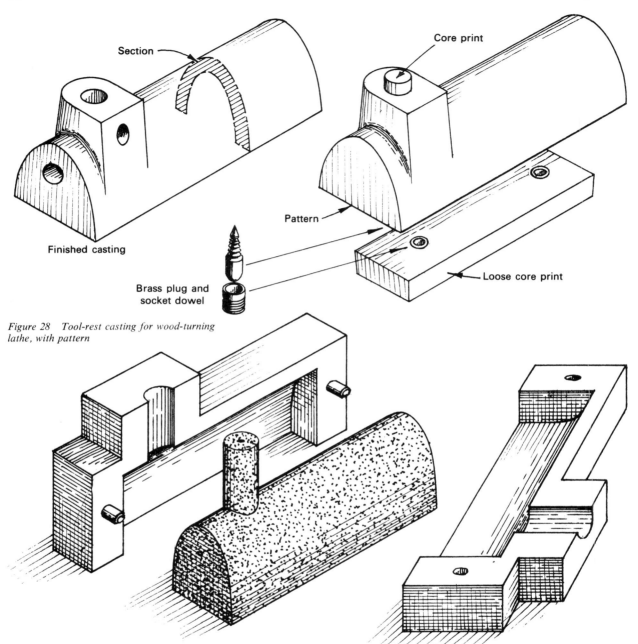

Section

Core print

Pattern

Loose core print

Finished casting

Brass plug and
socket dowel

*Figure 28   Tool-rest casting for wood-turning
lathe, with pattern*

*Figure 29   Split core box and core for lathe tool-
rest. See Fig. 28*

In Fig. 28 is a drawing of a tool-rest casting for a wood-turning lathe, together with its pattern, and in Fig. 29 are shown the core box and the core produced. It will be noticed that only one of the holes required in the casting is cored, the others being left for drilling out. These other holes could, of course, be cored, but it would mean a lot of extra work in the core box and extra trouble in making the core. The pattern would also need to be split so that the core could be entered in the mould. Balanced against the few extra minutes needed to originate the holes by drilling, this extra work on the pattern and core box is not really justified on a job which is not exactly mass production work.

Cores and core boxes

Core boxes need special care in their making, not only in the provision of taper so that the core can be removed easily, but also as regards dimensions since the core must fit exactly into the recess left by the core print in the moulding sand.

The core box shown for the lathe tool-rest is a 'turn over' box in which the core sand is rammed firmly and then strickled off. Vents are formed by piercing or by including wires when ramming up and then withdrawing them. A core plate (usually of cast iron), is placed on top of the box and both are turned over. The box is rapped and lifted off, leaving the core on the plate, ready for drying or 'stoving'. Small cores are often rammed up with short lengths of wire in them to act as reinforcement whilst large cores are strengthened with 'grids' of cast iron, 'special made' for each core shape. Where the venting in a core cannot easily be done by piercing, it is often accomplished by including a special waxed string as the core is rammed. When the core is stoved, the wax melts, leaving a vent hole from which the strands of cotton are withdrawn easily.

Oil sand cores have been replaced to a great extent by a core material which can be hardened whilst still in the core box. The sand contains sodium silicate, and after the core is rammed, carbon dioxide is blown through the core box and a chemical reaction hardens the core which does not require drying.

Cods

It is not always necessary to use dried cores for forming holes or recesses, and in Fig. 30 is an example in which a sand projection is formed by the pattern as it is moulded, the projection being known as a 'cod'. A cod can be formed in either cope or drag and in some cases it is better in the top of the mould because venting can be arranged to better effect there. In all but the smallest cods formed in the cope, some kind of reinforcement is needed to give support and this must be arranged to suit each individual job. In the industrial foundry, the reinforcement is usually made in cast iron.

Figure 30   Section through mould, showing a cod

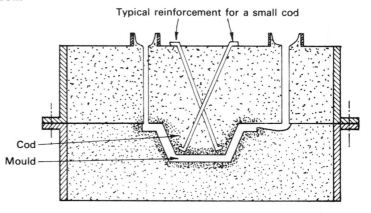

Typical reinforcement for a small cod

Cod

Mould

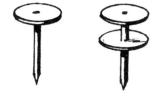

Pipe nail and spiked stud for pressing
into side of mould

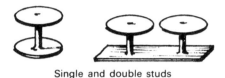

Single and double studs

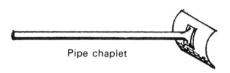

Pipe chaplet

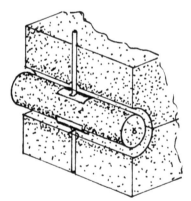

Cut-away of mould to show
how pipe chaplets can be used

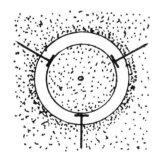

Pipe nails (or spiked studs) can
be used to hold a vertical core

Figure 31   A small selection of chaplets

Chaplets

It is always necessary to guard against the movement of cores and in many cases, the core itself is strong enough to resist the tendency to float when the metal is poured, whilst ample core prints hold it in position. With long, or slender cores, or where perhaps a core can be located with only one print, it is necessary to hold it in place by other means and this is done with chaplets. These are, in effect, distance pieces made of metal. Many kinds of chaplet are used and a selection is shown in Fig. 31. All require careful fitting so that they just bridge the gap between mould and core without damaging either.

Loose pieces

It is often necessary to incorporate loose pieces in patterns in order to mould over-hanging parts which would otherwise prevent the pattern from drawing without breaking the mould. An example of such a pattern is shown in Fig. 32. The example is 'typical' and does not represent any particular component. The pattern would be moulded with the loose parts in position, and on drawing, these pieces would remain in the mould, being removed later with a sharp spike or with the fingers.

Plate moulding

A great saving of time is effected by the use of plate moulds in repetition work. The split pattern is mounted, one part on each side of a pattern plate of wood or metal and this plate is sandwiched between the cope and drag when moulding. The plate over-hangs the box sides for ease of lifting and is located by the box pins which pass through suitably placed holes. With cope, drag and plate assembled, the drag is moulded in the usual way, with parting, facing and backing sands, is rammed up and strickled off. The assembly is then turned over and the cope is rammed up, and when the boxes are separated and the plate removed, the two halves of the mould will match exactly. Because of the difficulty of drawing the cope away cleanly from the pattern in hand moulding, the double sided plate is used only where the top half of the pattern does not stand very high and involves a shallow draw. Where both halves of the pattern involve deep draws, it is better to use two separate plates with one half of the pattern on each.

Where large numbers of small castings are required, several castings can be made as a 'spray' on the same plate as in Fig. 34, runner, in-gate (and sometimes a channel where the patterns are in line), are also mounted on the plate and are moulded at the same time.

Much of the hard work of moulding is done nowadays by machine moulding, boxes being rammed by squeezing or by jolting under power. Turning over and the withdrawal of pattern plates is also an automatic process. This subject cannot be pursued further here, but it will be of interest to know that such mechanical aids exist.

Figure 32   Pattern with loose-pieces

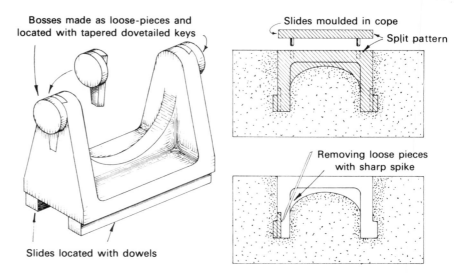

Bosses made as loose-pieces and located with tapered dovetailed keys

Slides moulded in cope

Split pattern

Removing loose pieces with sharp spike

Slides located with dowels

Figure 33   Plate moulding

Where both halves of a pattern involve a deep draw, they are mounted on separate plates

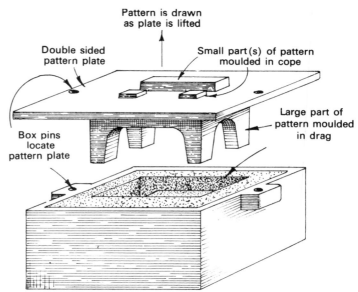

Pattern is drawn as plate is lifted

Double sided pattern plate

Small part(s) of pattern moulded in cope

Box pins locate pattern plate

Large part of pattern moulded in drag

Figure 34   Plate moulding with 'spray' patterns

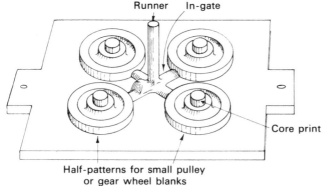

Runner   In-gate

Core print

Half-patterns for small pulley or gear wheel blanks

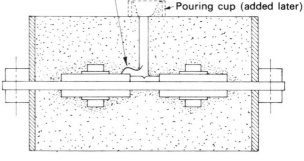

Trap for sand inclusions (when no riser is used)

Pouring cup (added later)

Box is sectioned to show plate and patterns

(1) Odd-side (drag) is rammed up and strickled off.
(2) Pattern is bedded in to joint-line at both
ends. (3) Joint face is then made up and
trowelled off firmly to joint line along handle

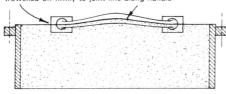

Odd-side (drag)

(4) Cope is positioned and is rammed up properly
i.e. parting sand, facing sand and backing

Pattern shown 'solid' for clarity

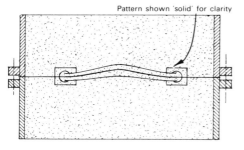

(5) Both boxes are turned over, odd-side is removed and
knocked out. (6) Drag is replaced and properly rammed
up. (7) Runner can be moulded with sprue-pin or cut
with a tube, with in-gate behind the hand-grip.

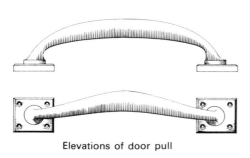

Elevations of door pull

Figure 35   Example of the use of an odd side

Odd sides

It is not always essential to use split patterns for moulding in two boxes for it is possible to make a mould from a one-piece pattern and in some cases it is the only way in which a mould can be made. The process involves the making of an odd side, the purpose of which is to support the pattern up to its joint line, in sand or any other convenient material, whilst the other part of the pattern is moulded.

An example is shown in Fig. 35 in which the joint line is not in a flat plane and moulding procedure would be as follows. The drag is rammed up with floor sand and is strickled off level at the joint. A suitable recess is then made in the sand and the pattern is bedded in, the sand face being formed up to the joint line, trowelling it neatly and firmly exactly half way. The cope is then put in position and normal moulding procedure is followed. The runner can be moulded with a sprue pin or tube. Both boxes are then turned over, the odd side is lifted off and the sand is knocked out. The drag is then replaced and normal moulding procedure followed once again and after strickling, both boxes are turned over and the cope is lifted off. The pattern is removed after cutting the in-gate and the mould prepared for closing in readiness for casting.

Fettling

When cold, moulding boxes are knocked out and the castings are fettled, i.e. they are cleaned, cores are broken out and unwanted metal is removed, viz: runners, risers and flashes. A 'flash' is formed when metal creeps between the moulding sand faces. Fettling is an important stage in the preparation of castings for the machine shop and large foundries always have fettling shops, specially equipped with mechanical aids for this work. Large castings are often cleaned by pressure washing and by shot blasting. In the small foundry, wire brushes, old files and hack saws will be much in evidence for this work.

Melting

In the melting of non-ferrous metals, crucible furnaces heated by gas, oil or coke may be employed or they may be of the indirect arc type, (usually tilting furnaces) depending on the capacity of the foundry and the metals melted. Small gas-fired crucible furnaces are available and are suitable for the small shop in melting in small quantities from ingot or scrap.

It is important that the metal is at the right temperature before pouring and this is checked in the crucible by means of a pyrometer which is a high temperature thermometer. There are several kinds of pyrometer and, of these, two in common use are: (1) the thermo-electric pyrometer, and (2) the optical pyrometer. The first applies the principle that when two wires of dissimilar metals are joined together to make a complete circuit, a difference in temperatures at the two junctions will cause an electric current to flow in the circuit. At the 'hot' junction, which is inserted in the hot metal, the wires are joined by welding and at the 'cold' junction (at the instrument end of the circuit) the connection is made through a galvanometer so that any current passing will register on the instrument which is calibrated to read in degrees of temperature and not in electrical units. The greater the difference between the temperatures of the hot and the cold junctions, the heavier the current will be, giving a higher reading and vice versa. In the optical pyrometer, the light emitted from a furnace or from molten metal is viewed through a telescope and is compared with the filament of an electric lamp which is alight in the path of the rays from the light source. The brilliance of the filament can be varied by means of a

Figure 36A   Foundry cupola

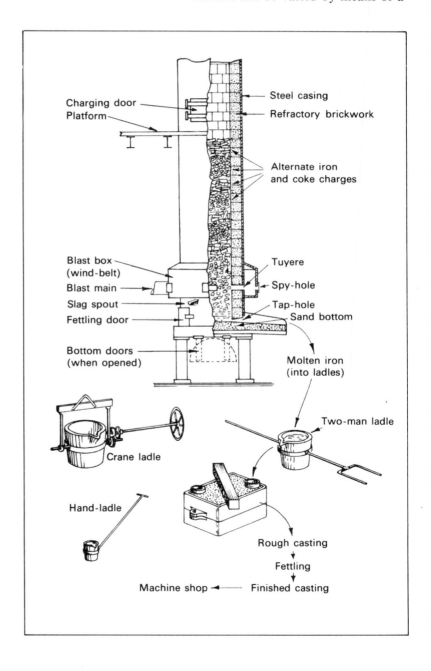

resistance and when the light intensities from both sources are equal, the filament disappears. A milliammeter, graduated in degrees of temperature, measures the current passing through the filament and gives a temperature reading.

The cupola is used in melting iron and its construction is shown in Fig. 36A. It resembles a small blast furnace but it does not work continuously, generally being used to produce daily melts according to the capacity of the foundry. Cupolas are usually operated in pairs so that maintenance can be carried out on one whilst the other is at work. The metal charge is of pig- and scrap-iron with steel-scrap included to help control the final carbon content by dilution. Small quantities of limestone are included in the charge to form a slag and any additives required to adjust the analysis of the iron are included in the ladle when tapping.

Figure 36B   Life-out furnace suitable for use in schools
(William Allday and Co. Ltd.)

5

Forgework

The effects of the hot working of steel have been discussed in Chapters 1 and 2, and in hand-forging the same things happen, but on a much smaller scale, of course. In forming and bending the metal whilst hot, its grain is made to follow the shape of the article and is not interrupted or severed. This is important in items which have to withstand stresses and examples of the effect of hot working on grain flow are shown in Fig. 37.

Figure 37   Three items cut from the solid, compared with the same things made by forging
Note the continuity of grain-flow in the right-hand drawings

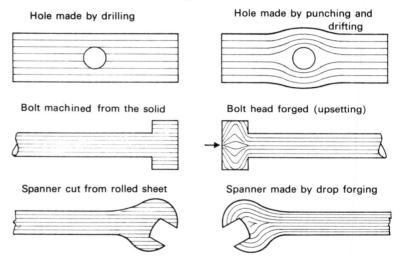

A great variety of items such as engine components and tools of all kinds, too complicated or too large to be hand-forged are made by drop-forging in which a billet of hot steel is squeezed to shape in two half moulds or 'dies'. One of these is stationary at floor level whilst the other, inverted and attached to the 'tup' or ram, takes the place of the hammer. The tup, often of many tonnes weight, slides between vertical guides and is dropped from a considerable height on to the billet in the bottom die. The metal is squeezed at each drop until it completely fills the cavity between the dies. A small gap is left between the die faces so that surplus metal can be squeezed out to form a 'flash' which is removed later.

Hand-forging equipment

The forge
The forge shown in Fig. 38 (B) is constructed in mild steel angles and sheet. The firepan (or hearth) is one metre square and 267 mm deep. The forge is fitted with a motor driven fan with a variable speed control and a slide valve for precise control of the blast. The larger

58

Forgework

A

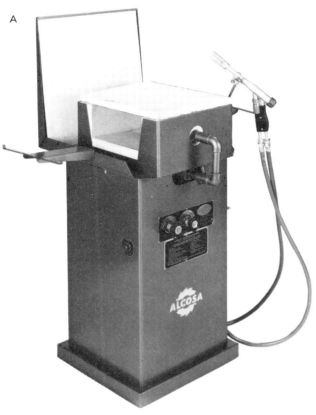

Figure 38   A. Gas-operated forge
B. Forge
(William Allday and Co. Ltd.)

forges can be obtained with movable gap pieces at the sides so that long pieces of metal can be placed correctly in the fire without being tilted.

Also shown in Fig. 38 (A) is an Alcosa gas-operated forge which can be used as an open-topped forge or as a closed heating chamber that can be adapted for large or small jobs by a suitable rearrangement of the fire-bricks inside.

The blast and tuyere

By directing a controlled air-blast through the fire the rate of combustion can be increased and governed, high temperatures being reached very quickly by this means. The blast-pipe, called a tuyere or 'tue iron' can be of the 'wet' or 'dry' type. The wet tuyere is commonly used today and is water jacketed so that it can withstand the high temperatures for lengthy periods before it becomes burnt out, always provided that it is looked after properly. The water jacket is connected to a water tank called the 'bosh' situated at the back of the hearth. The bosh should be kept covered to keep out dust.

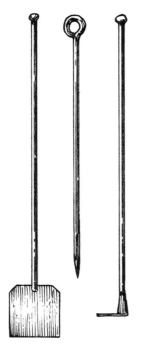

Figure 39 Smith's fire tools: slice, poker, rake

The Smith's fire

Before lighting the fire the water bosh should be topped up to within about 25 mm of the top and then a hollow is raked out in front of the tuyere, removing any clinker and ash. A few small balls of paper can be lit in the hollow and a handful of small kindling wood added. As soon as the wood is well alight, a very gentle blast can be turned on and fuel added a little at a time to build up the fire. Too fierce a blast may well blow the fire out at this stage, all that is required is a little patience whilst the fuel ignites.

As soon as the fire has a good heart, it can be built up over the tuyere, moving in fresh fuel with the rake and tamping it with the slice to form a blast barrier around the fire.

For most jobs, only part of the hearth is required for the fire and the remaining space can be filled with sand, coal- or coke-dust or even earth.

Fuels Several fuels are used: (1) coke breeze, which is the least costly, (2) smithy coal, a sulphur-free anthracite which burns readily and fiercely, and (3) Avenue (Sunbrite) beans, which are pellets made in two sizes and readily available in the UK.

Fire management During working, fresh fuel is raked to the middle to prevent a 'hollow fire' from forming as the heart burns away and since the cavity is often concealed by a crust of part-burned fuel, some gentle tamping with rake or slice is needed. Metal cannot be heated properly in a hollow fire because cold air will be blowing on to it. In addition, the blast, which should be diffused throughout the fire, will be concentrated on a small area giving intense local heating and hastening the formation of clinker. This will often adhere to the work in a treacly mass or perhaps accumulate round the tuyere and obstruct the blast.

It is good practice to turn off the blast at intervals during lengthy operation so that clinker can be raked out. An over-fierce blast with a small fire will make clinker form rapidly.

The anvil

This, the most important piece of equipment in the smithy, is made in two patterns. The *London* and the *Double Bick* anvils. A London anvil of 50 kg weight is quite suitable for the school handicraft room. The anvil is made of cast iron and has a hardened

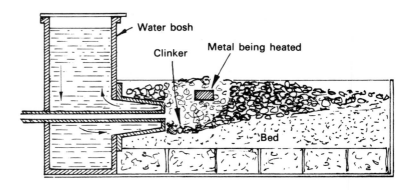

Figure 40 Section through hearth and fire
Note point at which clinker forms

Figure 41   The London anvil

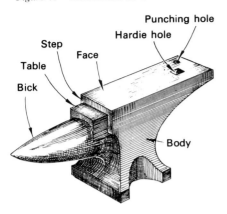

working face and this should always be kept clean. It should not be used for cutting or chiselling of any kind to avoid damaging the surface. At the arch end of the anvil are the punch and hardie holes, the first being there to receive the punch when holes are being made right through the metal, whilst the hardie hole, which is square, is used for holding various square shanked tools, viz., the hardie, the bottom fuller, the bottom swage and others.

One corner of the anvil face, near the bick, is rounded slightly so that bends can be made without the corner cutting into the metal. Just below the working face is the step or cutting table which is used mainly for cutting or chiselling, and being of softer metal, it does not damage the tool edge when metal is being cut right through.

The bick, or 'beak', tapers to a point but it is not a true cone. It is used in forming all kinds of bends and is particularly useful in forming rings or 'eyes'.

The leg vice

Being of robust construction, the leg vice is an essential in the smithy for the sort of jobs that would quickly spoil a fitter's vice. Located within easy reach, it should be fixed to a free-standing tripod-bench made specially for this purpose. The leg gives increased rigidity and transmits the shock of hammering to the floor. It is an integral part of a simple and robust construction.

Figure 42   Leg vice and tripod stand

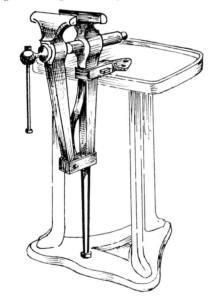

The swage block

On a heavy metal stand which raises it to a convenient working height, the swage block is one of the basic pieces of equipment. It is made in cast iron and has vee and half-round grooves on all four sides to accommodate different sizes and sections whilst the flat face is pierced right through with holes of various shapes and sizes. These holes are used to hold the stock whilst bending and other operations are carried out.

Metals used by the smith

Figure 43   Swage block and stand

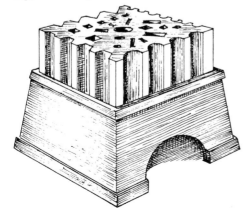

Although some of the smith's work will be in medium and high carbon steels, the greatest part will be in mild steel, used nowadays in place of the wrought iron of former years. The fact that decorative work is still referred to as 'wrought iron work' is not a misnomer, since the word 'wrought' means that the metal has been worked in some way, e.g., under the hammer.

The medium carbon steels are used where better mechanical properties are required and they are commonly used in drop forging. The hand forging of high carbon steel calls for special care since there is a restricted temperature range and the metal must not be heated above a cherry red or it will be spoiled. This steel should not be quenched during working or it will be left dead hard and may fracture.

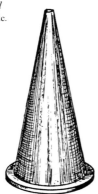

Figure 44   Floor mandrel
for truing up rings, hoops, etc.

Working heats

The correct judgement of temperatures is not made easier by their different appearances on bright or dull days or by artificial light. For this reason, the forge should always be sited away from large windows and in a place where the overall lighting is likely to remain fairly constant and not too bright. Under these conditions, the following may be taken as a guide:

Red heat   This is used for making easy bends in mild steel and for forging high carbon steels.

Cherry red heat   At this heat simple forging operations can be carried out on mild steel, for example, hot cutting and light punching. High carbon steels must not be raised above cherry red or they will lose their special properties.

Bright cherry red or near yellow   All principal forging operations are carried out at this heat on mild steel and wrought iron, viz., drawing down, upsetting, swaging, fullering and heavy punching.

Welding heat   As the metal approaches white heat, it becomes plastic or 'pasty' and is in a condition suitable for joining together by quickly hammering together on the anvil.

A few basic facts must always be borne in mind.

1. High carbon steels have restricted working heat ranges.
2. Too many heats in any ferrous metal will cause some deterioration, especially with the high carbon steels.
3. Very flat or gentle bends require less heat than that needed for extensive changes in section or size.
4. Even heating will help in making even bends.
5. Small sections will heat rapidly and will quickly burn if left in the fire too long.
6. The heating of work containing large and small sections must be done slowly to avoid burning of the small parts.
7. No time should be lost in transferring the work to the anvil and in getting the hammer at work.
8. At the risk of over-stating the obvious, the student is reminded that metal does not have to be red hot to cause severe injury. When the fire is alight, *all* metal lying on or around the forge is suspect.

Hand tools and basic processes

Apart from his marking out and measuring tools, the smith's hand tools can be divided into two broad groups, viz.: those which he can use on his own and those which need the assistance of a second person, his 'striker'.

Measuring and marking out tools

These are few in number and simple in form, viz.:

Rule   Usually 600 mm in length with a centre pivot and made of brass which is used because a steel rule would soon lose its temper and would become rusty through contact with water and hot metal.

Square Made in flat steel in a range of sizes up to 600 mm by 900 mm, usually with dimensions on each arm.

Centre punch Similar to the engineer's punch but much heavier as it is struck heavily to leave a large dot which can be seen easily when the metal is hot.

Calipers Of a large pattern, these are usually double-ended with one large and one small pair of jaws.

Tongs

Tongs are used when it is not possible to hold the work in the hand. In selecting a pair of tongs it is important to see that they really do grip the metal firmly and are not too large. If they are to be used for any length of time the strain on the hand can be relieved by slipping a ring over the handles to hold them together tightly.

Figure 45 Blacksmith's tongs

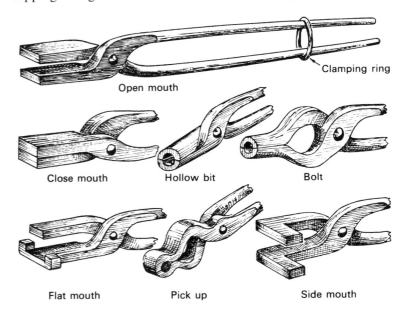

Clamping ring

Open mouth

Close mouth   Hollow bit   Bolt

Flat mouth   Pick up   Side mouth

Hammers

Two types of hammer are used at the forge, viz.: (1) the hand hammer, used when the smith is working alone, and (2) the sledge hammer, used by the striker when handling large work or when certain two-handed tools are in use. Hand hammers are made with ball, cross or straight pane (or 'pein') and from 900 to 1800 g in weight, whilst sledge hammers range from 1800 g upwards, a 3 kg sledge being of quite a useful weight where no very heavy work is undertaken. Hammers with split or unsound shafts or with heads which are loose or spreading are a source of danger and should not be used.

Setts

These are a special form of chisel (with handle or 'haft') for cutting metal with the aid of sledge, the sett being held in position by the smith whilst it is struck. Setts are made in two forms, viz.:

Figure 46   Smith's hammers

Sledge hammer heads

Double faced

Straight pein
(if holed as dotted, it
is a cross pein.)

Ball pein

the *hot* and the *cold* setts and they are for cutting hot or cold metals, respectively. The hot sett is ground to a cutting-angle of 30° with a slightly convex edge and is left untempered, this condition being quickly brought about by its contact with hot metal. This cutting-angle is quite suitable for cutting hot metal which is, of course, soft. The cold sett is more robust, is ground with a cutting-angle of 60° and is hardened and tempered to enable it to cut cold metal without fracturing.

Both the hot and cold setts can be used in conjunction with the *hardie*, as shown in Fig. 47, or the metal can be held flat on the anvil. No attempt is made to cut right through the metal, it is 'nicked' as deeply as possible (on all four sides if of large section) and is then broken apart.

Setts are often fitted with stout wire handles but the wooden haft is more satisfactory as it is rigid and the operator can place the tool more accurately and quickly. The smith often uses hand chisels for cutting small stock, those for hot cutting being much longer so that the hand can be kept well away from the work. Small stock can, if necessary, be cut right through on the anvil step.

Figure 47   A. Cutting with hot sett and hardie
B. Cutting on the hardie
C. Cutting-angles

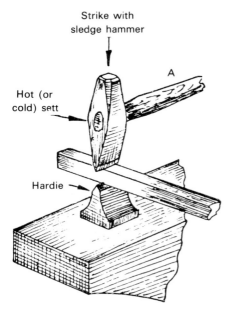

Strike with
sledge hammer

Hot (or
cold) sett

A

Hardie

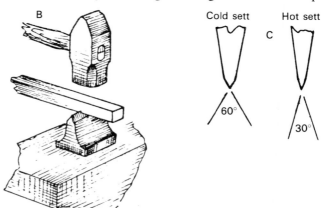

B

Cold sett   Hot sett

C

60°

30°

Figure 48   Upsetting

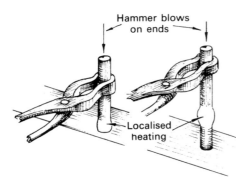

Upsetting

Also known as 'jumping up', this process is used for thickening the section of a bar and can be done at the end or anywhere along the length. The metal is brought to a full yellow heat at the desired point of upsett and the excess of heated metal quenched off. The bar is then bounced firmly, end-on, on the anvil which causes the metal to bulge all round. Alternatively, the bar can be held in the pick-up tongs and with one end on the anvil, the other is struck with the hammer. Upsetting is used for 'gaining' metal at any point for further forging; e.g., where a bar is to be spread (increased in width) without losing thickness or for making bends with sharp exterior angles.

Bending

A bright cherry red heat is necessary for satisfactory bending. Fig. 49 shows a right-angled bend being formed over the anvil and as with all forge work, this should be done with as little hammering as possible to avoid thinning the metal. The position of the bend can be located by marking with a chalk line which will show clearly enough when the metal is hot. Only a short portion needs to be heated, any great excess of hot metal being quenched off.

Figure 49   Forming a right-angled bend and the effects of bending

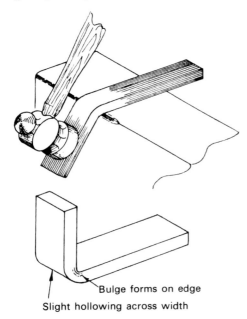

With the bar held flat on the anvil and square across it the end of the bar is quickly pushed downwards with the hammer face and the bend tidied up with a few light hammer blows, square to the anvil face and side. Care must be taken not to strike on to the corner of the anvil, for the stretching of the metal on the outside of the bend will already have reduced the thickness a little and this will make it worse.

If a sharp external angle is required then more metal must be worked up to the point at which the bend is to be made. This can be done by first upsetting and then moving the extra metal to the outside. On making the bend the extra metal in the bulge can be used to form the sharp corner. This is shown in Fig. 50. Bends in small sections can be made by gripping the hot bar in the leg vice, the bar is then pulled round with the tongs or by hand and the bend hammered lightly into shape. Right-angled bends can be checked with the smith's square and other angles by laying the job on a chalk-drawn angle on the bench top or with a sheet metal template.

Figure 50   Forging a sharp right-angled bend

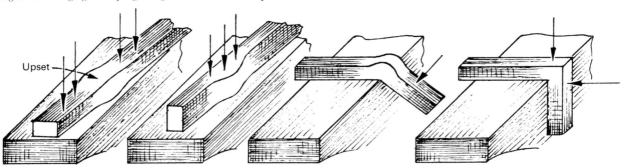

Work is hammered as indicated by arrows

Figure 51   Making bends

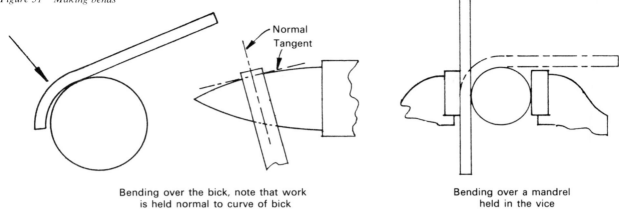

Bending over the bick, note that work
is held normal to curve of bick

Bending over a mandrel
held in the vice

Many different bends can be formed over the bick and it is well to remember always that the metal should be *bent* rather than *beaten*, for excessive hammering spreads and distorts the metal. Especial care must be taken with round stock which is not easily restored to its original section after being flattened. Excessive or uneven heating should be avoided as these will prevent the formation of smooth bends.

Figure 52   Stages in forging an eye

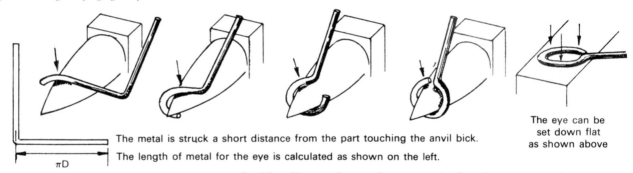

The metal is struck a short distance from the part touching the anvil bick.

The length of metal for the eye is calculated as shown on the left.

πD

The eye can be
set down flat
as shown above

Figure 53   Machine for bending cold metal
(Miracle Mills Ltd. London)

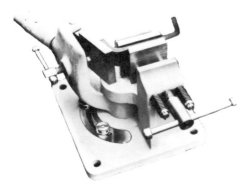

In Fig. 52 are shown the stages in forming an eye. Points to note here are: (1) the length of the metal for the eye is calculated on the neutral line at the centre, (2) a right-angled bend is made first, and then (3) the eye is formed over the bick commencing at the *end* of the bar.

It is not essential to form all bends over the bick, curves of specific radii can be made and repeated accurately over a mandrel of the correct size, the mandrel being a piece of solid bar or heavy barrel held firmly in the leg vice. See Fig. 51. A simple bending jig for small radii can be made up as in Fig. 54 and with this, small bends can be repeated accurately without using the hammer.

Drawing down

This is the reducing of the cross-section of a bar from any given point, resulting in an increase in length at the same time. Drawing down can be in the form of a taper or a parallel reduction shoul-

Figure 54   Bending devices for strip metal

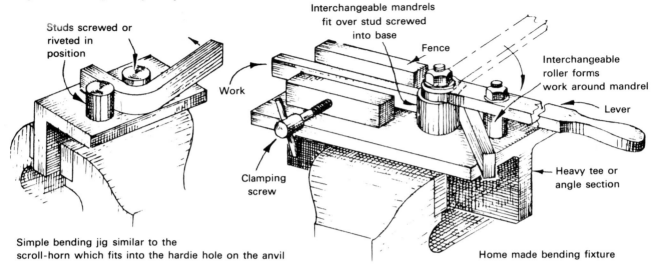

Studs screwed or
riveted in
position

Work

Interchangeable mandrels
fit over stud screwed
into base

Fence

Interchangeable
roller forms
work around mandrel

Lever

Clamping
screw

Heavy tee or
angle section

Simple bending jig similar to the
scroll-horn which fits into the hardie hole on the anvil

Home made bending fixture

dered at the change of section. The process is illustrated in Fig. 55 in which a square section is being drawn down to a taper. The end of the bar is brought to a yellow heat and, held square to the anvil edge, is hammered to a blunt point, the bar being turned through 90° after each two or three hammer blows. If drawing down is commenced with the end left square, the edges will be extruded and will form a hollow end which may split, this fault being known as 'piping'. The blunt point prevents this. The metal is reheated, held on the anvil at the required angle and hammering is commenced at the end with the hammer inclined at the angle of the taper. This is repeated with the metal turned through 90° until the taper is completed.

If a round taper is required the metal is first drawn down square and this square is then converted into an octagon and then into a round by hammering each corner in turn. Heavier sections are best drawn down on the bick in the early stages after which the work can be finished on the anvil face.

Figure 55   Drawing down

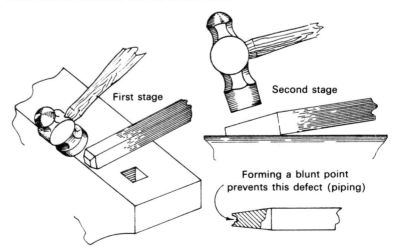

First stage

Second stage

Forming a blunt point
prevents this defect (piping)

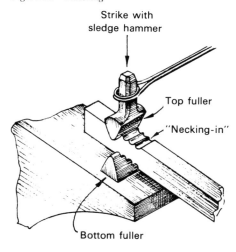

Figure 56   Fullering

Strike with
sledge hammer

Top fuller

"Necking-in"

Bottom fuller

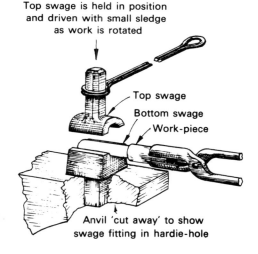

Figure 57   Pair of swages in use

Top swage is held in position
and driven with small sledge
as work is rotated

Top swage

Bottom swage

Work-piece

Anvil 'cut away' to show
swage fitting in hardie-hole

Fullering

Fullers are used in pairs, the bottom fuller in the hardie hole and the top one being held in position whilst struck with the sledge. The faces are half-round in section and range from a 12 mm diameter upwards. In Fig. 56 they are shown in use, the process being known as 'fullering' and used to assist in drawing down in the large sections. Where the drawing down is tapered, the fullering would begin with small indents, getting heavier towards the point and the work would be finished with the hammer on the anvil face. For parallel drawing down, the fullering would be of the same depth, the first impression at the shoulder being known as 'knecking in'.

Swages

Swages are forming tools which are used in pairs for finishing or smoothing round sections previously reduced from larger or different sections. The bottom swage is square shanked and fits into the hardie hole whilst the top swage is hafted or fitted with a wire handle. It is struck with the sledge. They are made to form rounds of 6 mm diameter and upwards.

Flatting

Flatters are used for finishing surfaces and are struck with the sledge. The faces are either flat or convex with sharp or rounded corners for various kinds of work. The *set hammer* is for the same work but has a smaller face. They are shown in Fig. 58.

Punching and drifting

Punches can be of any section, square or rectangular as well as round. Drifts are made with a long taper to one end and a short taper to the other and are used to open out holes which have been punched. The long taper is entered in the punched hole and the drift is then driven right through the hole which is opened out to

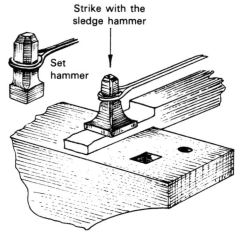

Figure 58   Using the flatter

Strike with the
sledge hammer

Set
hammer

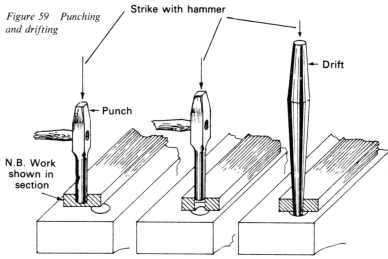

*Figure 59   Punching
and drifting*

Strike with hammer

Drift

Punch

N.B. Work
shown in
section

Figure 60   Forming a twist with a wrench and sleeve

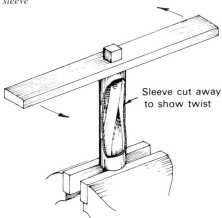

Sleeve cut away
to show twist

Figure 61   Flaring

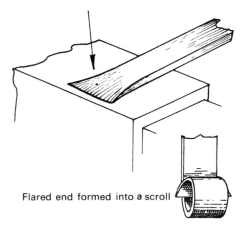

Flared end formed into a scroll

Figure 62   Fire-welding preparation

Preparation for scarf weld

size and smoothed in the passing. Drifting is done over the tool hole in the anvil.

In punching, the metal is brought to near-yellow heat, is laid on the anvil and the punch driven through as quickly as possible (withdrawing it at intervals for quenching) until it is stopped by the under surface-layer of the metal which has become cool and hard because of contact with the anvil. On turning the metal over the chilled disc will be darker in colour, is easily located and the punch can be placed accurately and driven through.

Twisting

Twisting is often used in decorative work and is very effective if nicely done. It strengthens the section in which it is made (squares and flats) by the turning of the diagonals in the cross-section.

For twisting to be regular, it must be done in one heat which must be even along the length for any hotter parts will twist more easily. When several pieces are to receive identical twists care must be taken to see that each in turn, is heated to the same temperature, and when gripped in the vice, a loosely fitting tubular sleeve will ensure that each twist is the same length. The twisting is best done with a two-handed wrench made from a length of flat bar with a square or rectangular hole at the centre. Small sections of up to about 6 mm square can be twisted cold. Twists can be made with $\frac{1}{4}$, $\frac{1}{2}$, $\frac{3}{4}$, or whole turns and are used in many different forms by the experienced smith.

Flaring or spreading

This is another form of decorative work used often with scrolls. The metal is hammered and is drawn down on two faces only, the other two faces being struck only enough to control the extent and the form of the flaring.

Fire welding

This is a process which calls for much skill and good judgement of the welding heat with the ability to maintain a clean fire with a good heart, free from clinker.

Parts to be welded need some preparation, the first thing being to form an upsett because some metal is 'lost' in the welding and next is scarfing which is shown in Fig. 62.

The parts are brought near to welding heat, are withdrawn from the fire and sprinkled with silver sand or a proprietary brand of flux. They are returned and positioned so that both will reach welding heat together. A few sparks emitting from the fire will indicate that this heat has been reached. The welding must be completed in the shortest possible time, both parts being withdrawn from the fire, knocked on the anvil edge to dislodge any scale and quickly positioned. The first blow is struck at the centre of the joint, a hard 'ring' indicating that the weld has not taken.

6

Marking out and measuring

Marking out is done by scribing fine lines on the metal and in a few cases some preparation is needed so that they will show clearly. On many of the non-ferrous metals and alloys, scribed lines show clearly and there is no need to prepare surfaces which are smooth and coated with a film of oxide. The bright surfaces of steel, when de-greased are prepared by brushing or swabbing on a solution of copper sulphate which immediately deposits a film of copper. The surplus solution is then washed off and when the metal is dry, scribed lines will show very clearly.

With iron castings, a thin coat of flat oil paint will suffice.

Tools in general use

Engineer's square

Squares with 100 mm blades and of 'workshop' grade are suitable for use in small fitting work. Made in bright steel and with hardened and tempered blades, these tools will give good service but must be looked after and not left lying about where they might be knocked on to the floor. A few larger squares will be needed for the occasional large job and a combination set, with adjustable blade, mitre square, protractor, level and centre square is undoubtedly a useful piece of equipment.

A small slot is cut in the stock of the engineer's square to avoid errors caused by filings or dirt which might be picked up, or from burred edges which have inadvertently been left on the work.

In testing surfaces for squareness, the stock is held firmly against the work face and with the blade held normal (at right angles) to the edge under test, the square is slid down so that the blade comes into contact. With the work held towards a light source, inaccuracies are clearly revealed.

Figure 63   Combination set
(Moore and Wright (Sheffield) Ltd.)

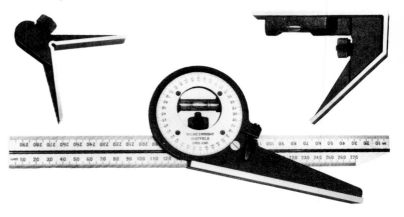

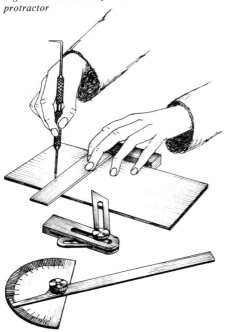

Figure 64   Scriber, square, bevel and bevel-protractor

Scriber

The scriber is used for marking out by scratching very fine lines and is used in conjunction with the square, straight-edge or bevel in the same way that one would use pencil and drawing instruments. It is made of tool steel, with hardened points. In squaring lines across the work, the scriber point is first placed exactly on location and the square is slid up to the scriber with the stock held firmly against the work.

Bevel and bevel protractor

The bevel is used in transferring angles and in marking them out but cannot be used for measuring them. For setting a bevel to a desired angle, a bevel protractor can be used and for very accurate settings, a bevel protractor with a Vernier attachment is needed.

Straight-edges

For most purposes in the small workshop, a good steel rule of 300 mm will serve as a straight-edge for testing and marking out on small work, but a few straight-edges of 'workshop' grade will occasionally be needed. These are available from 300 mm to 1800 mm in length, but it is doubtful if anything longer than 750 mm will ever be needed.

Figure 65   Bevelled straight edge and metric rule (Moore and Wright (Sheffield) Ltd.)

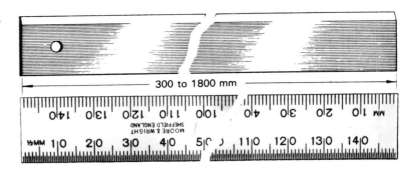

Figure 66   Spring dividers and wing compasses

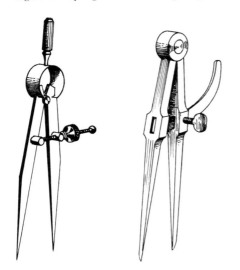

Dividers

With a fine adjustment, spring dividers are useful in the division of lengths into equal parts by trial and error. The knurled finger grip enables one to 'walk' the dividers along a line until the correct setting is obtained. The divisions can then be marked by striking an arc at each step. Dividers are also used in transferring lengths and in locating points with intersecting arcs. The wing compass is a more robust tool but with limited applications.

Calipers

Illustrated in Fig. 67 are the firm-joint calipers for inside and outside work with the spring type tool for the same work in Fig. 68. Outside calipers are for taking off sizes in all situations on round or other sections, for comparing objects in conjunction with the feeler gauge, and for testing parallelism, all with moderate precision. Inside calipers are for use on interior work of the same nature.

Figure 67   Setting (or reading-off) with calipers and rule

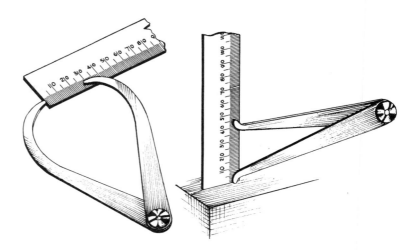

Figure 69   Scribing a line with the odd-leg calipers

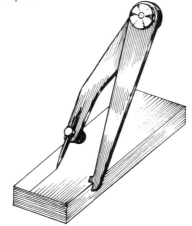

Figure 68   Spring calipers—outside and inside

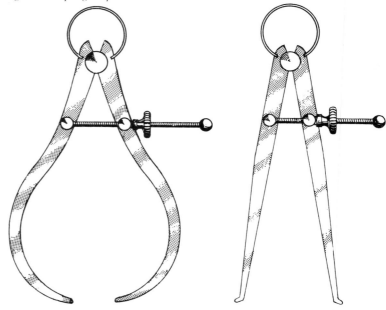

Figure 70   Locating a centre with odd-leg calipers

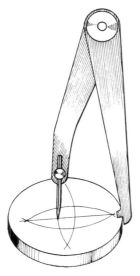

In taking off sizes with the firm-joint calipers, it is better not to close the points on to the work, but to set the calipers so that in drawing the points across the work, they are automatically adjusted to its size and can be felt to be in contact with the surfaces. Measurements from the calipers are taken as in Fig. 67. Spring calipers are moved across the work, adjusting a little at a time until the points can just be felt in contact with the surfaces.

Odd legs

Also called 'Jenny' calipers. These are used for scribing lines parallel to finished edges and are useful in finding the centres of round bars by striking arcs.

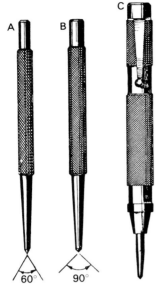

Figure 71   A. Dot punch (centre 'pop').
                B. Centre punch
                C. Automatic centre punch

Dot and centre punches

These two punches look alike, but the dot punch is often of lighter stock than the centre punch and is ground with a point at 60° whilst centre punches are usually ground at 90°. The dot punch is useful in locating hole centres accurately with a very small dot which can easily be drawn over with a second attempt if the first is not correctly positioned. This can then be followed with a heavier indent from the centre punch before drilling.

The dot punch can also be used for 'confirming' a scribed line with a series of dots as a guide when filing. A scribed line always seems to disappear before the filed edge reaches it, but the dots become visible at the crucial moment and give a positive guide. Work should be solidly supported for dot or centre punching.

The automatic dot or centre punch is a very useful tool with its adjustable control over the weight of the blow delivered when the body is depressed.

Surface plate and surface table

The surface plate provides a true 'plane of reference' for the testing of other surfaces and for measuring and marking out of all kinds. The plate is made from fine grade cast iron, is ribbed on the underside to prevent warping and is usually arranged to stand on three small feet to give stability and to ensure that no stresses are imposed when

Figure 72   Some of the tools commonly used in marking out and testing

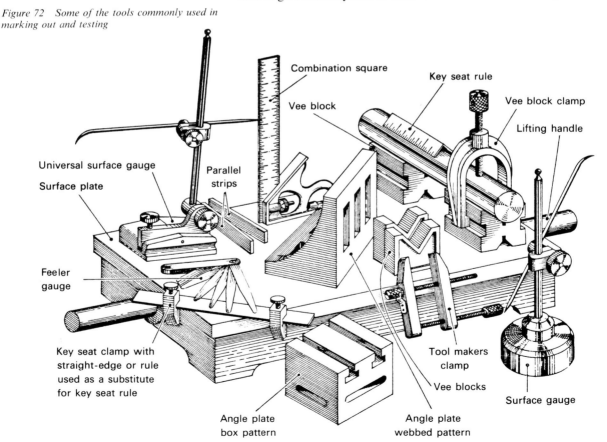

Figure 74   Finding a centre using the centre-square

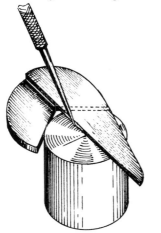

Figure 75   Locating a centre using the centre-head from a combination set

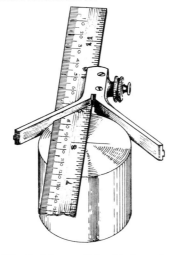

Figure 76   Scribing parallels with the surface gauge

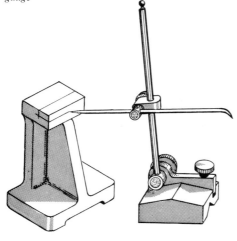

Figure 73   Locating a centre with surface gauge and vee blocks

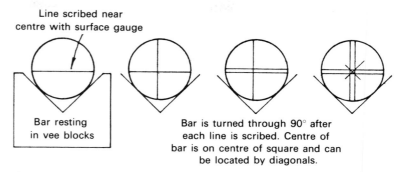

Line scribed near
centre with surface gauge

Bar resting
in vee blocks

Bar is turned through 90° after
each line is scribed. Centre of
bar is on centre of square and can
be located by diagonals.

the plate stands on an uneven surface. A great range of sizes is made from 100 mm × 150 mm upwards. The very largest sizes are often fitted with legs to stand on the floor and they are then known as *surface tables*.

The finishing of the surfaces is commonly done to two specified grades of precision, viz.: grades 'A' and 'B'. Grade 'A' plates are brought to a high precision by hand scraping and in grade 'B' plates, the surface is finished by accurate machining. Grade 'A' plates are naturally very costly items, but for general use and in the school workshop, Grade 'B' plates are sufficiently accurate. Surface plates and tables should be kept scrupulously clean and protected with covers when not in use.

Surface gauge

Sometimes referred to as the 'scribing block'. Two kinds are illustrated in Fig. 72, the simple tool shown is quite sound but restricted in its applications. The gauge can be set to scribe lines at any height above and parallel to the surface plate, its heavy base keeping it steady and requiring only a little hand pressure. If the scriber points are kept nicely sharpened only the lightest stroking action will be needed to scribe a clean line. Used in conjunction with the vee blocks the surface gauge can be used to locate accurately the centres of round bars as shown in Fig. 73.

Both the scriber and the pillar are held in adjustable clamps on the universal surface gauge, giving the tool an increased reach. Fine adjustments are made by turning the knurled screw which moves the rocker arm up or down. With the scriber pointing downwards, the surface gauge can be used to check work for parallelism by 'feeling' the surfaces and with the aid of the feeler gauge, discrepancies can be measured, the feelers being inserted singly or in groups until a combination is found which just drags slightly on being drawn through the gap.

Angle plates

Angle plates can be used for holding work for marking out or for machining and in Fig. 77 are shown two types not already illustrated, viz.: the open-ended and adjustable angle plates.

Figure 77   Angle plates: A. Open-ended
*   B. Adjustable*
(Neill Tools Ltd.)

Figure 78   Depth gauge in use

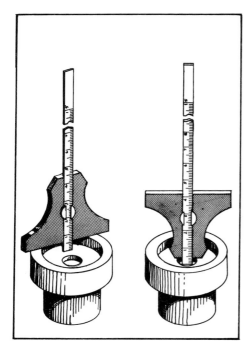

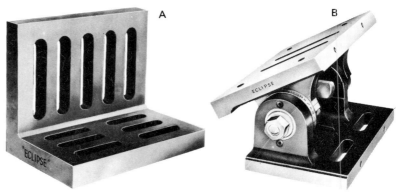

Vee blocks

Made in cast iron and accurately machined, vee blocks are made and sold in pairs. Two types are shown in Fig. 72, one being provided with clamps for holding bars in position for marking out, finding centres and holding work in position for drilling.

Key-seat rule and clamps

The key-seat rule is used for marking parallel lines (mainly for key-ways), on round bars whilst a pair of key-seat clamps used with a rule or straight-edge make a good substitute.

Depth gauge

Two typical uses of the depth gauge are seen in Fig. 78. The body of the Moore and Wright gauge can be reversed for working in restricted places. With two positions for the rule, the gauge shown in Fig. 79 can be used in restricted corners.

The Vernier caliper gauge

Named after its inventor, the Vernier scale is incorporated in many measuring instruments, the most commonly used of which is the sliding caliper gauge, seen in Fig. 80. It can be used for taking internal and external measurements. These gauges are made from fine quality alloy steels and are very accurately finished by grinding and lapping.

In measuring an object externally, the locking-screws A and B

Figure 79   Depth Gauge used in a restricted corner

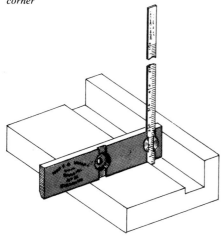

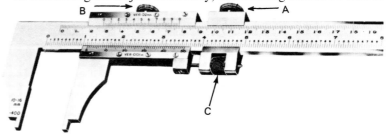

Figure 80   Vernier calipers
(Benson Verniers Ltd.)

Figure 82 Vernier height gauge
(Rabone Chesterman Ltd.)

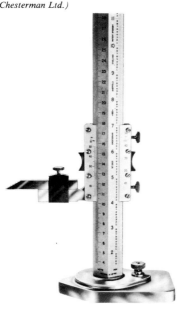

Figure 81 Metric Vernier scale
(Rabone Chesterman Ltd.)

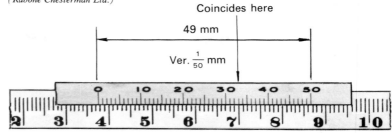

Scale divided into mms.

are both slackened off and the sliding-jaw assembly is moved along, almost on to the object. Locking-screw A is tightened down and then, by turning the knurled screw C, the jaws are gently closed on to the surfaces without putting any pressure on them. Locking-screw B is then tightened down and the calipers removed from the work for reading.

The jaw tips are stepped and rounded on the outsides so that internal measurements can be taken and to whatever reading is obtained, the widths of the jaws must be added. This measurement is found engraved on the jaw face for reference.

Reading the Vernier

In Fig. 81, we see part of the caliper main scale which is divided into centimetres and millimetres. The actual length of the Vernier scale is 49 mm and this length is divided into 50 parts. Each division of the Vernier will therefore be equal to 0·980 mm, i.e. each will be 1/50th mm shorter than each division on the main scale. The reading is taken as follows: reading along the main scale up to the Vernier zero, we can see the number of whole mm in the measurement and the line on the Vernier which coincides with a line on the main scale indicates the number of 1/50th mms to be added on.

In the illustration, the reading is 37·66 mm, i.e. 37 whole mms on the main scale, plus 33/50ths mm on the Vernier which equals 0·66 mm, giving a total of 37·66 mm.

Tools incorporating the Vernier are often provided also with scales in Imperial measure, the main scale inches sometimes divided into 1/40ths. With a Vernier scale of 24/40ths ins in length and divided into 25 parts, readings of 1/1000ths ins can be taken.

Figure 83 Vernier depth gauge
(Benson Verniers Ltd.)

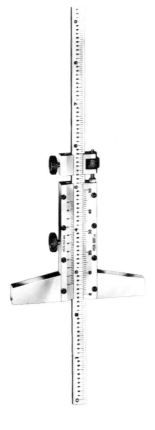

The micrometer

The micrometer is a precision-made measuring instrument in which a threaded spindle, passing through a 'nut' in the form of a tube, can be made to pass through very precise distances from a fixed point when it is rotated. The principle is very simple, single-start threads being used so that for one complete turn of the spindle, its axial movement will be equal to the thread pitch.

Micrometers measuring in millimetres are usually made with a

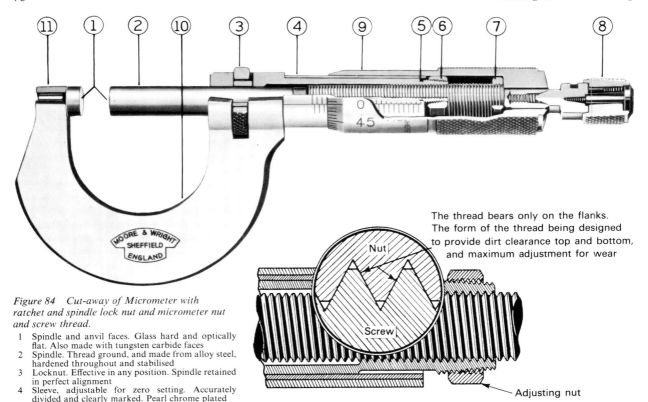

Figure 84   Cut-away of Micrometer with
ratchet and spindle lock nut and micrometer nut
and screw thread.

1   Spindle and anvil faces. Glass hard and optically
    flat. Also made with tungsten carbide faces
2   Spindle. Thread ground, and made from alloy steel,
    hardened throughout and stabilised
3   Locknut. Effective in any position. Spindle retained
    in perfect alignment
4   Sleeve, adjustable for zero setting. Accurately
    divided and clearly marked. Pearl chrome plated
5   Main nut. Length of thread ensures long working
    life
6   Screw adjusting nut. For effective adjustment of
    main nut
7   Thimble adjusting nut. Controls position of thimble
8   Ratchet. Improved design ensures even pressure
9   Thimble. Accurately divided. Every fifth graduation
    clearly numbered. Pearl chrome plated
10 Steel frame. Drop forged. Marked with useful
    decimal equivalents. Pearl chrome plated
11 Anvil end. Cut away frame can be used in narrow
    slots

(Moore & Wright (Sheffield) Ltd.)

The thread bears only on the flanks.
The form of the thread being designed
to provide dirt clearance top and bottom,
and maximum adjustment for wear

Figure 85   Micrometer
Internal tubular type
(Moore & Wright (Sheffield) Ltd.)

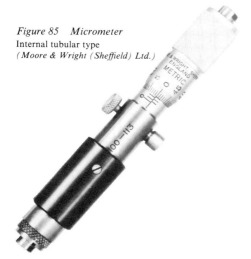

thread of 0·5 mm pitch, thus, the spindle will travel 1 mm if given
two complete turns, 0.5 mm for one turn and correspondingly
smaller distances for fractions of a turn.

Along the sleeve is scribed a datum line which is divided into
whole and half mms. To the outer end of the spindle is attached a
thin walled tube or 'thimble' which fits closely over the sleeve as
seen in Fig. 84. As the spindle is rotated, the thimble moves along
the sleeve, its bevelled edge registering the movement along the
datum, viz.: 1 mm for two turns, 0·5 mm for one turn and so on.
With the bevelled edge of the thimble divided into 50 equal parts
around its periphery, it is a simple matter to turn the spindle 1/50th
of a turn, producing a movement equal to 1/50th of 0·5 mm which
is 0·01 mm.

Objects are measured between the spindle and the anvil faces, the
spindle being rotated by means of the ratchet knob. This device
ensures that an even pressure is applied under all conditions. The
micrometer shown in Fig. 84, with a 'C' shaped frame, reads from
zero to 25 mm (or 1 inch in Imperial sizes), the next size up reads
from 25 to 50 mm, the next from 50 to 75 mm and so on up to 300
mm.

Before attempting to adjust the setting of a micrometer, the
locknut, which prevents accidental movement of the thimble, must
be released, and having set the micrometer for measuring or perhaps
for reading practice, the locknut should be tightened.

*Figure 86   Depth gauge micrometer
(Moore & Wright (Sheffield) Ltd.)*

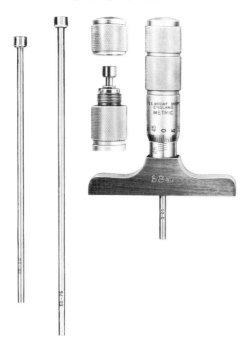

*Figure 86   Depth gauge micrometer
(Moore & Wright (Sheffield) Ltd.)*

Reading the metric micrometer

Fig. 87 shows a close-up of a sleeve and thimble reading in hundredths of a millimetre (0·01 mm). The datum line is graduated in millimetres on top and to avoid any confusion, half millimetres are marked below. The thimble edge registers the number of whole and half millimetres over which it has travelled from zero along the datum and the fifty divisions around the thimble indicate the hundredths of a millimetre to be added on, the reading being taken at the datum.

For example, in Fig. 87:

Above the datum line, 10 whole millimetres are visible,	= 10·00 mm
Below the datum line, 1 half millimetre is visible,	= 0·50 mm
Line on the thimble coinciding with the datum,	= 0·16 mm
Reading of measurement	= 10·66 mm

Fig. 88 shows a sleeve and thimble graduated to read to thousandths of a millimetre (0·001 mm) and this is accomplished by the addition of a Vernier scale on the sleeve, reading in conjunction with the thimble. On the sleeve and parallel to the datum are marked 5 equal divisions occupying the same space as 9 divisions on the thimble, each division on the Vernier scale representing 2 thousandths of a millimetre.

In taking a reading from this micrometer, a reading is first taken as previously described, in hundredths of a millimetre and then a note is made of which Vernier line coincides with a graduated line on the thimble and this gives the number of thousandths of a millimetre to be added.

For example, in Fig. 88:

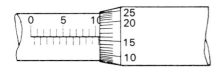

*Figure 87   Close-up of a sleeve and thimble
reading in hundredths of a millimetre*

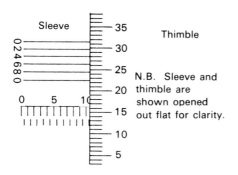

*Figure 88   Sleeve and thimble graduated to read
thousandths of a millimetre*

Sleeve

Thimble

N.B. Sleeve and thimble are shown opened out flat for clarity.

Above the datum, 10 whole millimetres are visible,	= 10·00 mm
Below the datum, 1 half millimetre is visible,	= 0·50 mm
Highest line on thimble below the datum is	= 0·16 mm
Vernier line coincident with line on thimble is 4,	= 0·004 mm
Reading of measurement is	10·664 mm

When there is no coincidence of lines when reading the Vernier, the intermediate thousandths can be estimated, i.e. if the reading lies between 4 and 6 (for example), then the additional thousandths reading would be 0·005 mm.

Care of micrometers

Micrometers should never be left laying around on benches or machines where they may pick up dirt or get knocked on to the floor and damaged. They should be cleaned and returned to their cases immediately after use. They should not be held in the hand too long as warmth will cause expansion and possibly faulty readings.

It is important that anvil faces should be kept clean by wiping lightly with absorbent paper and in the smallest sizes, where the two faces meet, a piece of paper can be lightly gripped and then withdrawn.

Zero readings should be regularly checked after closing the freshly cleaned anvil faces, not forgetting to use the ratchet. For this purpose, micrometers larger than 0 to 25 mm (or 1 inch) are provided with accurately made setting gauges on which the micrometer is closed. Any adjustment needed must be made in accordance with the maker's instructions.

The dial indicator

This is a delicate measuring instrument for checking on parallelism, on the flatness of surfaces and on the concentricity of round objects. It is also used extensively in setting up work for machining.

The dial or 'clock', seen in Fig. 89, is provided with several mountings for adaptability and in use, is traversed across the surface under test, contact being made via a spring-loaded stud or plunger protruding from the body. The slightest movement of the stud, in or out, as it traverses the surface is magnified through a gear train, causing a needle to move to right or left of zero on the dial face, thus indicating high or low spots. The dial face can be rotated independently of the body so that the zero mark can be brought round to the needle point wherever it stops after adjustment against the work face.

Mountings with powerful magnetic bases provide a ready means of mounting the dial gauge on machines in almost any situation.

Figure 89   Dial indicator and bench stand checking parallelism of gauge stands (Thomas Mercer Ltd.)

Gauges

Many kinds of gauges are used in engineering for the checking of sizes by comparing them with accurate dimensions between surfaces on the gauge. For checking external sizes, gauges incorporating holes or gaps are used whilst for internal sizes, they are in the form of plugs or distance pieces.

The measuring faces are always made with extreme accuracy

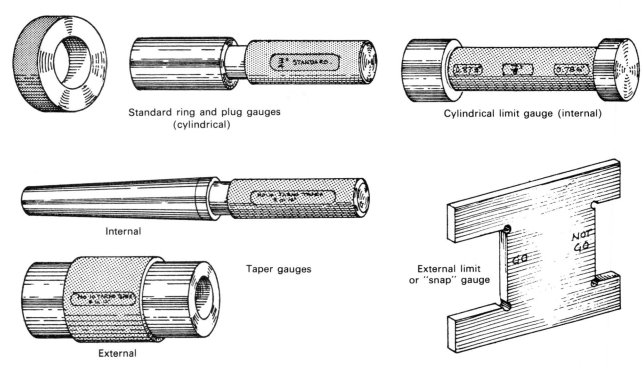

Standard ring and plug gauges
(cylindrical)

Cylindrical limit gauge (internal)

Internal

Taper gauges

External limit
or "snap" gauge

External

Figure 90   Ring and plug gauges, cylindrical and taper, limit gauges

and although the principle of checking by comparison is elementary, some care must be taken over the handling and using of gauges. Only the very lightest of pressure should be used to 'feel' a gauge over or into the work, taking care to offer it in line with the work to avoid jamming.

Plug gauges

Circular plug gauges are made in two forms, viz., *standard* and *limit* gauges. The standard gauge is made precisely to the nominal diameter and would be used when boring exactly to a given size, but quite often, small variations above and below nominal sizes are acceptable. Where this occurs in repetition work, limit gauges are used because they give immediate checks on sizes without having to spend time with measuring instruments.

The comparison of the work with the taper gauge calls for a fine sense of touch in judging whether the two are mating accurately. Whilst the angle of the taper is compared with the gauge, its size is gauged by the depth to which the plug enters and this is often indicated by a line scribed around the plug.

Ring gauges

These are made for testing parallel or taper turning and are shown in Fig. 90, they give a positive check of size and are usually made from mild steel and case hardened.

Parallels

Made of hardened steel and ground on all faces, parallels range from 100 mm to 300 mm in length and in a variety of square and rectangular sections between about 6 mm and 75 mm. They can be used in the setting up of work for machining, in marking out and in inspection. Parallels should not be confused with *slip gauges*, which are made in sets and very accurately ground. They are used in various combinations as references for standard sizes in the workshop.

Feeler gauges

These are comprised of sets of tempered steel blades whose thicknesses range from 0·03 to 1·00 mm and from 0·001 to 0·025 inches, the thickness being marked on each blade. Feelers are used singly or in combination to measure clearances between parts by touch and can be judged to fit a gap when a slight pull is felt on withdrawing them. See Fig. 72.

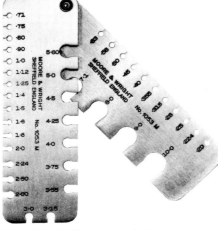

Figure 91   *Radius gauge and wire gauge
(Moore and Wright (Sheffield) Ltd.)*

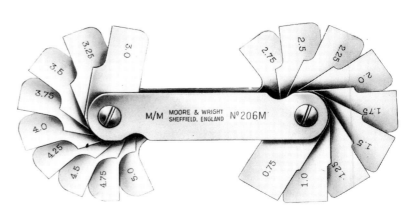

Trammels

For striking arcs beyond the capacity of the dividers, trammels are used. They are shown in Fig. 92. They can also be used in transferring measurements from one part to another or as inside or outside calipers for large diameters.

Figure 92   *Trammels*

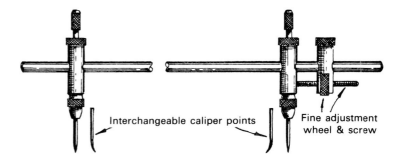

Interchangeable caliper points   Fine adjustment
                                           wheel & screw

7

Work at the bench

Vices

A variety of engineer's and fitter's vices are available for different classes of work and the mechanic's vice, seen in Fig. 93 is quite suitable for the school workshop. It is a plain vice with a cast iron body and will give good service, provided that it is not used as an anvil. Steel vices are much stronger but are more costly. The size of a vice is measured along the jaws (not the opening) and a 75 mm vice is a useful size.

Vices are fitted with hardened steel jaw-faces screwed in place and these are either smooth-faced or serrated, depending on the work being done. The serrated jaws grip firmly but mark the work unless vice clamps are used.

In the mechanic's vice the screw passes through a solid nut and all adjustments must be made by turning the screw, but in the instantaneous vice, seen in Fig. 95, the screw passes over a half-nut which can be disengaged from the screw thread by depressing a spring-loaded trigger. The vice is then free for quick adjustment after which the half-nut is re-engaged by releasing the trigger and the vice is tightened in the usual way. The thread-form used is the buttress thread which is designed specially for transmitting pressure in one direction only.

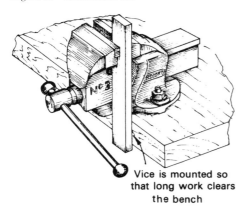

Figure 93   Mechanic's vice

Vice is mounted so that long work clears the bench

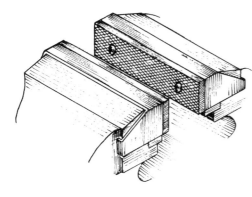

Figure 94   Vice clamps

Figure 95   Quick-grip vice
(C. and J. Hampton Ltd.)

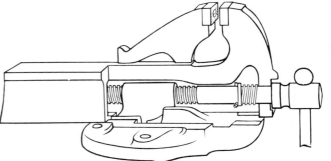

Figure 96   Mechanic's vice in section

Hand vice

This is a most convenient tool for holding small work at the drilling machine or for holding small parts for riveting and other similar jobs. Hand vices are measured over the length and range between 100 mm to 150 mm.

Figure 97   Pin vice, open jaw type. Pin vice, chuck type. Hand vice.

Tool maker's clamps

A tool maker's clamp is illustrated in Fig. 98 and these tools are made in a range of sizes from 50 mm upwards, the size being measured along the length of the jaw. These clamps have a number of uses, for example, holding parts together whilst marking out, whilst cutting out to shape or at the drilling machine.

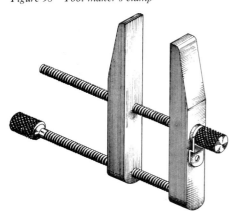

Figure 98   Tool-maker's clamp

Hack saws

Made with either adjustable or fixed size frames, the hack saw will take blades of 250 mm or 300 mm in length and these are tensioned by a wing-nut adjuster. In both types of frame the blade can be turned through 90° so that long cuts can be made.

Hack saw blades   These are made with a range of teeth sizes of 14, 18, 24 and 32 per 25 mm, cut on one or both edges and they are of either low tungsten or high-speed steels. The heat treatment is arranged to produce either 'flexible' or 'all-hard' blades, the flexible blades being hardened only on the cutting edges whilst in the all-hard blade the whole thing is hardened. With normal use, the flexible blades are unbreakable and for this reason are more suitable for use in school workshops.

All blades are used with the teeth pointing away from the handle and should be correctly tensioned. With the 'Eclipse' frame, this is done by first taking up the slack and then applying three full turns on the wing nut. This would probably apply also to other frames as well. The teeth size should be suitable for the work in hand, as follows:

14 teeth   This is a suitable size for cutting large solid sections in the softer metals, for example, aluminium, copper, brass and also mild steel.

18 teeth   Suitable for general use and for smaller sections in aluminium, copper, brass and mild steel.

Figure 99   *Metal-cutting saws*

Adjustable
hack-saw

Pad handle

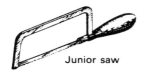

Junior saw

Figure 100   *A. The stance for hack-sawing*
B. Choosing correct size of saw-tooth

Figure 101   *Using the sheet-saw*

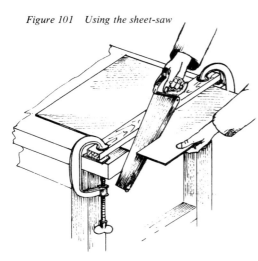

24 teeth   Suitable for plate up to about 6 mm and for thick walled tubes, large angle sections, etc. High-speed steel blades with 24 teeth are suitable for alloy, stainless and silver steel and for annealed tool steel.

32 teeth   For small angles and other sections, thin walled tubing and thin plate. The junior hack saw is often used on small sections.

Using the hack saw

A sound guide to the correct size of teeth for any job is the rule that at least three consecutive teeth should be in contact with the metal at all times. This ensures free action of the saw, avoids damage to the work and to the teeth and helps to avoid broken blades.

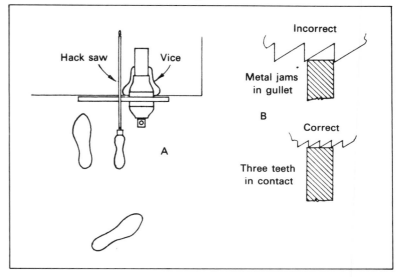

Cutting should begin on a flat surface with the saw tilted very slightly, and *not* on a sharp corner or the teeth may be stripped. Long, steady strokes should be made and the cut should be close to the line to reduce subsequent filing to the minimum. Over-tension on the blade, too-rapid cutting and excessive pressures are causes of broken blades which will cause injury if the knuckles strike the vice corners.

In hack-sawing, a good stance is important. The feet should be placed as shown in Fig. 100 with the body leaning slightly towards the work. The right leg is kept straight and with the left knee slightly bent, the balance of the body can be controlled and the weight brought to bear on the saw as required. Using steady strokes to the full length will give far better results than rapid, short strokes with the middle of the blade.

Sheet saw

In this saw the blade is tensioned along the edge of a stiff plate and is used for cutting sheet metal of any size.

Junior hack saw

A miniature hack saw in which the blade is tensioned by the spring steel frame. It is a very useful saw on small work and on thin-walled tubing.

Tension file
Fitted into the standard hack-saw frame by means of special clips, the 'Abrafile' tension file is round, thin and parallel and is very useful in cutting curves of any shape. Although this tool, strictly speaking, is a file, it is included with the saws since it does in fact cut out shapes in metal.

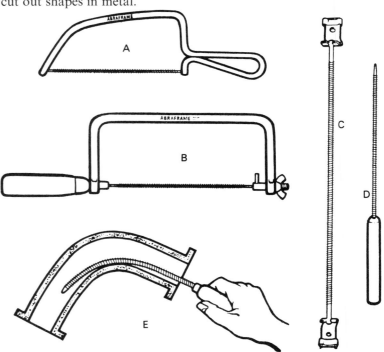

Figure 102   A few items from the Abrafile range of tools

A and B. Abraframes. C. Abrafile with adapting links for use with hack-saw frames. D. Abrafile 'Mousetail', 95 mm long.
E. Abrafile soft core file which can be bent to almost any shape.

(Abrasive Tools Ltd.)

Pad handle
Using short pieces of hack-saw blade, the pad handle is useful in piercing holes with straight sides and for other odd-jobs.

Hammers

Engineer's hammer
The ball pein hammer is the most commonly used, the cross and straight peins only appearing where it might be necessary to strike blows in corners or other restricted spaces.

Hammer heads are made from cast steel and the striking faces are ground with a slight dome-shape which helps in avoiding unsightly marks on the work and ensures that the force from the hammer blows is delivered by the centre of the face and not the edges which might ultimately fracture. The beginner is nearly always tempted to hold his hammers just behind the head because he feels that he is then more certain of striking accurately, but this habit must be resisted because it is not possible to strike squarely

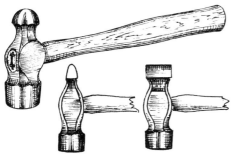

Figure 103   Engineer's ball pein hammer
Below: Cross and straight pein hammer-heads

or to use the full weight of the hammer in this way. The hammer should be held towards the end of the shaft and swung from the elbow.

Hammers are graded by weight between 112 g and 900 g. Handles are generally of ash for smaller hammers, but for heavier tools—sledges and other smith's tools—hickory is always used for it is the tougher wood.

Damaged hammer handles should be renewed without delay as they can cause serious accidents and great care should be taken in the fitting of new handles into the heads. The shaft-end can be reduced using a wood rasp, leaving a short parallel portion which is expanded by barbed steel wedges after the shaft is driven home securely and square to the head. Heads with mis-shapen or chipped faces should be discarded as they are dangerous—the hammer may be caused to glance off when striking, or chips of metal may fly off.

Soft hammers

Copper, lead and hide hammers are used in fitting so that work faces shall not be marked when assembling or adjusting component parts. They should be used with care and for delivering light blows only or they will soon become mis-shapen and useless.

Figure 104   Soft hammers

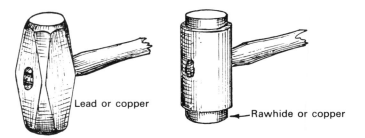

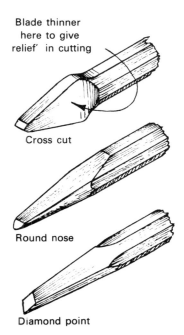

Flat chisel

Blade thinner here to give relief' in cutting

Cross cut

Round nose

Diamond point

Figure 105   Cold chisels

Cold chisels

Cold chisels, commonly forged from high carbon steel and of octagonal or hexagonal sections, are made in a variety of sizes and with four forms of cutting edges, viz.: the *flat*, the *cross-cut*, the *diamond point* and the *half-round* chisels. All are illustrated in Fig. 105 and are known as 'cold' chisels since they are used for cutting cold metal. After forging and grinding of the cutting-edge, only the blade of the chisel is hardened and tempered leaving the body (shank) of the tool softer so that it will not be liable to fracture in use. The cutting edge is normally ground to an angle of 60°.

Nickel chromium steels are used to make very tough chisels which are almost unbreakable. They can be re-forged and hardened without any special apparatus and can, if necessary, be sharpened with a smooth-cut file. Illustrated in Fig. 106 is a dome-head chisel in 3 per cent nickel chromium steel. The specially toughened head

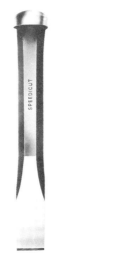

Figure 106 Domehead cold chisel
Made also as cross-cut, round-nose, diamond point
and hollow gouge

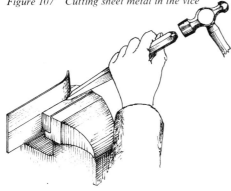

Figure 107 Cutting sheet metal in the vice

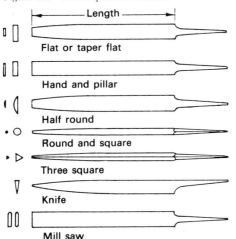

Figure 108 File shapes and sections

- Flat or taper flat
- Hand and pillar
- Half round
- Round and square
- Three square
- Knife
- Mill saw

spreads only very slightly under constant hammering and gives the chisel a much extended life.

Flat chisel

Made from 100 mm and upwards in length and from 6 to 25 mm in width, the flat chisel is useful in a variety of jobs in sheet, plate and cast metals. Sheet and plate can be cut edge-wise in the vice as shown in Fig. 107. The chisel is held askew to give a shearing action and at an angle which keeps it from running up out of the cut. The flat chisel can be used for cold cutting at the anvil and for jobs such as cutting away the waste metal from pierced holes already partly made by drilling.

Made with a broad blade-portion to give it strength, this narrow chisel is used in cutting key-ways and slots where other methods cannot be employed easily.

Half-round and diamond point chisels

These two chisels have similar uses in cutting of oilways in bearings and in other small jobs which do not justify the setting up of a machine. They are sometimes used in the difficult business of drawing over of large drilled holes which have started off-centre. (See under Drilling and Reaming.)

Files

Classification and cuts

The files in general workshop use are known as Engineer's Files and are made from high carbon steel in a great variety of forms and cuts to suit any kind of work.

The final heat treatment of files is carried out by heating them to between 760°C and 780°C in either a lead- or salt-bath and then quenching the blades in brine. There is no tempering process and the tangs, having received no quenching, are left in a comparatively soft condition which makes them less liable to fracture.

Files are classified by: (1) length, (2) section and shape, and (3) cut. Length is measured along the blade, as in Fig. 108 in which are shown the sections and shapes.

The cut (tooth form) is all-important, many different types being made which fall into two main groups, viz.: *single* or *double-cut*. In the single-cut file (sometimes called 'float'), one line of teeth is cut at an angle across the blade and these files are generally used in taking light, finishing cuts. In double-cut files, two lines of teeth are cut, one across the other at angles varying between 30 and 87°. A number of 'special' double-cut files are available for use exclusively on particular metals and some of these are shown in Fig. 109.

Also shown in Fig. 109 are the degrees of coarseness, viz.: *rough, bastard, second, smooth* and *very smooth*. Of these, only the bastard, second and smooth are likely to be used in the school workshop.

The grade of any cut is related to the size of the file, thus, the cut on a 300 mm bastard file would be coarser than that on a 200 mm bastard file and so on.

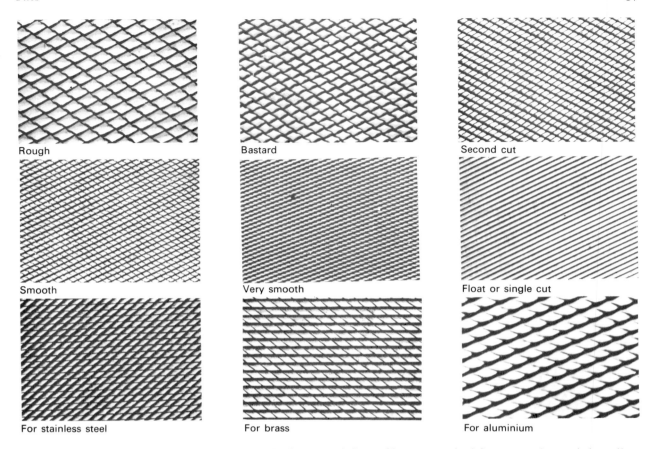

Rough

Bastard

Second cut

Smooth

Very smooth

Float or single cut

For stainless steel

For brass

For aluminium

Figure 109   File cuts and 'special' files

Unless 'special' cut files are stocked for use on brass, it is well to remember that any file which is first used on steel will not afterwards cut brass satisfactorily. Many people reserve sets of new files for use on brass and then pass them on for use on steel.

Hand flat files   These files are rectangular in section, parallel in width and tapered in thickness. Both sides are double cut and *one edge only* is single cut. The uncut edge is known as a 'safe edge' and the files are often referred to as 'hand safe edge files'. The safe edge is very useful when working into corners where one surface is to be left untouched.

Flat files   These are rectangular in section and taper in width and in thickness. They are double cut on both sides and single-cut on both edges. They should not be confused with the hand flat file.

Half-round files   With one flat side, the half-round file tapers in both width and thickness over about one-third of its length. It is not a true half-round, its section being a segment of a circle. The flat side of the file is double-cut and the curved side single cut.

Round files   With a taper over about one-third of the length, the round file can be used in pierced work, for enlarging holes and for rounding internal corners. The smaller round files are often referred to as 'rat tails'.

Square files   Tapered as with the round file, these are used in pierced work and in slots and corners where flat files cannot be

Figure 110   Dreadnought cuts

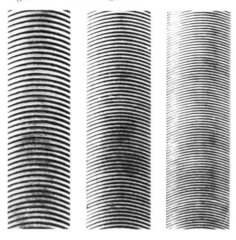

used. Care must be taken not to use too large a file in holes or slots or they may become jammed and broken.

Warding files   These are small files similar to the flat file but they are parallel in thickness. Double-cut on one or both sides and single-cut on the edges. They are used by locksmiths in ward and key cutting and in filing other work with narrow slots.

Pillar files   These are similar in shape to the hand file but are smaller in section.

Three square files   Triangular in section, these files taper over about one third of the length and are used for filing into angles. Similar to the saw file, but this latter file is usually made only with single-cut.

Milled tooth files   Files with milled teeth, sold under the trade names 'Millenicut' and 'Dreadnought' are very useful when cutting soft metals like aluminium which quickly cause clogging ('pinning') of other files. Of alloy steel, they are made in a range of cuts for use on wood, fibre, lead and other soft metals, brass, slate, marble, cast iron, stainless and high carbon steels.

Needle files   These are slender files from 12 to 18 centimetres in length made in the common sections together with the *knife, crossing, barrette, pippin, round-edge joint* and the *slitting* sections. A knurled hand grip is formed in place of the usual tang and these files are used on very small work as in decorative piercing, silver-smithing, and in model engineering.

Figure 111   Needle files
The thin lines in the knife and Barette files indicate non-cutting faces. All other files cut on all faces

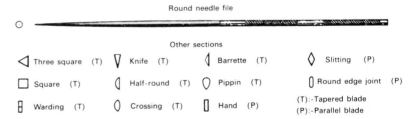

Rifflers   These are small bent files formed in pairs on a central hand grip. A great variety of sections is available for use in filing intricate shapes inaccessible to ordinary files. They are used extensively by diemakers.

Figure 112   A small selection of rifflers
A number of other shapes are available

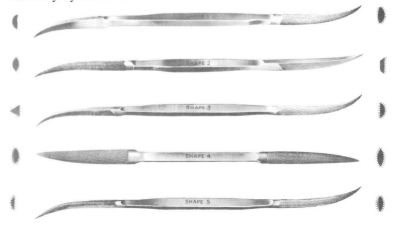

Figure 113   Holding the file

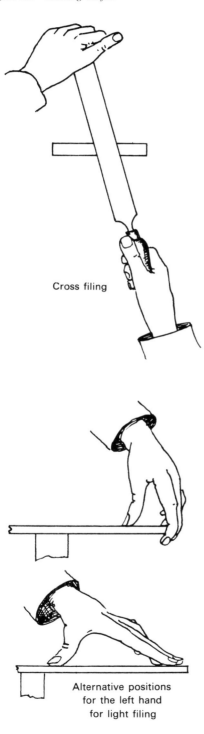

Cross filing

Alternative positions
for the left hand
for light filing

Care of files

Being very hard, the blades are brittle and the teeth are easily damaged by careless storage or rough handling or by being rubbed against other files. When in use, they should not be thrown down haphazardly on the bench, but should be laid side by side. They should not be allowed to touch the hardened steel vice jaws or used on hardened tool steel.

No file should ever be used without a handle, holding the tang could lead to injury. Handles should be of a suitable size, should be secure on the tang and should be discarded if split. They can be fitted by heating the tang of the file to a dull red and then driving the handle on a little at a time whilst the hot metal sears the wood to form a snugly fitting hole.

Filing

Cross filing

The file is one of the fitter's basic tools and mastery of its use calls for much careful practice. It is important that a good stance (as in hack-sawing) should be adopted from the very beginning, with the work set low in the vice to avoid vibration noise and at about elbow height.

Holding the file as in Fig. 113, the beginner should practise making long, steady strokes, concentrating on keeping the file level throughout its length of travel. This calls for flexing of the wrists to compensate for the pivoting movement of the right arm and for the forward extension of the left arm. Working with the file slightly aslant across the work will give a wider surface contact and if it is also traversed sideways a short distance along the surface, this will help in producing straight edges.

Work should begin with a coarse-cut file to remove waste metal quickly, changing to finer cuts as the finished size is reached.

Draw-filing

This is a finishing process which follows on after cross filing and is used to produce a fine surface. A smooth-cut file is held squarely across the work, and held steady with both hands, is drawn back and forth along the surface until the coarser marks disappear. Only a little metal should be removed by draw-filing as it is intended as a finishing process only.

Figure 114   Draw-filing

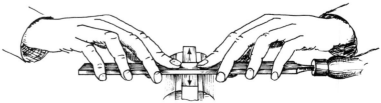

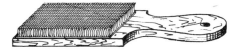
Figure 115   File-card

Pinning

Occasionally small particles of metal will pick up on the file and clog the teeth and this is known as 'pinning'. It occurs with all metals to some extent, but more so with the softer ones. A little chalk rubbed over the file will help to prevent these adhesions and when they do appear, the file should be cleaned at once to prevent the work becoming scored. The metal can sometimes be removed by brushing along the line of the teeth with a file card, but it is more effective if the edge of a piece of copper or soft brass strip is pushed across the file in line with the teeth.

Filing curves

In rounding external corners, the procedure is to remove as much metal as possible with the hack saw and then a number of flat surfaces are filed, each touching the curve and each removing one sharp corner until they blend to form a close approximation to the finished curve. It is then finished off as shown in Fig. 116.

Figure 116   Rounded corners

The curve
marked out

Corner sawn
off at 45°

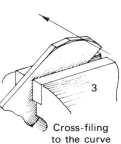

Cross-filing
to the curve

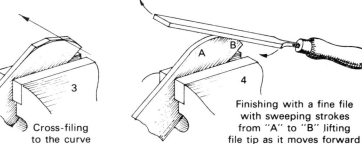

Finishing with a fine file
with sweeping strokes
from "A" to "B" lifting
file tip as it moves forward

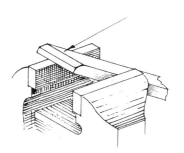

Edge chamfered at 45°
by sawing if large, and filing.

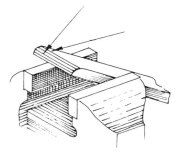

Corners of chamfer removed

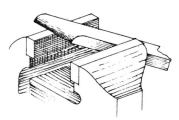

Taking light cuts with a fine
file, all corners are removed,
finishing as in no. 4 above.

Round and half-round files adapt readily in forming small internal curves but the filing of flat curves calls for a sweeping movement from side to side with the half round file and some care to produce a good curve. Such curves can often be finished by draw-filing with a small hand file.

Emery cloth

Emery is a natural abrasive material and in the manufacture of

Figure 117 Engineer's scrapers.
(Moore and Wright (Sheffield) Ltd.)

emery cloth the grains are graded in a range designated by numbers, viz.: No. 4 (very coarse), 3, $2\frac{1}{2}$, 2, $1\frac{1}{2}$, 1, F, FF, 0 and 2/0, the finest being known as 'flour'.

In the finishing of surfaces which have been nicely drawfiled, a start could be made with 'F' grade cloth which would remove file marks. The scratches from this grade of cloth would be removed with a finer grade and so on until the scratches become so fine that they are not visible, by which time, the surface will have become smooth and bright. The premature use of fine grades of cloth should be avoided, otherwise the surface, with a moderate polish, will still show score marks.

Scraping

The hand scraping of surfaces has been largely superseded by precision grinding but scraping is still commonly employed in the final 'mating' of machine parts such as lathe slides. Scraping is done with various shaped tools of hardened alloy steels with finely sharpened cutting edges, some of which are seen in Fig. 117.

In scraping flat surfaces, the work is mated to a surface plate on which has been rubbed a film of engineer's blue. In drawing the work across the plate, high spots pick up a little of the pigment and these are reduced by scraping. This is repeated until there is an even spread of the blue on the work.

Internal cylindrical scraping is done with three-square and half-round scrapers in such things as the fitting of split bearings to their shafts.

Riveting

The use of tinman's rivets in the joining of sheet metals is dealt with in Chapter 9, and here the joining of more robust materials is dealt with. In industry, the use of rivets on a large scale has been replaced by welding which gives a more satisfactory result in many ways but riveting still has its place in the school workshop.

In Fig. 119 are shown the more commonly used rivet shapes, one head being formed during manufacture and the other when the joint is being made. Riveting is regarded as making a permanent joint and can be used in structural work, connecting angle or other

Figure 118   Using the scraper

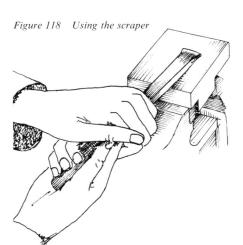

Figure 119   Small rivet forms

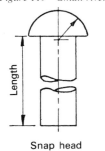

Snap head

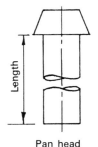

Pan head

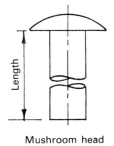

Mushroom head

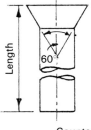

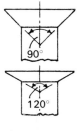

Countersunk heads

sections, or for joining plates either by overlapping them and inserting one or more lines of rivets, or by butting the plates edge-to-edge and riveting on straps on one or both sides.

Light riveting

Most of the riveting done in school workshops will be of a light nature, the rivets can be formed cold and provided that they are not beaten unnecessarily after the heads are formed, the results will be quite sound. Aluminium, brass, copper and iron rivets are readily available and are always supplied annealed and will, of course, work harden as they are formed.

Figure 120   Riveted joints

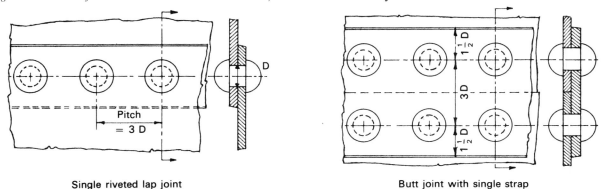

Single riveted lap joint

Butt joint with single strap

An approximate guide to rivet diameter for light work can be taken as $1\frac{1}{2}$ times plate thickness and provided that the pitch (see Fig. 120) is not reduced, this will be quite satisfactory for work not expected to be highly stressed.

Figure 121   Forming a snap rivet-head

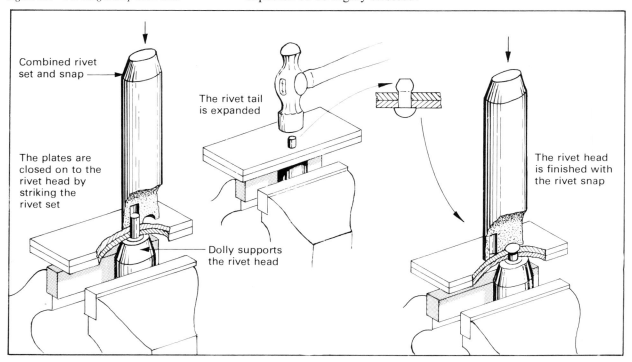

Combined rivet set and snap

The plates are closed on to the rivet head by striking the rivet set

The rivet tail is expanded

Dolly supports the rivet head

The rivet head is finished with the rivet snap

Figure 122 Pre-forming a snap-head on larger rivets

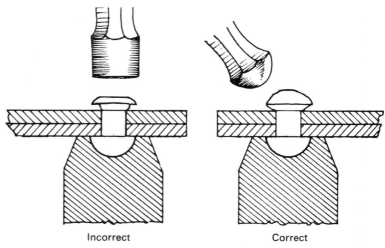

Incorrect   Correct

*Figure 123 Pop riveting
(Tucker Fasteners Ltd. Birmingham)*

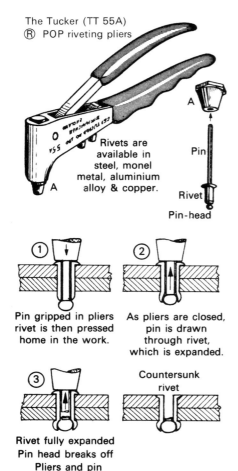

The Tucker (TT 55A)
® POP riveting pliers

Rivets are available in steel, monel metal, aluminium alloy & copper.

Pin

Rivet

Pin-head

① Pin gripped in pliers rivet is then pressed home in the work.

② As pliers are closed, pin is drawn through rivet, which is expanded.

③ Rivet fully expanded Pin head breaks off Pliers and pin withdrawn.

Countersunk rivet

Rivets should be cut neatly to length with a junior hack saw and should not be snipped off with pliers or cut roughly. If the end is left badly cut, the first blows with the hammer may cause it to bend and it will then have to be extracted. For forming a snap-head, an allowance of $1\frac{1}{2}$ times the rivet diameter on the rivet 'tail' will usually suffice.

Assuming two pieces of 3 mm plate 100 mm wide are to be lapped and joined together with one row of 5 mm snap-head rivets, the work would proceed as follows. Having marked the rivet line and the spacing (pitch) on one of the plates, each point is centre-punched and the two plates are aligned and held together with two hand vices. All the holes are drilled through at one operation, and taking the plates apart, all burrs are removed with a countersink. Riveting can then begin with the two outside ones.

With the dolly held securely in the vice to support the rivet head as shown in Fig. 121, the rivet set is positioned and one smart blow will set the plates together against the pre-formed head. Two or three blows on the rivet end will expand the tail tightly in the hole, and also produce a bulge as shown in the drawing. The other end rivet can be treated likewise and then each snap head can be formed with several solid blows on the rivet snap, which must be held upright to avoid forming a lop-sided head and perhaps damaging the work face. The centre rivet can be dealt with next, followed by the other two.

A similar order of work would apply to a longer line of rivets. It is not advisable to work straight along a line of rivets as there could be a tendency for a slight movement between the parts, resulting in misalignment of holes as work proceeds.

Each rivet head must be closed down just enough to bring the two plates together tightly, remembering always that excessive hammering will distort the work, especially if one happens to be working in a ductile metal such as copper. With rivets larger than about 5 mm diameter, it will not be easy to form heads using the snap only, and it will help if the head is partly formed with a small pein hammer as in Fig. 122, and then finished with the snap.

When forming countersunk heads, care must be taken to avoid striking the face of the work, for in addition to looking unsightly, the metal will be stretched a little and if this goes on all along the line of rivets, the finished work is certain to be distorted. It is better, perhaps to allow a little excess metal for the heads which can be filed down flush afterwards.

Removal of rivets
The removal of rivets is best done by first centre-punching the heads and running in a drill of the rivet diameter to the depth of the heads. The machine-made head is more likely to be accurately centred than the hand-made head and is best for this purpose. The rivets can then be punched out with a drift, the work being solidly supported close to the rivets. Snap-heads which do not come away readily on drilling can be removed easily with the cold-chisel.

Screw threads

The inclined plane and the helix
The value of the wedge as a means of transmitting motion is well known. For a constant effort applied in driving a wedge, a smaller

Figure 124   Transmission of motion with the inclined plane in the form of a wedge

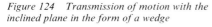
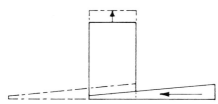
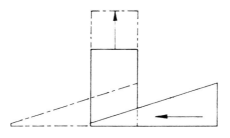
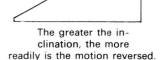

Transmission of motion with the inclined plane in the form of a wedge

The greater the inclination, the more readily is the motion reversed.

Figure 125   A helix

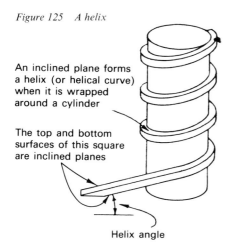

An inclined plane forms a helix (or helical curve) when it is wrapped around a cylinder

The top and bottom surfaces of this square are inclined planes

Helix angle

angle of inclination between the planes will cause a greater force to be exerted through a shorter distance, whilst conversely, a larger angle will cause less force to be exerted through a greater distance. Whilst the wedge is generally used as a means of transmitting motion, it must be remembered that this can be reversed and the wedge itself caused to move when a force is applied to the inclined surfaces. This is readily appreciated when the angle is large, as seen in Fig. 124, but, however small the angle, the resultant of forces applied will tend to produce movement although in fact, friction between the surfaces may prevent this from taking place.

From Fig. 125 it will be seen that the inclined plane, when formed around a cylinder, produces a spiral properly known as a 'helix'. The helix angle is important in screw threads, for a nut turning on a thread with a small helix angle (a *fine* pitch thread) will exert a greater pressure than one turning on a thread with a larger angle (a *coarse* pitch thread), always provided that equal forces are

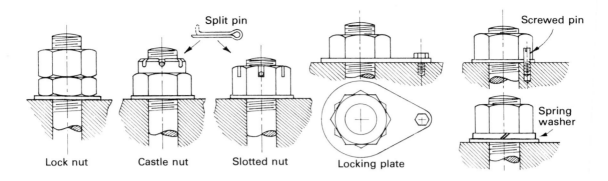

Split pin

Screwed pin

Spring washer

Lock nut   Castle nut   Slotted nut   Locking plate

Figure 126   Methods of locking nuts

Figure 127   Standard screw thread forms

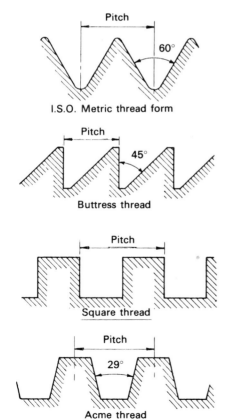

Pitch

60°

I.S.O. Metric thread form

Pitch

45°

Buttress thread

Pitch

Square thread

Pitch

29°

Acme thread

applied in turning both nuts. Pitch affects thread size, fine pitches being associated with small thread sections and in soft materials this can be a source of weakness with an increased risk of the metal shearing under stress. A good example of this influence on the choice of thread size is to be seen in the motor engine where the cylinder head is often secured to the block by means of steel studs and nuts. The studs, threaded at both ends, are screwed into the 'soft' cast iron block with a coarse thread whilst the nut is screwed on to the stud with a fine thread. Engine components are usually assembled with fine pitch threads on screws, bolts and nuts, largely because there is less danger of slackening off when they are subjected to constant pressure and vibration. Even so, nuts holding engine parts together are usually locked in some way and a few of the accepted methods are shown in Fig. 126.

Screw thread forms

The most commonly used thread forms are the 'V' threads used in constructional and engineering work where parts are assembled with screws or with nuts screwed on to studs or bolts. Where a screw thread is used in transmitting motion or power in machines, buttress, square and Acme threads are used. See Fig. 127.

Following on the introduction of the Whitworth screw thread with a V angle of 55°, developed by Sir Joseph Whitworth in 1841 and later to become the British Standard Whitworth (BSW) thread, a number of other V threads were standardised to meet various requirements and amongst these are the British Standard Fine (BSF) and the British Association (BA). The BSW is a coarse thread. With the adoption of the ISO Metric Screw Thread Standards in the UK, these original screw threads are not commonly used now, but it seems unlikely that they will disappear completely, because of present trade requirements. The appropriate threading tools are still in good supply.

ISO metric screw threads

The basic form of the ISO metric thread is shown in Fig. 127, nominal diameters ranging from 1.0 mm upwards in two series, 'fine' and 'coarse'. It is important that the designation of these threads is understood, viz:

Figure 128   Screw thread terms

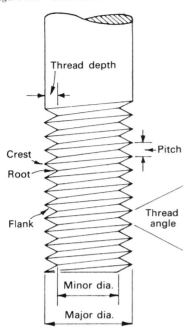

The letter **M** is followed by the nominal diameter and the pitch, both in millimetres.

> e.g. M6 × 0.75   i.e. nominal diameter, 6 mm and pitch, 0.75 mm.
> (This is in the fine series.)
> e.g. M6 × 1   i.e. nominal diameter, 6 mm and pitch, 1 mm.
> (This is in the coarse series.)

Where a coarse thread is intended, the pitch need not be indicated. Thus, M6 × 1 can be shown simply as M6.

Other thread forms

In Fig. 127 are shown the Acme and square threads which are used in machinery to transmit motion. The buttress thread is used in vices and presses for applying pressure in one direction only. Screw threads are usually made right-handed ('RH') so that they screw *in* when turned clockwise, but tools are made also for cutting left-handed ('LH') threads for special purposes.

Screw threads may be cut in a number of ways, viz.: with hand tools, in screwing machines or in the screw-cutting lathe, whilst for special purposes they are made by grinding, milling and rolling in industrial processes. Hand screw-cutting is done with *taps* which are held in wrenches for cutting internal threads and with *dies* which are held in stocks for cutting external threads.

Figure 129   Nuts, bolts and screws

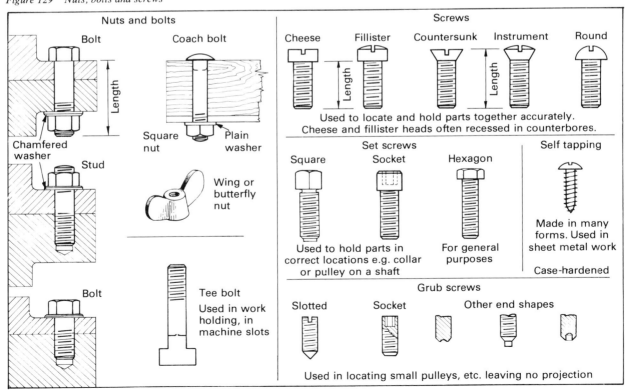

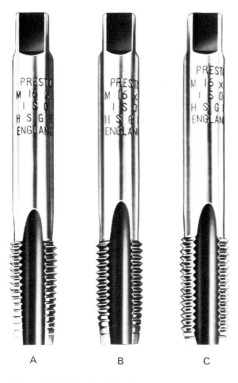

Figure 130   Standard hand taps.   A. Taper
B. Second
C. Bottoming
or plug

(Easterbrook Allcard and Co. Ltd.)

Figure 131   Tap wrenches.
A. Bar type
B. Chuck type.
C. American type.
(Neill Tools Ltd.)

Cutting of screw threads

Hand screw-cutting

Hand taps   These are known as *hand* taps to distinguish them from those used in screwing-machines and for other purposes. Made in either carbon or high-speed steel and left in a hardened state, a tap is a very accurately made 'master' screw along which are cut grooves or 'flutes' to form cutting-edges on the thread and at the same time provide room for the waste metal as it is removed. The hole into which a tap is screwed *must* be of the correct size to obtain a full thread and to avoid tap breakages. The tap is tapered to provide a 'lead' into the hole and is made in three forms, (1) the *taper* tap in which the taper extends over eight or nine threads, (2) the *second* tap with a taper over only three or four threads, and (3) the *plug* or bottoming tap in which there is no taper over the threads but only a small chamfer on the first thread to provide a lead-in. Wherever possible the three taps should be used in the order given, the taper tap being the most efficient of the three because of its *progressive* cutting action due to its long taper. The taper tap, however, cuts a full thread for only part of its length and where this is insufficient for the thickness of the metal being tapped, it is followed up by the second tap and, if necessary, the plug tap. The second and plug taps are also used in tapping blind holes where the taper tap cannot be used at all.

Tapping sizes

The importance of using the correct tapping drill has already been mentioned and at the end of the book will be found tables giving tapping and clearing drill sizes.

Tapping an internal thread

It is safer for the beginner to make his first attempt at tapping with a thread of moderate size to avoid breakages and to get the feel of cutting a thread. Let us assume a hole through a piece of 9 mm mild steel plate is to be tapped M10. An 8·5 mm tapping hole is drilled through the plate which is then held in a vice. With

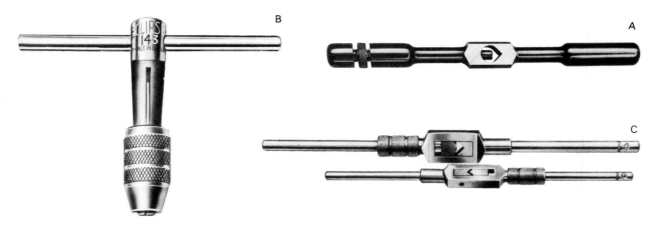

Figure 132   Tap extractor (made with 3 or 4 flutes)

the tap secured in the wrench and some lubricant on the threads, it is entered squarely and turned clock-wise with slight pressure to start it cutting. Quite soon, solid resistance will be felt and at this moment, it must be turned back about a half-turn to clear the cuttings. It is again turned in until resistance is felt and then eased back, and working in this fashion, the tap will cut the thread, a little at a time until the full thread is made. The tap can be turned in almost to the end of its thread to ensure a clean thread in the hole. It should be possible to tap this particular hole in one operation, but with smaller holes or thicker plates the flutes may become choked and it will be advisable to remove the tap from the hole for clearing at intervals. The tap should be cleaned before it is returned to its box.

Tapping a blind hole
The tapping of blind holes calls for much care and wherever possible, the hole should be drilled deeper than required so that the *second tap* can be used for getting the thread started, finishing with the *plug tap*. The procedure is the same as before but more care is needed as the second tap will offer much more resistance than a taper tap and must be eased back at shorter intervals and withdrawn more frequently for clearing the chippings. The tap must be kept well lubricated and when the full depth has been reached it is followed by the plug tap for finishing off the last few turns. Holes which are too shallow for the second tap must be started with the plug tap and the most difficult part here is in getting it started off straight. A small block of wood with a clearing hole drilled through it is of some help in this respect and can be dispensed with as soon as cutting is properly started.

*Figure 133   A. Circular split die
                B. Hexagon die nut
(Easterbrook Allcard and Co. Ltd.)*

A

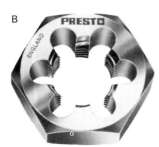

B

Broken taps
Broken taps always present a problem as there is rarely enough tap left protruding for easy extraction with pliers. If the tap extractor shown in Fig. 132 fails, then other means must be found, success depending largely on one's ingenuity in devising ways of getting out of trouble. Sometimes it may be possible to punch the tap out from the opposite side or the tap may become loose enough for extraction when the job is heated. The tap can be annealed by heating after which it might be possible to drill it and loosen it with small punches.

External threads
External threads are cut by hand with a specially designed nut, called a 'die' and made from either carbon- or high-speed steel. The die is gripped and turned by means of a stock and both are made in various forms, some of which are shown in Figs. 133 to 135.

Figure 134   Circular die stock

Figure 135   *Stocks and dies.*
    A. Angular pattern stock and dies.
    B. American pattern stock and dies
    for pipe threads.
    C. American pattern stock and dies
    (2-piece in collet) for standard threads

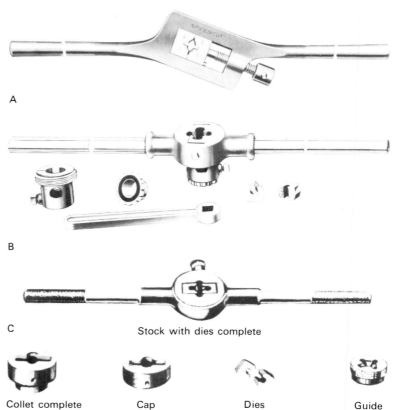

As with taps, the die is fluted to form cutting-edges and to provide room for the chippings as the thread is cut. With circular split dies, a small amount of adjustment can be made by means of three set screws. If the centre screw is turned in a little after the other two are slackened off, the die is sprung open and will cut a larger thread and vice versa. The hexagonal die nut is not used for cutting threads but is for re-shaping and cleaning up threads which are bruised or rusty.

Stocks with loose dies are shown in Fig. 135 and with the two-piece dies opened out a little, light cuts can be taken at first and with this adjustment, it is possible to cut threads to mate very snugly with the internal thread when required. Also shown, is a stock with guide bushes to help in aligning the dies with the work. These are commonly used in pipe-threading.

The cutting of external threads proceeds much the same as for tapping, and using a cutting lubricant, the die is eased back at intervals to ensure undamaged threads and for clearing of the swarf. Care must be taken to start the die off square or a 'drunken' thread will be formed. To obtain a clean start to the thread, the bar end must be square and neatly chamfered. Dies are made with the thread opened out at one side to provide a lead and they must always be started this way round. Hand screw-threading can be done in the lathe, and is described in that section.

Figure 136   Taps   A. Spiral flute tap
B. Spiral point tap
(Easterbrook Allcard and Co. Ltd.)

Other screw-threading tools

A large selection of taps and dies is made for special purposes and with *cut* or *ground* threads, according to the class of work to be done. Cut taps and dies are most commonly used and are quite accurate enough for use in school workshops. Ground threads are finished to much finer tolerances and are used on precision work.

Of interest is the spiral fluted tap, seen in Fig. 136. This type is specially suitable for blind tapping as it cuts freely and ejects the chippings, preventing clogging. The spiral point (gun-nosed) tap is used in through-tapping at high speeds, the spiral point forcing the chippings forward, thus preventing clogging in the flutes.

Table 7   Lubricants for Hand Screw Cutting

Material	Lubricant
Aluminium	Paraffin or soluble oil
Brass	Dry or soluble oil
Copper	Paraffin or soluble oil
Iron:	
cast	Dry or soluble oil
Steel:	
mild	Soluble oil or sulphurised oil
carbon	Soluble oil or sulphurised oil
stainless	Sulphurised oil
Gun metal	Soluble oil or paraffin

The reader is referred to p. 151 for further information on cutting fluids.

8

The joining of metals

Soft soldering

In soft soldering, metals are joined by melting a solder (or 'filler' metal) which flows into fine gaps between them by capillary attraction. The solders are based on tin–lead alloys with low melting points and can be melted with a heated copper 'bit' (soldering 'iron') which, in small jobs, heats the parent metals sufficiently to produce a good bond. Soft soldering is used in tinplate work and is equally effective on copper, brass, gilding metal, zinc, iron and steel. Because of a relatively low joint strength, the surfaces should be as large as possible; this can be achieved with laps or seams. A flux is always used to ensure that the solder flows over chemically clean surfaces, an essential feature to ensure satisfactory results.

Soldering stoves
A number of kinds of stove are available and two of these are shown in Fig. 137. These stoves are specially designed to heat soldering bits quickly and economically.

Soldering bits
Illustrated in Fig. 138 are the two common patterns of soldering bits. The bit is made from copper for two reasons: (1) copper is an excellent conductor of heat which is readily transferred to the solder and to the work, and (2) solder and copper have a great affinity which causes the bit to 'tin' readily when at the correct heat, i.e. to become coated with solder. It will then hold the solder in a molten state ready for transfer to the work. Over-heating will cause pitting and the bit will not tin properly. The surfaces will then have to be restored by filing. The correct heat can be judged by the appearance of a green tinge in the gas flame.

The straight soldering bit is used in general work and for getting into restricted places whilst the hatchet bit, with its blade-like edge, is suitable for making long joints. Electric soldering bits are commonly used today and the smaller sizes are specially suited to small electrical work.

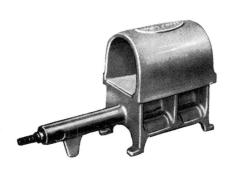

Figure 137   Soldering stoves
The smaller one is unlined *(William Allday & Co. Ltd.)*

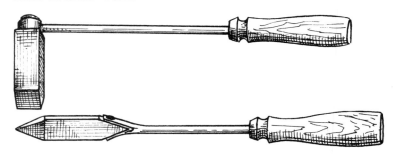

Figure 138   Hatchet and straight soldering bits

Soft solders

A range of alloys is available, some being for special purposes such as machine soldering and dipping. Those of immediate concern are shown in Table 8. Soft solders can be obtained in the form of sticks or as a paste or a powder. In the last two forms, the flux is generally already mixed in, and the mixture is spread on the surfaces and heat applied until the solder flows. Resin-cored solder is in the form of small tubes with a resin flux inside and is used mainly in electrical and radio work.

Table 8   Soft solders (Tin-Lead Alloys)

Solder	Percentage of tin	Percentage of antimony	Percentage of lead	Melting range in °C	Remarks
Tinman's fine solder 'A'	64–65	0·6 max.	Remainder	183–185	A free-running and quick-setting solder. Useful in radio and electrical work.
Tinman's solder 'B'	49–50	2·5–3·0	Remainder	185–204	Longer melting range. For bit-soldering of copper, tinplate and general purposes.
Tinman's solder 'C'	39–40	2·0–2·4	Remainder	185–227	With a long melting range. General purposes and for blow-pipe soldering.
Plumber's solder 'D'	29–30	1·5–1·8	Remainder	185–248	Very long melting range. This long pasty stage enables the plumber to make wiped joints on lead pipes. Also used in cable jointing.

'B', 'C', and 'D' are antimonial and not recommended for zinc or galvanised metal. Soft solders with higher melting points are made and these contain small proportions of silver, 1·4 to 1·6 per cent. With short pasty stages, their melting points are from 243 to 310°C.

Table 8. The reference letters, percentages and melting ranges are extracts from B.S. 219 (1977). The remarks have been appended by the author.

Fluxes

The purpose of a flux has already been touched upon, and whilst the object is the same in each case, different substances are used for different metals and for different kinds of work. Some fluxes are in liquid form and are swabbed on to the work whilst others are in powder or paste form and these melt at temperatures lower than the melting-points of the solders, protecting the surfaces from the atmosphere.

The fluxes in common use fall into two groups: (1) the 'passive' fluxes which serve only to exclude the atmosphere from the clean metal, preventing the formation of oxides, and (2) the 'active' fluxes, which, in addition to excluding the air, also play an active part in the removal of oxides by chemical action. Whichever flux is used, the work should always be cleaned before soldering is attempted.

Zinc chloride is probably the most commonly used of the active fluxes. It is known also as 'killed spirits' and can be made by dissolving zinc in hydrochloric acid, an operation which should be carried out in the fume cupboard. Zinc, in small pieces, is added to the acid until no more will dissolve and when all effervescence has ceased, the liquid is filtered and diluted a little. It is then ready for use and should be stored in a strong bottle and clearly labelled. Killed spirit should always be washed away from finished work so that no further action takes place and so that it does not get on the skin.

Resin, which is a passive flux, is quite commonly used in powder or paste form and is always employed in electrical work because there is no risk of any chemical action before or after joints are made.

The following table shows the fluxes suitable for a number of metals:

Table 9 Fluxes for soft solder

Metal	Active fluxes		Passive fluxes
Copper	Killed spirit	Powdered sal-ammoniac	Resin powder or paste
Brass	ditto	ditto	ditto
Steel	ditto	ditto	ditto
Iron	ditto	ditto	ditto
Tinplate	ditto		ditto
Pewter			Gallipoli oil
Lead			Tallow
Zinc and galvanised iron	Dilute hydrochloric acid		

Fluxite and Baker's Fluid are two well-known brands of passive and active fluxes, respectively.

Using soft solder

Let us assume a simple lapped joint in tinplate is to be soldered.
1. If the bit needs tinning, it is heated until the gas flame shows a greenish tinge and is then rubbed firmly on a sal-ammoniac block together with a bead or two of solder which will quickly flow and coat ('tin') the bit. Tinning can also be done by dipping the bit into a shallow dish of killed spirit or Baker's fluid and then touching it on the solder stick. This is quick and effective but care should be taken to avoid splashes.
2. The parts should be cleaned, tinplate needing only wiping with a clean rag, whilst other metals can be filed, scraped or rubbed with emery cloth. The surfaces are then coated with the flux.
3. With the parts held firmly in position, a small dot of solder is melted on at each end of the joint to locate the parts. To do this, a little solder is melted on to the hatchet bit which is then held on the joint whilst the metal is heated. The solder will then run into the joint. Then starting at the end, the bit is drawn slowly along the joint, allowing time for the metal to become heated sufficiently. The bit can be taken off for re-charging, but after some practice it will be found possible to feed the right amount of solder on to the bit without stopping until the bit becomes too cool. If it is arranged that one bit is heating whilst the other is used, there need be no delay. If on completion, the solder is unevenly spread, the bit can be drawn along the joint to remelt the solder and leave a cleaner finish.

Sweated joints

It sometimes happens that large surfaces are to be soldered together or the work may be so small or delicate that it is inconvenient to use a soldering bit at all. In such cases, sweating can be employed to make the joints, and this involves first the tinning of the parts

Figure 139 Soldering ring-base with gas flame

Both joint faces are tinned and fluxed, or coated with solder paint before heating. Ring and pot are heated evenly all round until the solder melts.

which are then brought together under light pressure and reheated until the solder runs. Solder paints are very useful in making sweated joints and, for that matter, all soldered joints. It is possible to place exactly the right amount of solder in position, and with a flux ready mixed in, all that is needed is to heat the work until the solder runs.

Figure 140   Tinning and sweating

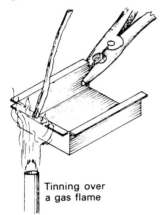

Tinning over
a gas flame

Tinning with
the soldering bit

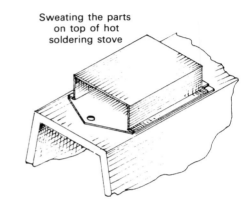

Sweating the parts
on top of hot
soldering stove

Silver-bearing soft solders

A number of alloys in this group of solders offer two advantages over ordinary soft solders, viz: (1) with higher melting points their range of applications is wider and includes uses in electrical control gear, electric motors and in steam control equipment, and (2) with high resistance to corrosion, some of the alloys are specially suited to use in certain water supply systems.

Although superior in strength to ordinary soft solders, these solders do not come up to the strength and other properties of the silver brazing alloys. Application is by the same methods as used in soft soldering, with fluxes based on resin or on zinc chloride.

Brazing (Low temperature brazing)

In brazing, just as in soft soldering, we use a filler metal which, on melting, is drawn by capillary attraction into a small gap between the joint faces where it forms a bond with the parent metals. The difference is that in brazing, the filler metals have higher melting points and make stronger joints. The term 'low temperature brazing' differentiates between brazing with filler alloys based on silver, copper and zinc, and other brazing processes employing filler alloys based on copper and zinc which have higher melting points.

The silver brazing alloys cover a melting range from about 600 to 890°C in low temperature brazing to which the terms *silver brazing*, *silver soldering* and *hard soldering* are equally applicable.

Corner fillets may be formed, but the main object in brazing is to ensure complete penetration of the joint gap, which should be of a size to suit the particular alloy being used. The parent metals must be properly cleaned (not polished) and fluxed and then heated to the melting point of the filler metal, which will melt and flow into the joint.

The silver brazing alloys are suitable for most of the common engineering metals in like, or unlike, combinations.

Features of the silver brazing alloys which make them widely adaptable are: (1) those with low melting-points are suitable for school use, (2) they can be used on most of the base metals, (3) they make strong and ductile joints with good corrosion resistance, and (4) they can be used on work which is to be plated.

One very useful application of these solders is in the assembly of composite jobs which cannot be soldered easily in one operation. In such cases, a short succession of joints can be made by using an alloy with a lower melting-point for each, so that those made previously do not melt.

Joint gap size

The phenomenon of capillary attraction is of great importance in silver brazing and, when preparing joints, care must be taken to provide a gap to suit the particular alloy being used, some requiring only a small gap whilst others are suitable for wider gaps. The manner in which the alloy melts determines the gap size. Some are quick running, for example, 'Easy-flo' No. 2, which has a short melting range, beginning to melt at 608°C and becoming liquid at 617°C, other alloys have long melting ranges, e.g. silver-flo 24 which begins to melt at 740°C and is liquid at 780°C. The quick (or 'free') running alloys are solid at one moment whilst heating and in the next they are molten and running freely. These call for small joint gaps whilst the long-melting range alloys are used with larger gaps and can be used to form fillets along the joints for extra strength.

Table 10   Silver brazing alloys (Hard, or silver, solders)

Solder	Melting range in °C	Flux	Characteristics
Easy-flo	620–630	Easy-flo	Low melting points, quick running and ductile. Close fitting joints required. Available as strips, rods, wire, foil, powder and as a paint.
Easy-flo No. 2	608–617	Easy-flo	
Silver-flo 67E	705–723	Easy-flo	This alloy is substantially white. It has a higher silver content.
Silver-flo 24	740–780	Easy-flo	These Silver-flo alloys are from a long list, all with different melting temperatures, providing a range suitable for stage brazing.
Silver-flo 16	790–830	Tenacity flux No. 4a	

The above solders are from the Johnson Matthey range of silver brazing alloys. All have a slightly yellowish tinge except the Silver-flo 67E. Easy-flo No. 2 is excellent for use in schools, it is cheaper than the Easy-flo but this latter alloy contains more silver, is more ductile and produces neater joint faces. Both alloys are useful in small and delicate work and, for this reason, are made in a variety of forms to suit all requirements.

Two alloys made specially for brazing copper are 'Sil-fos' and 'Silbralloy' and both are self-fluxing, the work only requiring to be cleaned. Sil-fos is the more ductile and Silbralloy the less expensive alloy. Many other alloys are made for special purposes in industry, but are of no direct concern here.

Hall marking quality silver solders

Used in silver-smithing, these solders all match the colour of standard silver and will satisfy the requirements for the Hall Marking of silverware. These solders should all be used with the recommended fluxes.

Table 11   Silver solders (Hall marking quality)

Solder	Melting range in °C	Recommended fluxes	Characteristics
Extra easy	667–709	Easy-flo	For general soldering. Strong ductile joints.
Easy	705–723	Easy-flo	
Medium	720–765	Tenacity flux. No. 5	Also a general-purpose solder. Higher silver content than 'easy'.
Hard	745–778	Tenacity flux. No. 5	For use in two-stage soldering where second joint is to be made with 'easy' solder.
Enamelling	730–800	Tenacity flux. No. 5	For work that has subsequently to be enamelled. Also for first soldering operations.

Fluxes

Parts for brazing or hard soldering must be quite clean, with bright metal exposed by filing, scraping or cleaning with emery cloth. The most careful cleaning, however, will not stop oxides forming when the metal is heated and since the slightest oxide film will prevent wetting of the surfaces by the molten solder, we employ a flux which should fulfil the following conditions: (1) to melt at a lower temperature than the solder and to spread quickly over the surfaces, (2) to prevent oxidation by excluding the air, (3) to dissolve any oxides already present, and (4) to remain stable (not to deteriorate) even if the heating is prolonged.

Because of the wide range of conditions which apply and because of the different melting-points, no single flux is suitable for all purposes and so a number of different kinds are available. The recommended flux for each solder should always be used and these are generally made up into a water paste for application before heating. Fluxes for lower temperatures are usually fluoride based, and residues from these fluxes should always be removed and the flux kept away from the skin and from cuts. For brazing, borax-based fluxes (with higher fusing-points) are used and these are often more difficult to remove because borax forms a glass-hard skin on cooling. Many of the proprietary fluxes made today are soluble in water. Some require dissolving in warm, dilute sulphuric acid or dilute caustic soda solution but, where any difficulty is experienced, the flux residues can be removed by wire brushing after quenching.

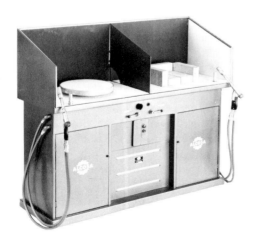

Figure 141   'Alcosa' double brazing hearth
One revolving and one fixed hearth
(William Allday and Co. Ltd.)

Figure 142   Revolving pan brazing hearth
(William Allday & Co. Ltd.)

Figure 143   Typical designs for brazed joints

Figure 144   Hard soldered joints

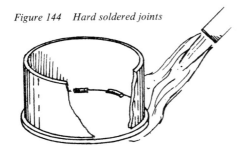

Drawing the solder through
a joint from outside

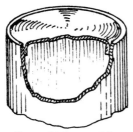

Flanged joint used in a
small boiler construction

Brazing equipment

Gas-air torches of the kind seen in Fig. 142 are commonly used in general brazing processes. With interchangeable air nozzles of different bores and with gas and air controls, the flame size and intensity can be adjusted to suit any particular job. The revolving pan hearth is a compact unit where work can be turned around without handling it.

Joints for brazing

Although butt joints are commonly used in decorative metalwork so that they will be unobtrusive, it is better, when maximum strength is desired, if the joint area can be increased. This can often be done by flanging the edges of sheet metal (folding them over) or by incorporating a simple structural joint of some kind. A few examples are shown in Fig. 143.

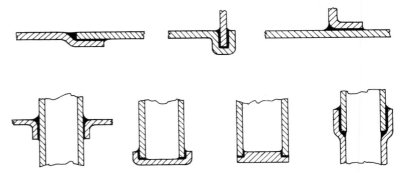

The solder can sometimes be melted on to a job from the end of a rod or strip and sometimes it can be placed over the joint before heating. An example is shown in Fig. 144 in which it is not touched by the flame at all, being drawn through the joint from the outside. Flux and small pieces of solder are put in position before heating.

The brazing process

For successful brazing, the following points should be observed: (1) the correct joint gap should be provided, (2) joint surfaces must be quite clean, (3) a suitable flux must be used, (4) parts should be wired together where necessary, (5) after a brief preliminary warming up of the whole job, the joint should be heated quickly to the melting point of the solder, at which moment it is applied to the work.

All but the smallest jobs will require packing around with fire brick and work with flat bases should be raised a little so that the flame can penetrate underneath. Where a job contains large and small (or thick and thin) parts, the flame should be concentrated on the larger masses to ensure even heating and it may be necessary to protect small or thin components with pieces of fire brick or sheet iron.

Figure 145A   Brazing a seamed cylinder

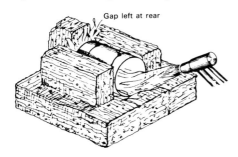

Gap left at rear

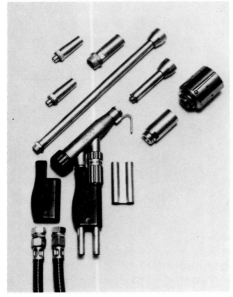

Figure 145B   The parts of the 'Alcosa' blowpipe seen in Fig. 142, showing interchangeable nozzles (William Allday and Co. Ltd.)

The silver brazing of a butt jointed cylinder (Fig. 145A) is taken as an example. Before rolling up the cylinder, the joint edges must be filed quite straight, square and parallel. The metal should then be annealed and thoroughly cleaned and can then be rolled into shape, the joint being closed with several soft iron wire bindings. The annealing removes any stresses which might later cause the joint edges to distort during the brazing process.

The joint is coated with flux paint and after a preliminary heating of the whole piece, the flame can be concentrated on the joint area. As soon as the flux is seen to run freely, the solder strip or wire is touched on to the joint, when a little will melt off and quickly flush along and into the joint. As soon as this happens, the flame should be removed. The flame should not be used directly to melt off solder from the strip otherwise a large piece might come away which, if the work is not hot enough, will roll away, perhaps adhering in the wrong place or disappearing into the hearth. This is messy and wasteful and will happen very readily if the solder strip is slender.

Before allowing the work to cool, the solder must be seen to have run along the whole length of the joint. If it has not done so, more local heating may be needed and, if necessary, a little more solder can be melted off into the joint. When adding more solder, it sometimes helps if a little flux is first picked up on the hot tip of the solder strip. Prolonged or excessive heating must be avoided.

Most flux residues are slowly soluble in water and can be loosened by soaking but their solubility may be reduced considerably if overheating has occurred. Careful quenching when the work has cooled to well below black heat will often help in loosening flux residues.

Silver brazing alloys used in schools will be mostly in the forms of rods, strips or wires but other forms are available, mainly for industrial use. Among these are foil, washers, wire rings, powder and easy-flo paint.

Lead and soft solder should never be used at the brazing hearth for even the smallest spot getting on to brass or copper will cause deep pitting of these metals at red heat. Lead should not be used in the bending of brass or copper tubes if they are to be hard soldered afterwards.

Safety precautions

Apart from the common-sense precautions which should be taken when lighting and handling gas torches and in dealing with hot metal, there are some hazards which are not quite so obvious. These are concerned with the fluxes, and the following points should be noted: (1) brazing should always be done in a well-ventilated room so that fumes from molten fluxes are dispersed quickly, especially those produced when fluxes are over-heated, (2) to avoid inhaling fumes, one should not lean over the hearth when brazing and (3) fluxes should be kept off the skin, taking great care not to get any on unprotected cuts or scratches nor into the eyes or mouth from one's fingers. As soon as brazing work is finished, the hands and finger nails should be scrubbed clean. Flux containers should be stored out of reach of children.

9

Sheet metalwork

In the working of sheet metals, the techniques and tools employed are specially adapted for the needs of the craft which is mainly concerned with the use of tinplate, terneplate and galvanised or plain sheet iron. The metal is folded to make boxes, trays and containers of all kinds, or is rolled to form cylinders, cones and other forms.

Sheet metals

Tinplate

Tinplate is made by coating thin sheets of steel with a protective layer of tin which makes it resistant to corrosion.

Until a few years ago, tinplate was made by hot dipping, i.e., immersing the sheets in a bath of molten tin, followed by rolling to remove excess tin and leave an even coating. This method is now outdated in the tinmill, but hot dipping is still employed in the tinning of made-up articles such as copper saucepans. Nowadays tinplate is made by electro-deposition, an efficient process which is economical of tin, a costly metal. It is possible to deposit a controlled weight of tin very evenly on both sides of the sheet, or where required, more on one side than on the other.

Low carbon steel is used in tinmill products and is made in the basic oxygen process. The steel must have physical and chemical properties suitable for the articles to be made, with ductility for deep drawing, with strength and hardness for large packaging and for pressurised containers such as aerosols, beer cans and so forth, or with specially good resistance to corrosion.

Hardness of the steel is controlled in the finishing processes in the rolling mill, cold rolling producing hardness which can be adjusted to varying degrees by heat treatment. Three kinds of steel are commonly used, one for general purposes, one for deep drawing and one which has good resistance to corrosion and is suitable for food canning. The dimensions of tinplate are now fully metricated.

Terneplate

This is made by hot-dipping sheet steel in a molten alloy of tin and lead which is less costly than pure tin. The tin is necessary in the alloy to form a surface alloy with the steel. Terneplate has a dull surface and is not used in food containers because of the danger of lead poisoning.

Sheet iron

The term 'sheet iron' is commonly used but the metal is in fact steel of a very low carbon content. Sheet iron is available as

Figure 146   Tinman's snips.
A. Straight.
B. Curved.
C. For straight or
left-hand curves

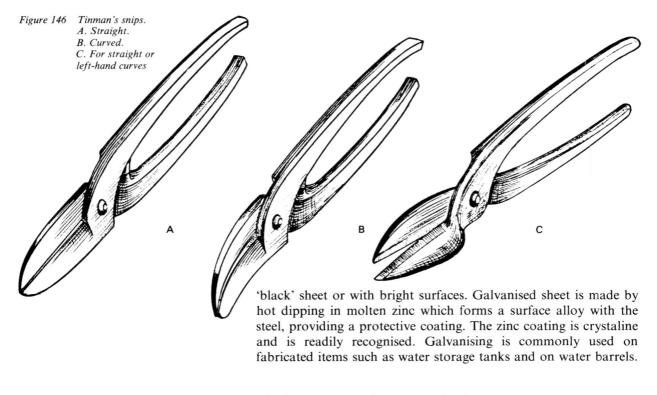

'black' sheet or with bright surfaces. Galvanised sheet is made by hot dipping in molten zinc which forms a surface alloy with the steel, providing a protective coating. The zinc coating is crystaline and is readily recognised. Galvanising is commonly used on fabricated items such as water storage tanks and on water barrels.

Marking out and cutting tinplate

Much of the marking out of tinplate can be done in pencil which shows up clearly enough for accurate cutting. The scriber can, of course, be used for indicating cutting lines, but bending lines should always be in pencil which will not damage the tin plating.

Shapes which have been developed on paper can be cut out and pasted on, taking care not to stretch the paper in the process. The shape is then cut with tin snips. Care should be taken to cut accurately at the first attempt as it is always difficult to remove slivers of metal afterwards. If the guillotine is to be used, it must be in good condition, viz., with properly ground blades which are closely adjusted so that the tinplate does not get drawn down between them.

Figure 147   Light-duty bench shears

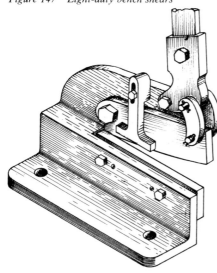

Tools used in sheet metalwork

Tinman's snips
A wide variety of snips are available for cutting thin sheet metal. A few of these are shown in Fig. 146. They should all be stored in racks and should not be used for cutting wire or anything other than sheet metal.

Tinman's mallet
Used in conjunction with stakes or folding-bars for shaping and

Figure 148　Creasing and paning hammer heads

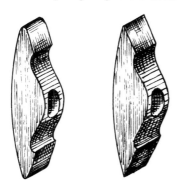

bending. The heads are made of box-wood or of tightly rolled hide which is sometimes enclosed in a metal sleeve. The handles are of cane.

Hammers

A few special hammers are used in tin-smithing:

Paning hammer　This has an acute-angled striking-edge and is mainly for tucking in the edge of the metal at the completion of a wired edge as in Fig. 164.

Creasing hammer　This has thin, rounded edges for use with the creasing iron in forming edges for wiring and for forming grooves.

Forming tools

Seaming tool　With a slotted end, it is used for neatly closing down seamed joints and is shown in Fig. 149. They are made in several sizes and can be made quite easily in the workshop.

Groove punch　Made with a rounded slot this tool (Fig. 150) is used for closing and neatly finishing off wired edges.

Figure 149　Seaming tool (left)
Figure 150　Groove punch (right)

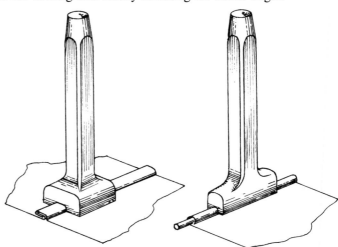

Folding bars　Two types are shown and these are used for making right-angled folds. In the bolted type of bars, one edge can be rounded off and is then useful in throwing rounded corners or for starting the rolled edge for wiring. (See 'Wired Edges'.)

Figure 151　Using the folding bars (left)
Figure 152　Two-piece folding bars (right)

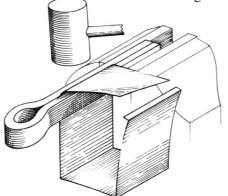

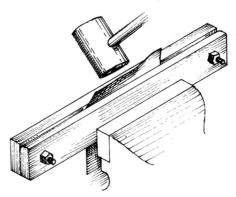

Figure 153   Tinman's horse and heads

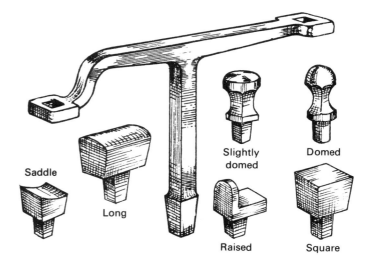

Figure 154   Making an acute fold on the hatchet-stake

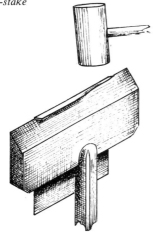

Figure 155   A. Hatchet-stake.
B. Half-moon stake.
C. Tinman's anvil.
D. Round-bottom stake

Figure 156   Bick-iron stake

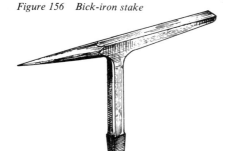

Tinman's horse   Used for mounting the various heads for forming sheet metal and also used in producing 'art' metalwork. As with other stakes and anvils these are sold by weight.

Hatchet stake   A 300 mm hatchet stake is a generally useful size and is used for forming bends at acute angles as shown in Fig. 154.

Half-moon stake   Used for 'throwing' up edges on curves as the first stage in wiring (see later) and for 'snuffing on' the bottoms of circular vessels, using the circular lap seam as in Fig. 163.

Tinman's anvil   The anvil has a polished face which can be used for a variety of purposes including the flatting and the stretching of metal whilst the edges can be used for angle-forming and for throwing straight or curved edges.

Bottom stake   Made with a round or oval face, the bottom stake is used in throwing the edges of bottoms for round or oval containers. The actual process is illustrated in Fig. 184, Chapter 10.

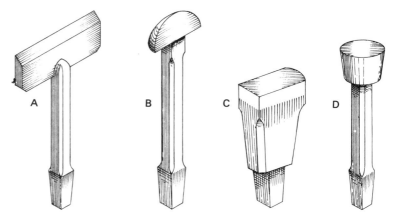

Bick-iron stake   For general use in shaping tapered work, for truing up rings and other curved work on the bick. The flat face can be used for angle-forming, flatting, light riveting, and a great variety of other small jobs.

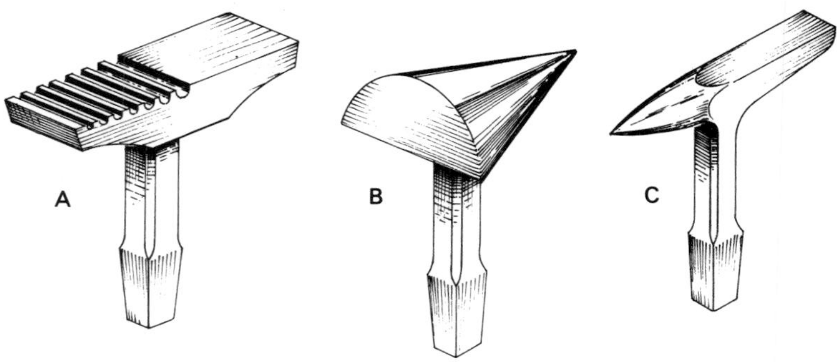

Figure 157   *A. Creasing iron.*
                 B. Funnel stake.
                 C. Extinguisher stake

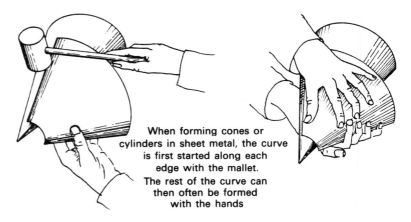

Figure 158   *Creasing iron and creasing hammer in use*

Figure 159   *Forming a cone on the funnel stake*

Creasing iron   With its selection of semi-circular grooves and the creasing hammer, this stake is used for forming beads and in the wiring of edges. See Figs. 157 and 158. Round wires of suitable size can be used instead of the creasing hammer in the forming of these sections.

Funnel stake   Designed for making conical shapes. It is also useful in forming and truing rings.

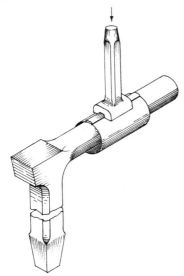

When forming cones or cylinders in sheet metal, the curve is first started along each edge with the mallet. The rest of the curve can then often be formed with the hands

Figure 160   *Closing a seam on the side stake*

Extinguisher stake   Also known as the bick-iron stake and with much the same applications as the larger bick iron.

Side stake   Illustrated in Fig. 160, the side stake, with round or tapered arm is used in forming tubes. It is shown being used in closing a folded seam.

Mandrels   Mandrels, up to about 1500 mm in length are held in the vice and are used in making pipes.

Joints used in tinplate work

Joints and seams

Lap joint   A very simple form of joint relying entirely on solder for its strength.

Creased lap   Another joint which relies on solder for its strength but showing a flush face on one side.

Folded seam   The edges to be joined are first turned over at right-angles in the folding bars and then closed down with the mallet

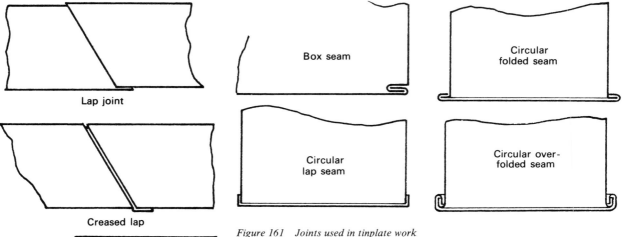

Figure 161   Joints used in tinplate work

onto a strip of metal of the same thickness which acts as a gauge. The two edges are then hooked together, dressed down firmly with the mallet and finally soft soldered.

Grooved seam   After assembly as in the folded seam, the face of the work is set down with a seaming tool to complete a strong and stiff joint which is finished by soldering. Allowances for the bends must be made carefully if the work is to finish to specified sizes.

Box seam   A strong joint for box corners which leaves both faces flush. If soldered neatly it gives a very good appearance on the outside.

Circular lapped seam   A joint used for the bottoms of cylindrical vessels, known also as a 'snuffed bottom' it requires soldering to complete it.

Figure 162   Making a box-seam (below)

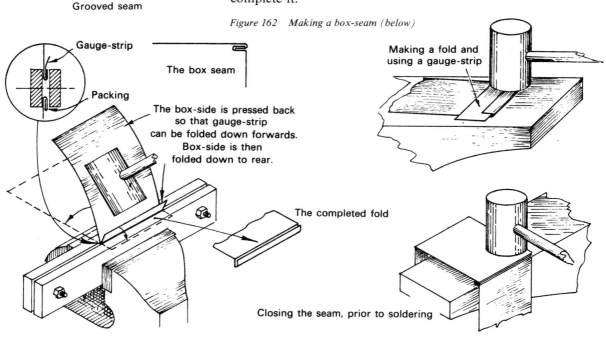

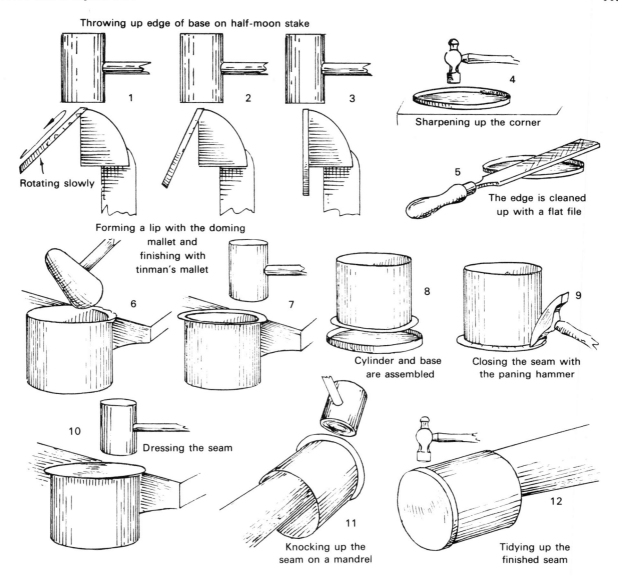

Throwing up edge of base on half-moon stake

1 2 3

4

Sharpening up the corner

5

The edge is cleaned
up with a flat file

Rotating slowly

Forming a lip with the doming
mallet and
finishing with
tinman's mallet

6 7

8

Cylinder and base
are assembled

9

Closing the seam with
the paning hammer

10

Dressing the seam

11

Knocking up the
seam on a mandrel

12

Tidying up the
finished seam

Figure 163   Forming a circular over-folded seam

Circular folded seam   Used for joining on the bottoms of cylindrical vessels, this joint calls for some measure of skill and patience. If knocked up as shown the joint is water-tight without soldering, and is then known as a circular over-folded seam.

Wired and safe edges

It is always desirable to form the edges of tinplate jobs to stiffen them and to avoid leaving sharp edges. In making a safe edge, the metal is first folded to an acute angle and is then dressed down gently with the mallet. The metal is left with a rounded edge and should not be beaten down flat or it will not be so stiff and may even distort.

The wired edge, shown in the making in Fig. 164 is a much more satisfactory job but requires a lot of care if it is to look respectable.

Figure 164   Making a tinplate box with wired edges

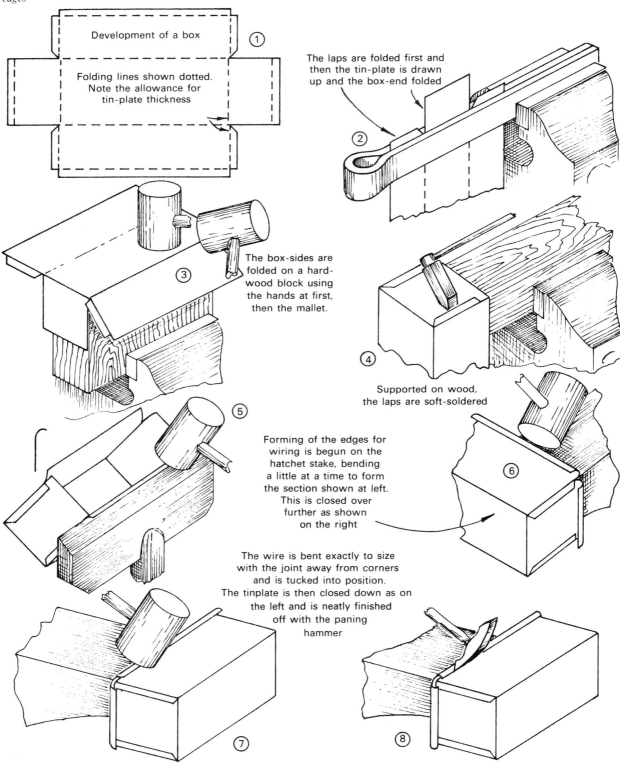

(1) Development of a box

Folding lines shown dotted. Note the allowance for tin-plate thickness

(2) The laps are folded first and then the tin-plate is drawn up and the box-end folded

(3) The box-sides are folded on a hard-wood block using the hands at first, then the mallet.

(4) Supported on wood, the laps are soft-soldered

(5) Forming of the edges for wiring is begun on the hatchet stake, bending a little at a time to form the section shown at left. This is closed over further as shown on the right

(6)

The wire is bent exactly to size with the joint away from corners and is tucked into position. The tinplate is then closed down as on the left and is neatly finished off with the paning hammer

(7)

(8)

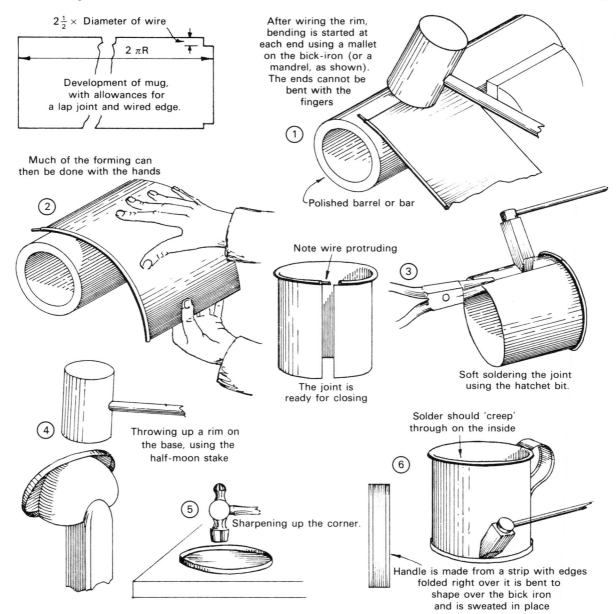

$2\frac{1}{2} \times$ Diameter of wire

$2 \pi R$

Development of mug, with allowances for a lap joint and wired edge.

After wiring the rim, bending is started at each end using a mallet on the bick-iron (or a mandrel, as shown). The ends cannot be bent with the fingers

① Polished barrel or bar

Much of the forming can then be done with the hands

②

Note wire protruding

③

The joint is ready for closing

Soft soldering the joint using the hatchet bit.

④ Throwing up a rim on the base, using the half-moon stake

⑤ Sharpening up the corner.

Solder should 'creep' through on the inside

⑥

Handle is made from a strip with edges folded right over it is bent to shape over the bick iron and is sweated in place

Figure 165   Stages in making a tinplate mug

An allowance of two-and-a-half times the diameter of the wire is required and care should be taken not to exceed this for surplus metal cannot be disposed of and spoils the finished job. Much care is needed in forming the bend along the edge of the tinplate which must be *rolled* over to accommodate the wire. If this bend could always be started off in folding bars with a rounded edge, the job would be simplified but this cannot often be done as many jobs have to be folded to shape before wiring can be started.

The tinplate can be fed, a little at a time over the corner of the bick iron or the hatchet stake, dressing the metal down only a few degrees each time it is moved forward. The creasing iron and

Figure 166 *'Home-made' dimpling punches*

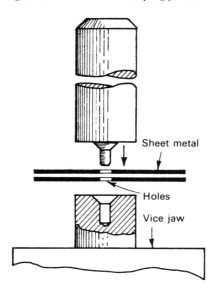

Sheet metal

Holes

Vice jaw

Figure 167 *Joining sheet metal with tinman's rivets*

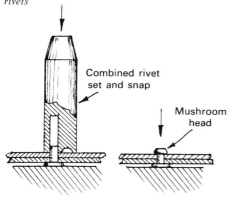

Combined rivet
set and snap

Mushroom
head

hammer can be used to shape up the bend when it is partly made and a short length of rod of the right diameter can be used to assist further in forming the bend. The closing of the metal over the wire is started with the mallet as in Fig. 164 and is completed with the paning hammer. The grooving punch can then be used as shown in Fig. 150 for a final tidying-up.

With cylindrical work the wiring is best done 'in the flat' and the metal afterwards bent up to shape as in Fig. 165. Where curved edges are to be wired, as in making a funnel, the edges are thrown on the edge of the half-moon stake as in Fig. 163.

In bending up tinplate for things like funnels and for cylindrical work much of the bending can be done with hand pressure only, coaxing the metal over bick iron, funnel stakes or mandrels. Folding can be done with hand pressure, the mallet being used only to sharpen up the corners.

Riveting of sheet metal
In the heavier gauges of sheet metal, joints are generally made by lapping over and riveting. In work such as trunking (air ducts), tinman's rivets are commonly used, and these, with plain, flat heads, do not need countersinking.

The preformed head is supported on the anvil, the sheets are closed with the rivet set and then one or two blows on the rivet tail form a mushroom shaped head which is quite strong enough for this kind of work.

Rivets with a 'flat' countersunk head (see Fig. 119) are available for sheet metals and where ordinary countersunk heads are to be used, a good method is to 'dimple' the metal with a pair of punches, one of which has a countersunk recess on the end and supports the metal whilst the other is made like a centre-punch with a locating pin in the centre.

Holes in tinplate can be made quite easily and neatly by punching on a smooth lead block, using a parallel punch which is struck smartly to pierce the metal in one blow.

10

Beaten metalwork

The forming of sheet metals with hammer or mallet is a traditional craft, seen to perfection in the work of the gold- and silver-smiths of present and bygone days. Gold and silver are the supreme metals for working under the hammer because of their high malleability and ductility, but they are precious metals and will not often be found in the school workshop.

Of the base metals, those most suitable for beating are aluminium, copper, gilding metal and brass. Nickel silver (an alloy of copper, zinc and nickel) is a bright and attractive metal but it is hard, even when fully annealed and is more suitable for work requiring only simple folding or a minimum of forming.

Sheet metal thickness is commonly measured in mm, 1.25, 0.90 and 0.71 mm (approximating to 18, 20 and 22 SWG, respectively) meeting most requirements in the school workshop. Most non-ferrous metals are available in degrees of hardness according to the final processes (rolling and annealing), and are classified as 'soft', 'half hard' or 'hard'. Half hard sheet is in a suitable condition for general use but will require annealing for beaten metalwork.

Metals for beating

For satisfactory results under the hammer, a metal must be: (1) *malleable,* i.e. readily formed whilst cold by hammering or squeezing without fracturing, and (2) *ductile,* i.e. readily formed whilst cold by tension as in the drawing of wires.

Aluminium
Whilst aluminium is very ductile and malleable, its use is confined to simple exercises largely because it is not so easily soldered in the assembly of composite jobs. Its annealing requires some care because of its low melting-point (around 660°C) and also unless anodised and coloured, it quickly acquires a thin oxide film which gives it a dingy appearance. This latter point does not apply to super-purity aluminium, used extensively in industrial processing of items which retain a high lustre without any protective coatings.

Copper
Of a warm, reddish colour, copper is specially suited to hammered work because of its high malleability and ductility. It is readily joined by brazing or by hard and soft soldering and its annealing is a simple process. It is a good metal for plating, its one disadvantage being that it is soft, lacking in rigidity especially when annealed. This makes it unsuitable for work which requires hard

Figure 168   A selection of hammers used in beaten metalwork

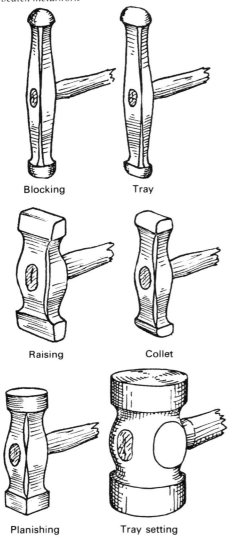

Blocking   Tray

Raising   Collet

Planishing   Tray setting

Figure 169   Mallets
The tinman's mallet is also used

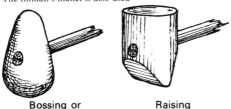

Bossing or   Raising
doming mallet   mallet

soldering in the later stages of a job which cannot be hardened again by hammering.

Gilding metal
This is a copper-zinc alloy of high copper content of between 80 per cent and 90 per cent. It is a little harder than copper but is nevertheless very suitable for cold working. With a rich, golden colour, it is used extensively in cheap jewellery, in architectural metalwork and in industrial production work.

Brass
The term 'brass' embraces a range of copper-zinc alloys of varying copper content (from about 55 to 80 per cent) and each brass has its own special properties, viz., for hot or cold working, for deep drawing, for good machining and so on. The hammering of brass must be done carefully to avoid uneven stresses which may cause fracturing to take place. The metal hardens more rapidly than copper or gilding metal and will require more frequent annealing.

Tools and equipment

Hammers
Some of the hammers used are mainly for shaping the metal whilst others are used in the finishing of surfaces by planishing.
Blocking hammer   This is used in the hollowing or sinking processes, also known as 'blocking'. The faces are of a full, rounded shape.
Tray hammer   This hammer has oval faces and is used in sinking and finishing of tray forms.
Tray setting hammer   A heavy hammer with one flat face and one slightly concave. It is used in 'setting' tray bottoms which involves the pulling out of buckles and tensions so that the tray does not distort.
Raising hammer   This is used in conjunction with the raising stake, its striking faces being oblong and flat with the edges rounded. Raising hammers are also made with only one face for raising, the other being slightly convex so that it can be used for stretching.
Collet hammer   This has oblong faces which are rounded across the width for working on the insides of rings and bands for bases, or on turned out edges. By careful control of the spacing and weight of the blows, the collet hammer can be used in the planishing of these shapes.
Planishing hammers   The planishing hammer is used in the finishing of surfaces by hammering the metal on suitably shaped stakes. The striking faces are always kept highly polished.
Mallets   Three kinds are used: (1) the doming or 'bossing' mallet with a stout, cane handle which can be used in hollowing, (2) the raising mallet with a wedge-shaped edge, and (3) the tinman's mallet, used for flatting and folding of edges.

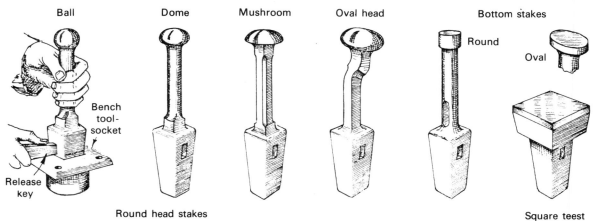

Ball
Dome
Mushroom
Oval head
Bottom stakes
Round
Oval
Bench tool-socket
Release key
Round head stakes
Square teest

Figure 170   Bench-socket and a selection of stakes (above)
(William Whitehouse & Co. (Atlas Forge) Ltd.)

Figure 171   Examples of the forms made by sinking, hollowing and raising (below)

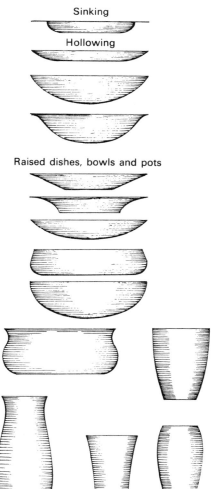

Sinking

Hollowing

Raised dishes, bowls and pots

Stakes

In addition to those stakes shown in Fig. 170, a variety of shaped heads are used in the horse (see Fig. 186). Their uses are dealt with as occasion arises.

Acid pickle bath

This is used for the cleaning of metal by 'pickling' in dilute sulphuric acid for the removal of oxides after heat treatments. The pickle is made by diluting one part acid in from eight to ten parts of water in a heavy earthenware or leaden container. The acid should be added to the water very slowly when diluting. Water should *never* be added to the concentrated acid because there is a very rapid generation of heat and water droplets, turning to steam, will cause spluttering. The acid bath should be near a sink and running water and it should be covered with a stout lid, labelled: 'Danger—Acid'. For inserting and removing work from the bath, tongs of brass or teak wood should be provided. Iron or steel will contaminate the acid and discolour every piece of metal subsequently pickled.

Beaten metal forms

In Fig. 171 is shown a selection of the various forms which can be made by hammering sheet metal. It will be noticed that in some cases, hollowing and raising produce very similar forms, but the processes themselves are in fact very different.

Processes

Preparation of the metal

Before marking out and cutting the blank disc, the sheet should be inspected so that any damaged parts can be avoided. After cutting to shape with the snips, the edges should be filed for safe handling and then any surface scratches can be removed with fine emery cloth, working through the grades down to No. 000. By constantly changing the direction of rubbing, all previously made

Figure 172   Holding tin-snips in the vice for ease of operation

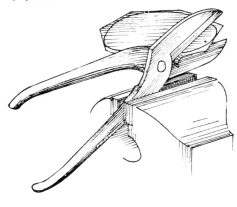

marks are removed. Metal in the hard or half-hard condition will require softening by annealing before work starts.

Annealing

This is an important and very necessary heat-treatment by which metals are restored to their original soft condition after becoming hard through being worked whilst cold. Annealing involves nothing more than heating the metal, in most cases to a dull red heat and allowing it to cool.

Copper is annealed by raising it to a dull red heat (between 500 and 600°C) and it can be allowed to cool slowly or it can be quenched after cooling to 'black' heat. Quenching saves time and also leaves the metal fairly clean as much of the oxide comes away on immersion. The metal should not be kept at red heat for any length of time or it may become pitted through excessive oxidation. Partial annealing can be brought about by heating to temperatures below the full annealing heat.

The annealing of brass needs more care because of lower melting points and also because prolonged heating may spoil the metal. Some of the brasses become brittle if they are quenched and it is generally safer to allow all brasses to cool slowly.

Aluminium has a low melting-point (660°C) with a correspondingly lower annealing temperature. The metal is very easily melted, even over a gas-ring, but the annealing heat can be fairly accurately gauged if the surface is first rubbed over with soap which will turn brown as soon as the metal is hot enough. The metal is quenched and the soap washed away.

Copper and brass should be pickled after annealing to remove all traces of oxide, then washed to remove the acid and scoured with a paste of fine pumice powder and water, then rinsed and dried.

Hollowing (blocking)

This is a simple method for forming shallow dish or bowl forms. The metal, after preparation, is beaten with doming mallet or blocking hammer over a suitable depression in a wooden block (or on the end of a short length of tree trunk), or alternatively the beating is done on a leather-covered sand pad. The blocking hammer is generally used in smaller work on the wood block whilst the doming mallet is used in larger forms on the sand pad, but there is no hard and fast rule about this. The process involves stretching and thinning of the metal and hollowing is therefore restricted to making shallow forms.

Figure 173   Hollowing with doming mallet on the sand pad

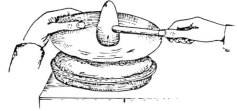

A series of concentric circles is struck on the blank as a guide to help in beating evenly. Hammering begins at the outside edge and each blow is delivered a little in advance of the point of contact with the wooden block in order to stretch the metal as it is pushed down. There is a tendency for the edges to wrinkle and this can be reduced by careful spacing of each blow and by light hammering. Any wrinkles that do form must be dressed down before they develop into folds. At the completion of each course of beating, the

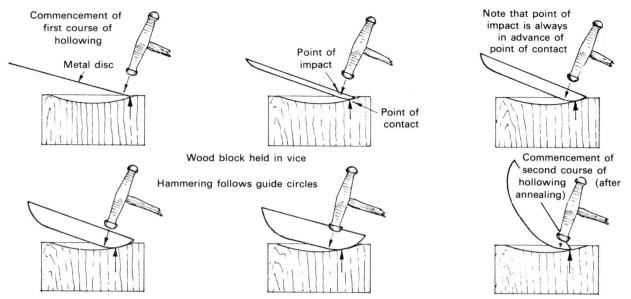

Commencement of first course of hollowing

Metal disc

Point of impact

Point of contact

Wood block held in vice

Hammering follows guide circles

Note that point of impact is always in advance of point of contact

Commencement of second course of hollowing (after annealing)

Figure 174   Forming a shallow bowl by hollowing on a wood block

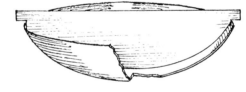

Figure 175   Checking a bowl-form with a template

Figure 176   A doming block

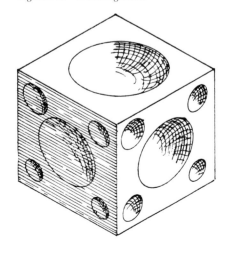

form can be pulled into shape with the hands and as soon as work hardening becomes apparent, the metal must be annealed.

Hollowing is illustrated in Figs. 173 and 174. As soon as the bowl approaches the required shape it can be checked with a template (or 'templet') made from thin card or tin-plate. On completion, the bowl is annealed, pickled and scoured thoroughly in readiness for the finishing process of planishing. This is dealt with under a separate heading.

Small hollowed forms such as ball feet for dishes, can be made on a brass doming block. The annealed disc is beaten into the depression with a wooden punch. In the absence of a doming block, suitable depressions can be beaten in a lead block.

Sinking

The forming of a plate or tray with a flat rim is done by sinking as illustrated in Fig. 177. Two small nails serve as guides in keeping the sinking parallel to the edge. With the annealed blank held very firmly in position, the metal is lightly struck with the blocking or tray hammer just inside the line, working steadily around the disc. After each course of beating, the rim is dressed down and the corner sharpened up with the mallet. Distortion of the rim happens very readily, and this can be rectified by dressing with a small hard-wood block and hammer as shown. The bottom of the sinking will also need flatting with the mallet as work proceeds. The corner can be finally sharpened up by working on the corner of a flat stake with the blocking hammer and mallet, but care must be taken or the underside of the work will be damaged if the stake corner is too sharp or the beating too heavy. The work is finished by planishing after annealing, pickling and cleaning.

Raising

This is the ideal method by which forms of all shapes can be made

Figure 177   Sinking

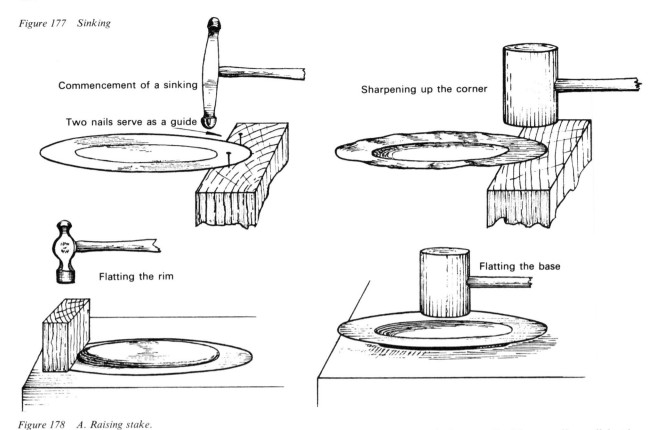

Commencement of a sinking

Two nails serve as a guide

Sharpening up the corner

Flatting the rim

Flatting the base

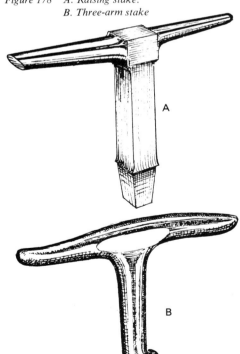

Figure 178   A. Raising stake.
B. Three-arm stake

from the flat disc, the process being applicable equally well in the making of bowl forms, deep pots and narrow-necked vases. Raising can be regarded as the 'ideal' method because, in addition to the form being made in one piece, there is no thinning or stretching of the metal which there always must be in hollowing.

Two methods of raising are employed, viz: with the *raising mallet* and with the *raising hammer*. In either case the process is commonly preceded by a slight hollowing of the form which makes the commencement of the raising easier. From then on, all hammering is done on the outside, starting along the base circle and working outwards along concentric guide circles.

With the work supported against a suitable stake, the metal is *pushed* inwards with hammer or mallet along the guide lines. The movement of the metal in this way causes some contraction together with a slight thickening of the metal and a wave-like depression travels out and up towards the rim. In this way, the periphery of the disc is progressively reduced during each complete course of hammering, the bowl or pot being literally 'raised' from the disc. Since the movement ('working') of the metal is considerable, frequent annealing will be necessary if progress is not to be slowed down by work-hardened metal.

The manner of striking the metal is most important, each blow striking a little in advance of the point of contact between metal and stake. Each blow must be controlled so that it does no more than push the metal on to the stake. If the hammering is heavy, each blow will first push the metal down on to the stake, causing the desired contraction but this will immediately be followed by squeezing against the stake which will cause expansion, defeating the object.

Raising with the mallet

This method is usually adopted for shallow bowl forms and is done on a round ended stake with the wedge-shaped raising mallet. After preparation and annealing of the disc, the base circle is struck and outside this, concentric guide circles at about 12 mm intervals. If the bowl is first hollowed slightly, this gets over the difficulty of striking into a flat surface with the straight edge of the mallet.

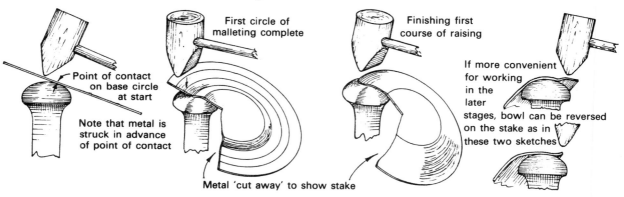

Figure 179   Raising with the mallet

Working as in Fig. 179, the disc is rotated slowly as evenly spaced blows are delivered with the wedge shaped mallet along the first guide circle. This will form the depression which will travel out and up as contraction takes place along each circle. When the edge is reached, the periphery will have been reduced and a shallow dish form produced. The process is repeated and at the first signs of work hardening, the work should be annealed, pickled and scoured clean. The work is finished by planishing which is described later.

Raising with the hammer

This method is used in forming deeper work on a raising stake, an example of which is seen in Fig. 180. The metal is prepared as for mallet work but with the guide circles a little closer, at about 9 mm spacing. The disc can first be hollowed slightly on the sand pad, after which the base may need flattening with the mallet on a round bottom stake.

At the commencement of raising, the base circle must always be held in contact with the corner of the raising stake during the first circle of hammering to ensure a clean start to the work. With the disc held at an angle of about 30° and rotating slowly, the flat face of the raising hammer will push the metal on to the stake, forming the wave which will travel upwards with each succeeding course of hammering.

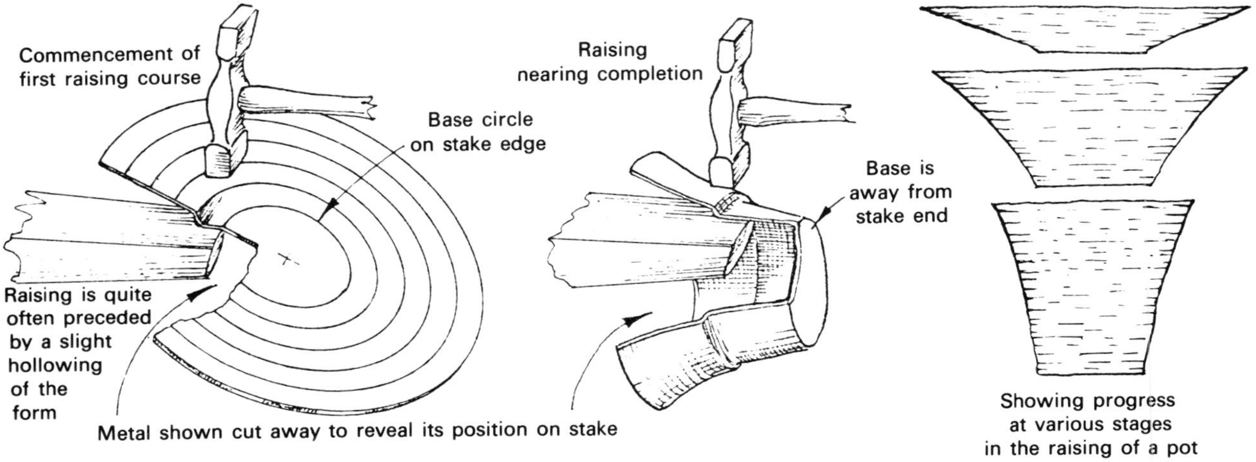

Commencement of
first raising course

Raising
nearing completion

Base circle
on stake edge

Base is
away from
stake end

Raising is quite
often preceded
by a slight
hollowing
of the
form

Metal shown cut away to reveal its position on stake

Showing progress
at various stages
in the raising of a pot

Figure 180   Raising with the hammer

The guide circles should be followed carefully and the weight of
each blow controlled so that it does no more than push the metal
down to the stake. As the hammered depression advances, the work
should be drawn away from the end of the raising stake to avoid a
constant pressure against the base as this would produce some distortion locally.

The raising of vertical sides calls for considerable skill, because
excessive hammering around the base will eventually cause stretching rather than contraction. It then becomes necessary to commence
the circles of hammering at carefully chosen intervals upwards
from the base.

Raising shaped profiles

Being flat over its length, the raising stake is not altogether suitable
for the forming of shaped profiles of any depth. Concave forms are
straightforward and can be produced by reducing the amount of
contraction. Convex profiles can be made by spacing the courses at
higher levels leaving a series of steps approximating to the finished

Figure 181   Snarling

form. These can be run together by malleting on a shaped stake or
the snarling iron can be used to stretch the metal from the inside as
in Fig. 181. The work is rotated slowly over the ball-end of the
snarling iron whilst the shank is struck with the ball pein hammer.
This causes the ball-end to rebound and strike the metal.

Stretching (expanding)

In stretching, contoured forms can be produced by expanding

Figure 182 Stretching

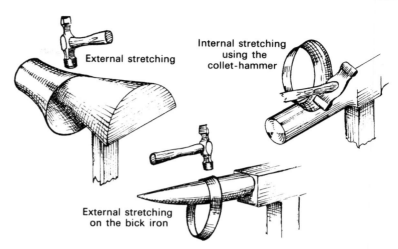

External stretching

Internal stretching using the collet-hammer

External stretching on the bick iron

the metal, its surface area being increased by squeezing and thinning it. This is done by hammering on a stake, the spreading action being helped by the convex face of the hammer.

Figure 183 Contracting on a stake

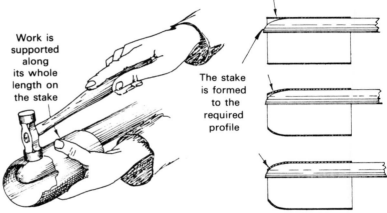

Work is supported along its whole length on the stake

The stake is formed to the required profile

Figure 184 Contracting a rim

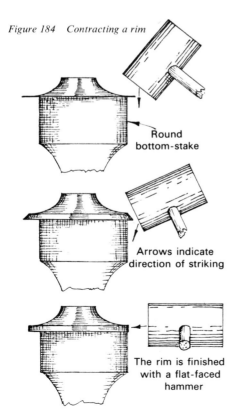

Round bottom-stake

Arrows indicate direction of striking

The rim is finished with a flat-faced hammer

Contracting

This involves a reduction in the diameter of a cylindrical form and this can be done as in Fig. 183. The metal is struck a little in advance of the point of contact with the stake, working around the cylinder as it is turned. Contracting is used in the forming of rims as shown in Fig. 184, working on the round bottom stake and striking light, glancing blows with the mallet.

Planishing

With a piece of work brought to its final shape by sinking, hollowing or raising, there should remain only minor imperfections of form and after annealing, pickling, scouring and washing, the job is ready for planishing. The metal must be quite clean, for any foreign matter left adhering will be hammered into its surface.

The objects of planishing are (1) to correct small irregularities of form, (2) to close the grain of the metal, especially where it has been stretched by hollowing, leaving a good, hard surface, and (3) to leave the work partly work-hardened so that it has some rigidity.

Figure 185 *Examples of planishing*

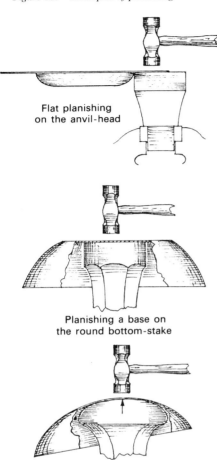

Flat planishing
on the anvil-head

Planishing a base on
the round bottom-stake

External planishing
on the mushroom stake

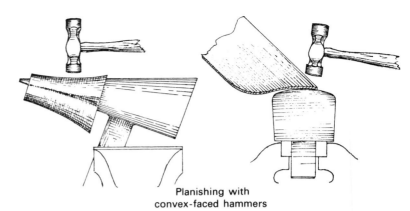

Planishing with
convex-faced hammers

Hammers and stakes (or heads) must be smooth and polished if they are to produce good surfaces. The stake should be a close approximation to the contour of the work with flat faced hammers being used on external surfaces. Collet hammers can be used on sharp internal surfaces. The work is rotated slowly under the hammer which should fall always on the same spot on the stake with carefully regulated blows. Variations in weight or spacing will tend to produce distortion of the work. The hammering should be quite light, heavy hammering causing the metal to expand and this will alter the shape or cause distortion.

Planishing will leave the surfaces with small facets, each of which should just overlap its neighbours and where a smooth finish is desired, the planishing should be as light as possible so that the facets are very small and these can be removed on the buffing-wheel.

Figure 186 *Horse and horse-head stakes (right)*
Figure 187 *General purpose planishing stake*
(William Whitehouse & Co. (Atlas Forge) Ltd.)

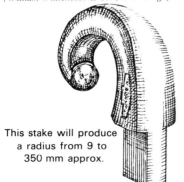

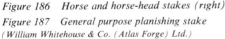

This stake will produce
a radius from 9 to
350 mm approx.

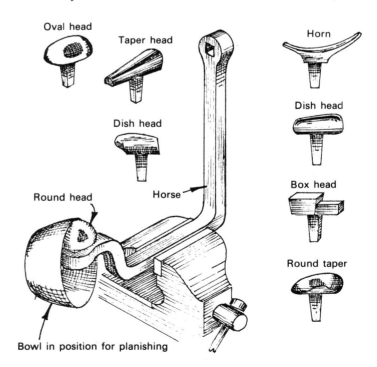

Figure 188   Caulking

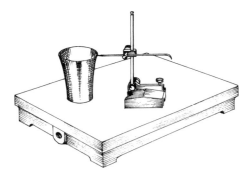

Figure 189   Scribing a rim, ready for trimming

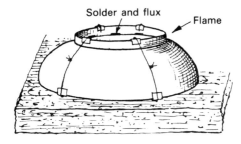

Figure 190   Silver soldering of seams

Figure 191   Silver soldering of ring base

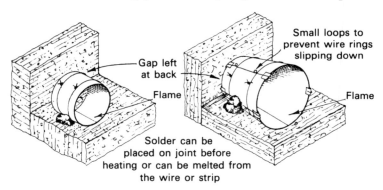

Figure 192   Silver soldering of recessed and flush bases

Bowl forms are planished from the centre outwards, working in circles whilst flat surfaces are best planished radially, from the centre outwards, to avoid distortion.

Caulking

This is an operation by which the edges of raised work can be progressively thickened as the form is raised. It is done by hammering with a convex-faced hammer as shown in Fig. 188. The metal is struck edge-wise in between each course of raising and before the metal is annealed. It is very effective in stiffening the edges of large bowls and articles such as chalices and beakers.

Truing of edges

Following on the planishing operation, the edges of the work are trued up after first marking out with the surface gauge as in Fig. 189. Surplus metal is trimmed off with the universal snips, the edge is lightly filed and is then rubbed on the 'emery board'—a piece of stout plywood onto which is glued a sheet of fine emery cloth. After this, the edge can be rounded with fine emery cloth, followed by burnishing with a piece of hardened and polished silver-steel rod.

Soldering of beaten metalwork

The main problem in hard soldering the shaped forms in beaten work is that of holding parts securely in position for the process.

Balancing one part on another or weighting down with odd bits of fire-brick are risky methods, something always slipping at the

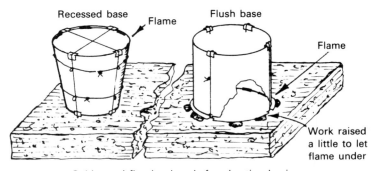

Solder and flux in place before heating begins

Figure 193   Silver soldering a spout (left)
Figure 194   Silver soldering a handle joint (right)

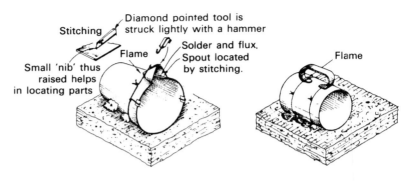

crucial moment. Various methods of securing with soft iron wire are shown in Figs. 190 to 194. The wires should not be pulled over-tight or they may distort parts of the job which become soft on heating. It is a good plan to anneal work-hardened parts to relieve stresses which might cause distortion during the actual soldering.

Figure 195   An example of 2-stage hard soldering, followed by soft soldering

1. Silver brazing alloy C4 740°–780°C or 'easy' silver solder G6 705°–723°C. 2. 'Easy-flo' No. 2. Silver brazing alloy 608°–617 C. 3. Soft soldered sweated joint

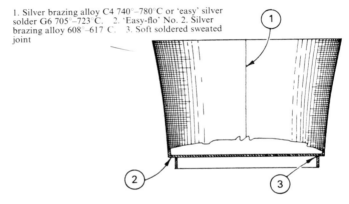

There is always a danger of melting off too much solder from the wire or strip and it is safer to snip off small pieces which are placed over the joint before heating. An excess of solder in an awkward spot can cause a lot of unnecessary work.

The flame should be removed as soon as the solder is seen to flush along the joint and this will help to prevent it from creeping over surfaces.

Figure 196   Folding a handle in thick metal

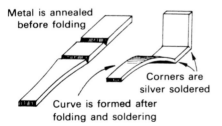

Seaming
A simple method of making cylindrical and conical forms is by seaming which involves rolling up a flat blank and hard soldering the butt joint to make a seam. Seamed work can be hammered

Figure 197   Seamed work

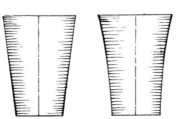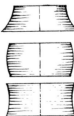

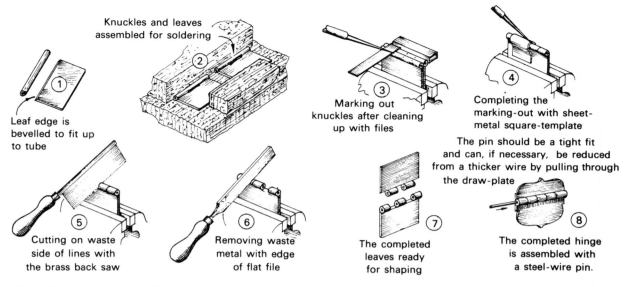

Knuckles and leaves assembled for soldering ②

① Leaf edge is bevelled to fit up to tube

③ Marking out knuckles after cleaning up with files

④ Completing the marking-out with sheet-metal square-template

⑤ Cutting on waste side of lines with the brass back saw

⑥ Removing waste metal with edge of flat file

The pin should be a tight fit and can, if necessary, be reduced from a thicker wire by pulling through the draw-plate

⑦ The completed leaves ready for shaping

⑧ The completed hinge is assembled with a steel-wire pin.

Figure 198   Making an applied hinge

Figure 199   Drawing wire with tongs and draw-plate

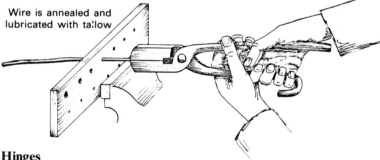

Wire is annealed and lubricated with tallow

quite safely provided that an Easy-flo solder is used and if the work is annealed whenever necessary. Seamed work always requires the soldering on of a separate base and the method is usually confined to elementary practice.

Hinges

The making of a simple hinge which can be applied to box or casket lid is shown in Fig. 198. One edge of each leaf is bevelled so that it fits snugly against a length of small-bore tube to which it is joined with hard solder. The finished hinge can then be joined to the box and lid with Easy-flo solder.

Piercing

Sheet metal jobs can be decorated very effectively by piercing but

Figure 200   Piercing

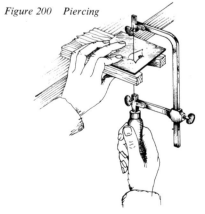

Figure 201   A selection of edge decorations for bowls

Figure 202   A. *Making a ring in strip metal.*
                B. *Making a number of wire rings*

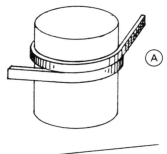

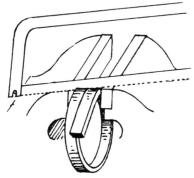

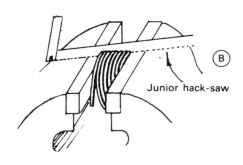

Junior hack-saw

this is work which calls for much patience and very intricate designs are best avoided. The saw blade is entered through a small drilled hole with the teeth pointing downwards and because the blades are very fine, the saw must not be forced at work. The frame is adjustable so that broken blades can be used again. Pierced work can be finished with needle files.

Repoussé

This is a form of decoration in which designs are raised by embossing from the back of the work with shaped punches and the repoussé (or 'chasing') hammer. The annealed metal is held on

Figure 203   *Repoussé or chasing hammer*
               The handle is of lancewood which is very elastic and
               reduces fatigue when used for long periods

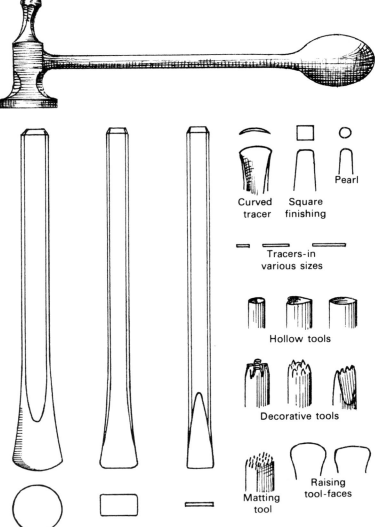

Curved tracer   Square finishing   Pearl

Tracers-in various sizes

Hollow tools

Decorative tools

Matting tool   Raising tool-faces

Round raising tool   Finishing tool   Tracing tool   Finishing tool-face

Figure 204   *Repoussé punches*

a bed of prepared pitch to which it adheres, the pitch supporting the metal and yet being soft enough to receive the impressions formed by the punches.

Copper of light gauge (22, 24 and 26 S.W.G.) is very suitable for repoussé work. The punches, a few of which are shown in Fig. 204, are of tool steel and the shaped ends are mostly of rounded form so that they do not cut the metal, doing no more than impress the shape. They are easily made in the workshop from square steel. Many different compositions are used for the pitch bed and the following is suitable for general use:

Material	g
Pitch	2000
Plaster of Paris	1500
Resin	250
Tallow	250

The pitch and resin are melted together in a bucket and the plaster is then stirred in and is followed by the tallow. This compound can be used in shallow boxes or hemispherical bowls for small work as shown in Fig. 205. The metal, with corners turned down a little to form a key in the pitch, is lightly smeared with tallow or grease and this helps in removing the pitch afterwards. The metal is pressed into the previously warmed pitch and this, oozing up over the edges, holds it firmly. When the work is complete, it is released by warming it gently with the gas blowpipe.

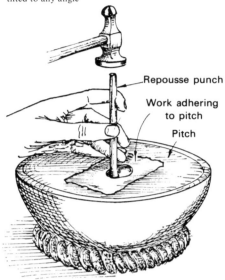

Figure 205   Repoussé modelling
Hemispherical bowl rests on rope ring and is easily tilted to any angle

Repousse punch

Work adhering to pitch

Pitch

11

The finishing of metals

The finishing of metals is important, not only in making articles look more attractive but also in providing some protection against tarnishing and corrosion. All metals show varying resistances to atmospheric and chemical actions, gold and platinum showing remarkable permanence whilst silver, which takes a beautiful lustre, quickly tarnishes if the air contains traces of sulphur compounds.

Of the base metals, it is unfortunate that the least costly of the ferrous metals, whilst possessing so many valuable properties, so readily revert to oxides on exposure to the weather. This can be prevented with metallic coatings or paints but they must remain unbroken if they are to be effective. Some metals quickly acquire a film of oxide on exposure and this protects them by inhibiting further atmospheric action. Notable among these metals are aluminium, copper, lead and zinc. Copper soon acquires an attractive green 'patina' on exposure and is then permanently protected. Tin, which tarnishes only very slowly in the atmosphere, is highly resistant to meat and fruit juices and for this reason is used in the plating of sheet iron for the canning industry.

Although the term 'finishing' is rightly taken to refer to the final stages in manufacture, viz: (1) cleaning and polishing, (2) plating with other metals, (3) painting, and (4) chemical colourings, the finishing of surfaces also calls for consideration in the early stages of manufacture. For example: (1) the deep forming of bowl shapes by hollowing is not a good thing because excessive stretching of the metal may cause hair cracks which cannot be rectified by planishing, (2) in hammered work, the preparation of the metal and its cleansing and scouring after annealing are essential to obtaining a good finish, and (3) in forge work, the hammering of hot metal into shapes is really part of the finishing process, expecially in decorative work.

When bright surfaces are required after filing and draw filing, they can be finished with the fine grades of emery cloth, but only after the best possible finish has been obtained with finer files. It is unlikely that emery cloth coarser than 'F' will be required in the school workshop. The change to finer grades of cloth must not be made prematurely or the surface will take only a moderately bright finish, marred by minute scratches. In the finishing of hammered work, crocus cloth, which is very fine, produces good surfaces.

Polishing

Final polishing is usually done on mops (or 'buffs') made up from calico discs 200 to 250 mm in diameter, stitched together or gripped between washers and mounted on spindle extensions in place of grindstone wheels. These tapered spindle extensions should never be left exposed whilst running as there is a very real danger of loose clothing being wound in rapidly.

Various grades of polishing compounds are made in the form of bars containing lubricant and abrasive, the buff being charged with the compound whilst it is turning. Work should always be presented a little below centre and the wheel must never run into an edge or corner, otherwise the work may be snatched violently. The wheel should always *trail* across edges and the work should be held quite firmly. If the work becomes too hot to hold in comfort it should be allowed to cool and not held with a cloth or with the apron one might be wearing. When buffing is finished, the work can be cleaned with a soft cloth and a fine powder such as Sheffield or Vienna lime.

Burnishing

This is a polishing process in which the metal surfaces are rubbed with a burnisher made from a very hard material with a highly polished surface. Burnishing produces a deep lustre, not by abrasion (as with polishing compounds on the buff), but by compacting the suface through the steady pressure on the burnisher which smooths down small irregularities and scratch marks and closes small pores.

Copper and brass can be burnished with tools made from hardened and polished tool steel, a short piece of polished silver steel rod being quite effective in finishing the lips of mugs and bowls. Agate and bloodstone are used in burnishing gold leaf, e.g. in book binding.

The work surface is wetted with a cream of tartar solution (13 g per litre) and the burnisher, after dipping in dilute acetic acid (vinegar), is rubbed with a steady pressure over the surface.

Electroplating

This is a process by which metalic coatings are deposited on other metals through an electrolytic action. The work, forming part of an electrical circuit, is suspended in a solution containing the appropriate metalic salts and known as the *electrolyte* which acts as a conductor. The article for plating is in the negative side of the circuit and is the *cathode* whilst the positive side of the circuit is connected to a plate or rod suspended in the electrolyte, and this is the *anode*. The anode is usually of the metal to be deposited, but in chromium plating, it is of antimonial lead. A current, passing through the electrolyte causes the metallic elements to separate from the solution and the particles migrate to the cathode, forming a deposit of pure metal. Whilst this is going on, particles from the anode pass into the solution, replacing the losses from deposition.

The preparation for plating involves very careful cleaning,

polishing and de-greasing followed by acid 'dips' for giving a bright finish to the plating or treatment with fine brass wire brushes for producing satin (matt) finishes.

Metal colouring

The term 'bronzing' is commonly used in reference to metal colourings generally, the chemicals used being known as 'chemical bronzes'.

Bronzing does not alter the character of the metal surfaces which should first be brought to the desired finish. A polished surface will be bright after treatment and likewise, scoured or scratch-brushed surfaces will retain the matt finish. Thorough cleansing of the work is essential before bronzing.

A good selection of prepared chemicals is marketed by W. Canning and Co. and these are identified by names such as 'Brown Bronze' which produces shades from rich brown to deep chocolate on copper; 'Florentine Bronze' which is used on copper (or coppered surfaces) to produce the brown shades seen on medallions, plaques, vases and such items; 'Oxidising Salts' which produce a film of copper sulphide ranging from dark brown to a black 'oxidised copper' finish. 'Black Bronze' is used on matt or satin finished articles used in photographic, optical and electrical instruments. This gives an ebony black finish and it neither brightens matt surfaces nor dulls polished or burnished surfaces.

A great many chemical formulae are to be found for producing a wide range of colours and a few of these are listed:

Green patina on copper
The solution indicated in the formula is brushed over the surface at about 2-hourly intervals during the daytime and can be repeated the following day if desired. The work is then put aside for 24 hours, at the end of which it should have acquired a good patina and can then be lacquered or wax polished.

Formula:		
	Ammonia ·880	3 cm^3
	Common salt	55 g
	Ammonium chloride	55 g
	Ammonium acetate	55 g
	Water	42 cm^3

Colouring of brass and copper
Various shades can be produced by immersion in a weak solution of ammonium sulphide, extreme dilution giving a golden colour to brass and reddening copper. Colours ranging from yellows and red to brown and black can be obtained by strengthening the solution and by variations of the immersion times.

Antique finish on brass
A greenish-brown finish can be achieved by repeated brushing of a solution of 283 g of copper nitrate in 30 cm^3 of water at a temperature between 49°C and 65·5°C over the article. When the desired

shade is reached, the work is dried by warming and is then brushed with French chalk on a soft brush. It is then protected by clear lacquering.

An alternative formula for antiquing brass, giving slightly different shades of colour is:

Copper nitrate	850 g
Hydrochloric acid	565 g
Water	90 cm^3

This is used at between 49°C and 65·5°C the work being immersed for a few seconds only, then swilled, dried and lacquered.

Dead black finishes

Brass and copper can be given dead black surfaces by a few minutes' immersion in a solution of 28 g of copper nitrate in 9 cm^3 of water. Copper will assume a slightly shiny black surface when immersed in a solution of 1 part ammonium sulphide and 4 parts water. This same solution will impart a steely grey colour to brass.

Colouring of iron and steel

These metals can be given a blue-black colour by immersion in a hot solution of sodium thiosulphate ('hypo') to which a small quantity of lead acetate has been added. The blueing of steel can, of course, be brought about by heating the work slowly on a hot plate. Mild steel articles blued in this way can be dipped in oil of a high flashpoint until cool and then wiped dry. A black finish on steel is obtained with Canning's 'Black Oxidising Salts' in a hot solution in which the work is immersed but because this solution is highly caustic and used at high temperature, its use in schools is open to question.

Silvering on brass for clock faces, etc.

Silvering can be done with a paste made up from the following constituents: 28 g of silver chloride, 56 g of cream of tartar, and 85 g of common salt. These are pounded together and enough water is added to make a creamy paste which is rubbed over the work with a soft cloth. When silver is deposited satisfactorily, the paste is washed away and the surfaces lacquered after drying.

Frosting of aluminium

Aluminium of high purity can be given a frosted surface by immersing for a few seconds in a hot and moderately strong caustic soda solution after which the metal is washed in warm water. If the aluminium is not of high purity, it will be discoloured by the solution but this can normally be removed by using dilute nitric acid.

Lacquering

In the preservation of finished surfaces, lacquers provide a very effective medium and can be applied by spraying, dipping or by brushing. They fall into four groups: (1) *hot lacquers* which require preheating of the work, some considerable skill being needed for successful results, (2) *gum lacquers* which are easily applied and which give a bright and glossy finish, some drying very quickly at room temperatures whilst some require stoving, (3) *cellulose lacquers*, formulated to give varying degrees of gloss and which dry very quickly in air, and (4) *synthetic lacquers* which generally require stoving.

Lacquers can be obtained either colourless or tinted, and of the four kinds mentioned, the cellulose and gum lacquers are most suitable for use in the handicraft room. Brushes of best quality soft hair are made specially for lacquering, wide and flat brushes for large surfaces and round brushes with square or domed ends for concave or shaped surfaces.

Lacquer should be used from an enamelled basin provided with a lid to prevent evaporation and with a draining wire over which excess lacquer can be removed from the brush. Lacquering should be done in a warm dust-free room, the charged brush being drawn steadily over the surface to spread an even film.

Spraying is a quicker and easier method of application, but is not suitable for use in schools for health and safety reasons. Dipping is employed more in the treatment of large numbers of small items.

Articles for lacquering must be absolutely clean and may require degreasing with white spirit or other cleansing fluid. The final cleaning can be done with clean, soft cloth and the work must not be touched by hand before the lacquer is applied.

12

Drilling and reaming

Accident prevention

Any special safety precautions are mentioned as the need arises, but at this point, a few general precautions are noted. It must always be borne in mind that *all* power tools can inflict serious injury if handled carelessly and they must be treated with profound respect at all times. Familiarity with a machine does not bring immunity from accidents, a momentary distraction or inattention bringing disaster to the experienced machinist as readily as to the novice. The beginner should seek instruction before attempting to use any machine with which he is unfamiliar, not only for his personal safety but to avoid damaging costly plant. He should be quite sure of the position of the 'stop' button on each machine and should never start one until he is sure that the guards are in position, that no one is touching or adjusting any part of the machine, that the cutter, drill or work is free to turn and that no rags or other obstructions are anywhere near rotating parts. Revolving parts should never be touched, however slowly they may be turning or however smooth they appear. Rags should not be used to clean moving parts.

Before making adjustments to working parts of machines or to cutters or gear trains, the machine should be isolated by throwing its main switch. Depressing the stop button is not sufficient safe-guard. In all machine shops there will be emergency 'stop' buttons, painted red and placed prominently at strategic points so that *anyone* can cut off the power in an emergency.

The human failings which lead to trouble in machine shops include: (1) *untidiness,* for example, long flowing neckties which can get caught up in revolving parts, especially when leaning over a lathe, also long unkempt hair, loose clothing and unbuttoned shirt cuffs; (2) *over-confidence,* which leads people to use machines they do not understand without first seeking instruction; (3) *inquisitiveness,* which makes people do silly things like taking the headstock guard off to watch the gears running, over-confidence perhaps prompting them to do some oiling at the same time; (4) *thoughtlessness,* which lets people touch rotating work in the lathe to see if it is smooth, or perhaps to clean the oil or swarf away with a rag or the fingers; (5) *forgetfulness,* which lets people do silly things like leaving the key in a chuck, with the risk of its being thrown out violently when the machine starts; (6) *inattentiveness,* which enables one to do two things at the same time for a very short time, e.g. screw cutting and gossiping, followed by trouble; (7) *the adventurous and inquiring nature,* which urges people on to dismantle and repair the electric motor or to investigate the switch gear without first turning off the main switch and so on. Then, of

Figure 206   Hand drill and breast drill
(Stanley Tools)

course, there is the *fool,* who treats the workshop as his playground in a light-hearted fashion. He should be barred from entering.

Drilling

In the course of his work the fitter uses the drilling machine whenever possible, but on the odd occasions when the job cannot be taken to the machine, he uses the hand-drill, breast-drill or the electric hand-drill. The hand-drill has a capacity of up to about 8 mm, whilst the breast drill, with a choice of two speeds has a capacity of up to about 12 mm. Electric hand-drills are a great boon but as many of them still have only one speed, care must be taken if drills are not to be spoiled by over-heating them. This can be avoided by easing the drill back at regular intervals when working and, of course, the use of coolant would help but this is not always possible in awkward spots. The work must be properly supported and should never be steadied with one hand whilst the other holds the drill. This practice is dangerous, for the electric drill would run out of control if the drill itself should break whilst under pressure.

Twist drills

Drills are classified by several features, the first considerations being: (1) *drill diameter,* from 0·30 to 100 mm, (2) the *steel in the drill,* either carbon or high-speed steel, (3) the *type of shank,* either parallel or tapered, and (4) the *length* of the drill. For general purposes, the *jobber's* drill is used in sizes up to 16 mm diameter.

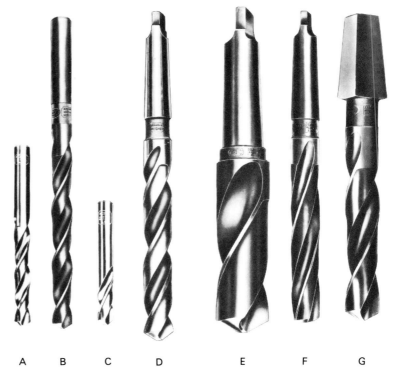

Figure 207   Twist drills.
    A. Jobber's.
    B. Long series.
    C. Stub.
    D. and E. Morse taper shank
    F. Core drill.
    G. Square taper shank for ratchet
      brace.
(Aurora P.L.C.)

A   B   C   D   E   F   G

Figure 208 Drill spirals.
A. Normal spiral or helix (normal lead and helix).
B. Slow spiral or helix (lead longer than normal).
C. Quick spiral or helix (lead shorter than normal).

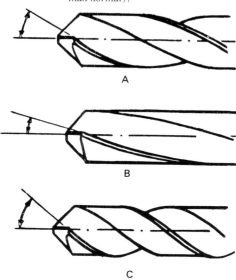

A

B

C

(Aurora P.L.C.)

Figure 209 Modifying a standard drill to produce a slow helix

Small flat ground in flute gives effect of slower helix

Figure 210 Morse taper sleeve and sockets for taper shank twist drills.
A. Sleeve.
B. Socket with unturned end.
C. Socket with taper shank
(Aurora P.L.C.)

The *long series* and *stub* drills would be used for special jobs and on production work.

Twist drills are also made with different spirals as shown in Fig. 208 and unless specially requested when ordering, it is always assumed that the standard spiral is required. The slow spiral is for use on brass, gun-metal, phosphor bronze and on plastics, whilst the quick spiral is for use on copper, aluminium and other 'soft' metals. A quick-spiral drill should never be used on brass or it will almost certainly dig-in and the job may be thrown if it is not secured firmly to the drilling table. In the absence of a slow-spiral drill, a standard-spiral can be converted by altering the helix angle at the cutting-edges. This is done by grinding on a round-edged stone, but it must be done very expertly if the drill is not to be spoiled.

Parallel-shank drills can be used only in chucks and are dependent for alignment on the condition of both chuck and drill shank. Taper shank drills are more satisfactory in this respect. At the end of the taper shank is a small flat tang which engages with a slot in the spindle, as shown in Fig. 221. The taper is the Standard Morse Taper, in sizes ranging from No. 1, the smallest, to No. 6. Where the drill taper shank is smaller than the taper in the spindle, the two can be matched by fitting a sleeve to the drill shank so that a drill with a No. 1 Morse taper, for example, could be fitted into a spindle made with a No. 2 Morse taper. Sockets with taper shanks can also be used for this purpose and these are made also for *reducing* the taper so that a drill with a No. 2 taper shank, for example, could be adapted to a spindle with a No. 1 taper. The socket with an unturned end, as seen in Fig. 210, is of a type which would be used in holding taper shank drills and other tools in turret and capstan lathes. Sleeves, sockets and taper shanks are all very accurately ground and if damaged, they will not run truly and may become jammed together.

In assembling taper shank tools and sleeves or sockets, it is permissable to tap them home with a soft hammer and for separating them, a tapered key (drift) is used and this is seen in Fig. 221, being used to eject a drill from the machine spindle.

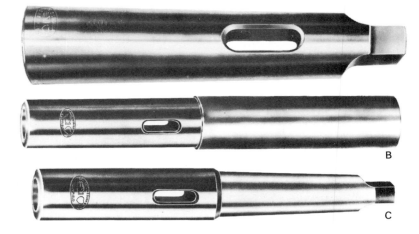

B

C

Figure 211   Drill nomenclature (right)
(Aurora P.L.C.)

Figure 212   Twist drills. Faulty point grinding

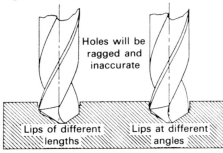

Holes will be ragged and inaccurate

Lips of different lengths   Lips at different angles

Figure 213   Drill point angles (standard drills)

Point-angle gauge

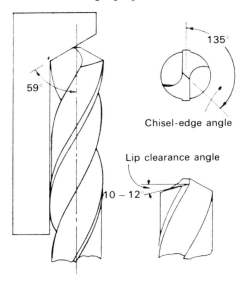

59°

135°

Chisel-edge angle

Lip clearance angle

10 – 12

Figure 214   Drill grinding jig
(H. D. Murray, Ltd.)

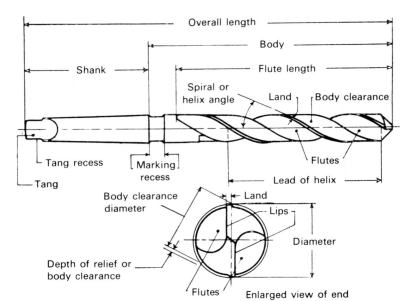

Overall length

Body

Shank

Flute length

Spiral or helix angle   Land   Body clearance

Tang recess   Marking recess   Flutes

Tang

Lead of helix

Body clearance diameter   Land

Lips

Depth of relief or body clearance   Diameter

Flutes   Enlarged view of end

Core drills are made with either three or four flutes and are for use in opening out holes already made by coring (as in casting), by punching or by smaller drillings. Opening out a hole with the normal double-fluted drill often results in digging-in by the drill lips or it may lead to inaccurate drilling. The modified lips and extra lands in the core drill obviate these troubles.

Drill maintenance   Figure 211 gives details of drill nomenclature and this should be studied carefully. The web thickness increases from the drill tip to the run-out of the flutes to give extra strength, but this has the effect of increasing the length of the chisel edge as the drill is worn away by re-grinding. This longer edge calls for extra feed pressure to overcome the resistance offered by this part of the drill, but this trouble can be rectified by reducing the web thickness by grinding on a thin, round-edged wheel.

Twist drills should be re-ground immediately there is any sign of inefficient working which will be revealed by: (1) the need for excessive feed pressure to make the drill cut, (2) the ejection of scored cuttings which indicates chipped cutting-edges, and (3) chattering or screaming from the drill when pressure is applied. This is caused by the drill rubbing instead of cutting and will quickly cause overheating.

Faulty grinding is indicated by: (1) two cuttings of unequal thickness, or only one cutting being ejected, (2) over-size holes which are caused by unequal lip length or unequal lip-angles, and (3) broken lips or digging-in which may be caused by excessive clearance angles.

Standard drill tip-angles are shown in Fig. 213 and these must be ground accurately on a fine grade wheel. This is best done with the aid of a grinding jig, one of which is shown in Fig. 214. Drill grinding can be done 'off hand' (free hand) but this requires a lot of practice before it can be done satisfactorily. Drills should always be kept in the drill stand, taking care not to mix different types

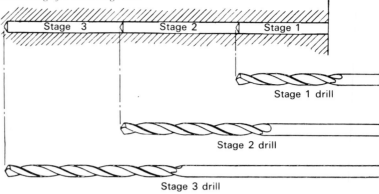

Figure 215 Recommended drill points for various metals (Aurora P.L.C.)

Figure 216 Deep drilling. Diagrams illustrating the drilling of a three stage hole *(Firth Brown Tools Ltd.)*

Brass
130° incl. Lip
clearance
angle: 12–15°

Aluminium
140° incl. Lip
clearance
angle: 12°

Stage 1 drill

Stage 2 drill

Stage 3 drill

Copper
125° incl. Lip
clearance
angle: 12–15°

Cast iron
90° incl. Lip
clearance
angle: 10–12°

together. A drill gauge is useful in identifying sizes especially where markings have been obliterated by chuck slipping on parallel shanks. High-speed drills can be identified by the letters 'HS' stamped on the shank.

Chip-breaking drills

These drills give increased efficiency by chip control, the effect of which is seen in Fig. 218. The swarf is broken into small chippings and this brings several advantages: (1) there is no danger to the operator from long coils of swarf as with the ordinary drill, (2) faster drilling speeds are possible because there is no swarf-clogging in the flutes, (3) the drill can be sharpened by standard practice and equipment, (4) the stiffer web gives greater rigidity, (5) the drill is suited equally well to precision and heavy constructional work, and (6) it costs no more than other drills.

Figure 217 Speedicut 'chipbreaker drill' (Firth Brown Tools Ltd.)

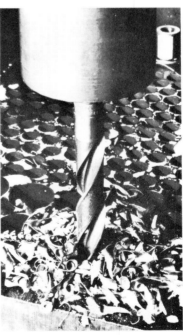

*Figure 218 A. Standard drill in action
B. Speedicut 'Chipbreaker' drill in action
(Firth Brown Tools Ltd.)*

Figure 219   A 19 mm capacity bench drilling machine
This is shown fitted with a tapping attachment, used in production work
(Kerry's (Gt. Britain) Ltd.)

Drilling machines

Bench drill

A modern bench drilling machine is shown in Fig. 219 and this one is shown fitted with a tapping attachment where the chuck would normally be. This device is used in production work, the tap automatically reversing when it is withdrawn. The machine spindle is usually bored with a No. 1 or No. 2 Morse taper and these machines are commonly fitted with four-step vee pulleys which give a speed range from about 500 to 3 000 rev/min. As with all motorised machines, they are equipped with a 'no volts' release switch and this, in the event of a power failure or switching off at the main, automatically breaks the circuit. There is then no danger of the machine re-starting on its own when the power is restored.

The drill table should be firmly supported before the locking bolt is slackened when adjusting the table height. It is a heavy component and could cause serious injury if allowed to drop, apart from the damage it might cause to the machine. When adjusting the height of the machine head, the tool tray with which most machines are fitted, should be first adjusted to serve as a stop before the locking bolt is slackened just enough to permit of the head being moved.

The machine illustrated is a 'sensitive' drill, it is sensitive inasmuch as the human touch is used in controlling the feed pressure. Feed is controlled through a rack and pinion and an automatic return is effected by means of a strong coil spring enclosed in a case and which operates on the pinion spindle. An adjustable depth-stop is provided so that drillings to any pre-determined depth can be made. The table can be tilted for angular drilling or can be swung aside so that large work can be accommodated on the machine base.

Pillar drill

The pillar drill, in a range of larger sizes, resembles the bench drill but has a longer column and stands upon the floor. When fitted with a gear reduction which gives a range of low speeds, it is a very useful machine. As with the bench drill, the spindle is bored to a Morse taper. The same precautions are necessary when adjusting the head or the table.

In another kind of machine—the *radial* drill—the head can be moved along an arm which pivots sideways on the column enabling any point on the table to be covered without moving the table or the work. Drilling machines are also made with *geared heads,* speed changes being made by operating gear levers. These machines are of larger capacities and are usually provided with power feeds.

Drill speeds

To ensure good work, without damaging or breaking a drill, it is important that the correct speed is used and this will depend on the metal being drilled and on the type of drill (carbon or high speed steel). Suitable cutting speeds for various materials are always

Figure 220 A. Pillar drilling machine
B. Radial drilling machine
C. Geared head drilling machine

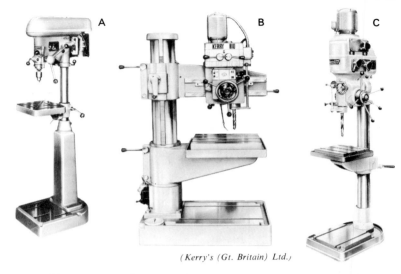

(Kerry's (Gt. Britain) Ltd.)

quoted in metres or feet per minute and these must be related to the drill periphery (circumference). Therefore, to maintain a constant cutting speed for different drill sizes, it will be obvious that the rev/min must *increase* as the drill size *decreases* and vice versa.

Speeds quoted in the tables in Ch. 16 are for high-speed drills and all must be reduced by about 50 per cent for carbon steel drills. From the table it will be noticed that the brasses and aluminium are among those metals drilled at the highest speeds, followed by copper and certain alloys. Carbon steels and alloy steels are among those drilled at the lowest speeds. Speeds for cast iron depend on the type of iron.

The location of holes

The precise location of a hole can be fixed by scribing intersecting lines after which the centre is very lightly dot-punched. A small dot can be drawn over quite easily if not accurately placed, and this is followed by centre-punching. The spring-loaded dot-punch is very useful as it can be placed accurately and set to give a small indent. With small holes it is quite satisfactory if the drill is run straight in on the centre dot, but with larger holes it is good practice to drill first of all a small 'pilot' hole which not only helps to keep the drill on course, but also removes the metal which would offer resistance to the drill web.

Holding work for drilling

It is very important that work should be held securely by clamping it to the table to avoid inaccurate work and to avoid accidents. When the drill is breaking through on the underside, the feed pressure may cause the point to push through before cutting is quite complete and two small 'ears' of metal are left in the hole. These catch up in the drill flutes but if the work is fastened properly they will be taken off by the drill. If the work is not secured properly, it may run up the drill and be thrown aside or spin until the machine is stopped. All work should be bolted down unless it is so large and

Figure 221   Using taper drift to remove drill from machine spindle

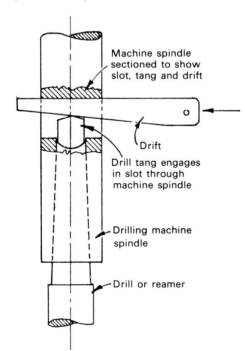

Machine spindle sectioned to show slot, tang and drift

Drift

Drill tang engages in slot through machine spindle

Drilling machine spindle

Drill or reamer

Figure 222   Machine vices
   A. *Record No. 643*
   B. *Taylor's No. 861*
   C. *Eclipse composite Vee vice*

(*C. Hampton & Co.*)

heavy that it could not possibly give trouble. It is always a good thing to ease off feed pressure as the drill nears the point of breaking through.

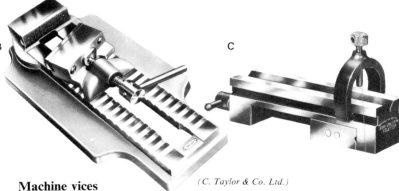

(*C. Taylor & Co. Ltd.*)

Machine vices

In Fig. 222 are shown two types of vice suitable for holding work for drilling. These can easily be bolted to the table and when in use care should be taken to avoid damaging them with the drills. Also shown is a combined vice and vee block.

Vee blocks, angle plate and clamps

These tools are shown in use in Figs. 223, 224 and 225. A method of scribing the centre line on the round bar is shown in Chapter 6. The line is taken along the bar whilst still in the vee blocks and the holes are located by dot- and centre-punches. A pilot hole is a great help in starting holes on curved surfaces. Work may be held in clamps adapted to suit the job or it can be bolted straight down if suitable holes or openings can be manoeuvred over the tee-slots in the drilling table. Clamps should always be arranged to grip as near as possible to the drilling and the free end of each

Figure 223   *Set-up for drilling a round bar*

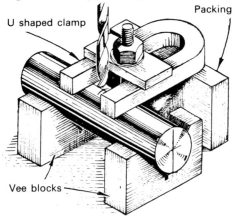

U shaped clamp

Packing

Vee blocks

Figure 224   *Work clamped to angle-plate for drilling*

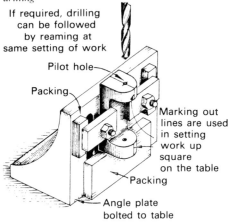

If required, drilling can be followed by reaming at same setting of work

Pilot hole

Packing

Marking out lines are used in setting work up square on the table

Packing

Angle plate bolted to table

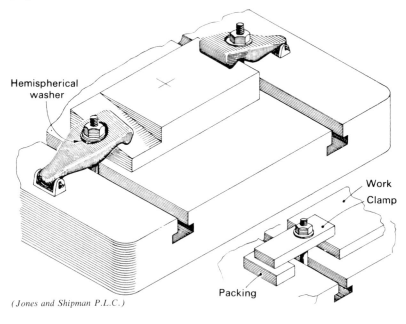

Hemispherical washer

Work

Clamp

Packing

Figure 225   *Universal machine clamps in use*
These clamps are self adjusting to height and tilt of work and require no packing. The inset shows a 'home-made' clamp.

(*Jones and Shipman P.L.C.*)

Figure 226   Drill point for sheet metal

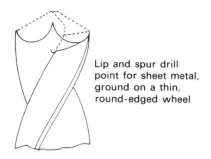

Lip and spur drill
point for sheet metal,
ground on a thin,
round-edged wheel

Figure 226   Drill point for sheet metal

Figure 227   Chassis punch, shown in part section

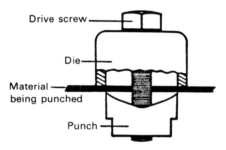

Drive screw

Die

Material
being punched

Punch

Figure 228   Drill-point modifications

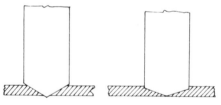

Drill-point breaking
through before
drilling full diameter

Obtuse point angle
avoids premature
breaking through

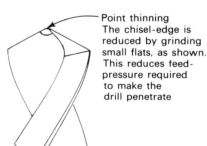

Point thinning
The chisel-edge is
reduced by grinding
small flats, as shown.
This reduces feed-
pressure required
to make the
drill penetrate

clamp should be packed so that it is level. The work also, may require packing to leave clearance when the drill breaks through or to bring it up level if the bottom surface is shaped in any way.

Drilling in sheet metal

It is not easy to drill through thin metal without the drill snatching or the hole being distorted and this is more noticeable with larger holes. One way of overcoming this trouble is to sandwich the thin metal between two stouter pieces and to drill through all three or the drill point can be ground in the form commonly used by sheet metalworkers, this is shown in Fig. 226. The point is ground to leave a pointed centre and the lands in the form of scribers which cut the hole by removing a disc. Another way of reducing the danger of snatch is to grind a more obtuse point-angle as shown in Fig. 228 so that the drill does not break through before it is cutting to its full diameter. The drill point should also be thinned, as shown.

Location of large holes

When large holes are to be accurately located, it is a good plan to scribe a circle of the hole size, from the centre dot. As the drill begins to cut, it is lifted two or three-times before cutting to its full diameter to check that the conical hole is running true. If it is off-centre, it can be drawn over by cutting a small groove with a diamond-point or a half-round chisel as in Fig. 229. This is, perhaps, a 'chancy' business, but it can be avoided by using properly ground drills and by drilling accurately-placed pilot holes.

Drilling for bolts and screws

When parts are to be held together by bolts or screws with nuts and washers, clearance holes are required through the components and this is best done with the parts located and held securely together whilst drilling.

When parts are to be screwed together, the top one will require clearance holes with tapping holes in the other. With the parts held together, this can be done effectively as shown in Fig. 230. The clearance drill point enters the lower part just far enough to leave a shallow counter-bore whilst providing a lead for the tapping drill. The counter-bore will leave a clean and neat finish after tapping.

Where components must be accurately located together, reamed

Figure 229   Correcting off-centre drill start

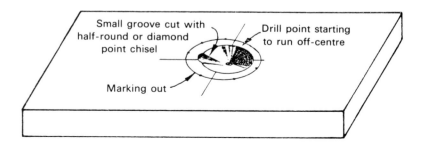

Small groove cut with
half-round or diamond
point chisel

Drill point starting
to run off-centre

Marking out

Figure 230   Drilling components for securing with screws

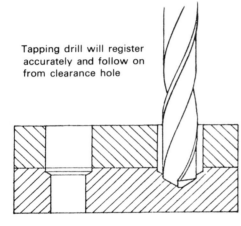

Machine depth stop is set so that clearing drill just enters lower component

Tapping drill will register accurately and follow on from clearance hole

The two components are clamped together for drilling

Figure 232   Countersink

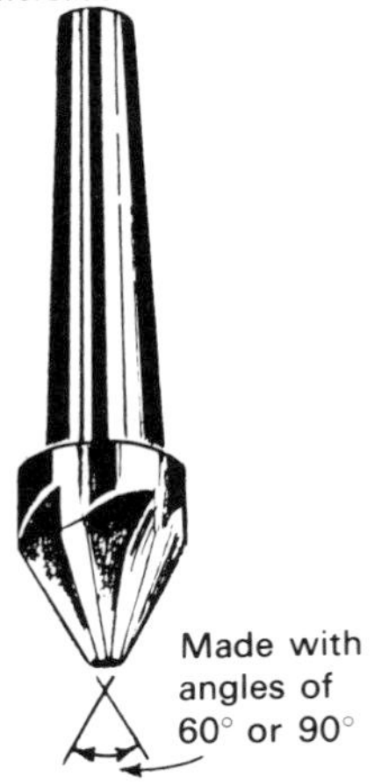

Made with angles of 60° or 90°

holes can be provided for the bolt shanks. Alternatively, the parts can be located with steel pins (dowels) in reamed holes but provision must be made for their removal, i.e. they should not be fitted into blind holes. Components can then be separated and replaced exactly. They would be held by screws or bolts in normal clearance holes.

Other processes

Counter-boring

This process is quite often used in order that the heads of bolts or screws can lay flush with the face of a job, the hole being opened out for part of its depth with a counter-bore as shown in Fig. 231. The

Figure 231   Counterbore with interchangeable pilot

tool shown has an interchangeable pilot for adapting to various sizes of holes and a solid type is made in which the pilot is made in one with the shank.

Spot-facing

In spot-facing, the surface around a hole is trued up so that bolt heads or other components can bed squarely. This is done with tools similar to those used in counter-boring but with teeth formed on the end face only. Spot-facing is commonly used on castings where it is desired to bed bolt heads squarely without machining a whole surface, small raised portions being left for facing.

Countersinking

To accommodate the countersunk (conical) heads of screws, chamfers are formed around the edges of the holes with the countersinking tool, one of which is shown in Fig. 232. These are made with included angles of either 60 or 90°. They should always be used at slow spindle speeds to get good results.

Reaming

The reamer is a cylindrical tool cutting along its sides and is used in opening out holes smoothly and accurately to size. Taper reamers are also available. The cutting edges are formed by either straight or spiral flutes, the latter being more favoured as there is generally less tendency to chatter which results from the long axial cut with straight flutes. Reamers are usually made with unequal spacing of cutting edges and this helps to obviate chatter whilst working.

Providing a quick and positive means for the repeated finishing of holes to fine limits, the reamer is used extensively in production

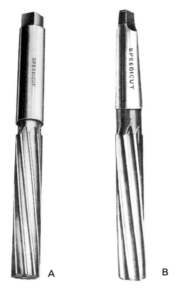

A   B

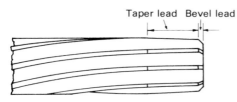

Taper lead Bevel lead

Figure 233B Taper and bevel leads

work as well as in the small workshop producing 'one off' jobs. Reamers are made with square ended shanks for hand use and with Morse taper shanks for use in machines.

For general purposes and in the smaller sizes, the reaming of drilled holes is an acceptable practice, but in larger sizes and for more accurate work, it is better if a drilled hole can be opened out by boring prior to finishing by reaming, all three operations being carried out at the same setting in the machine. This ensures true alignment in the hole and also makes it possible to leave only the lightest of cuts for the reamer.

These are both very desirable conditions since the reamer will not necessarily correct any misalignment in the hole whilst leaving only a light cut for the reamer is a great help in securing a good finish.

The reamer has to remove all the metal in one cut and a copious supply of the appropriate cutting fluid is an important feature when reaming—as in all machining operations.

Reamers are precision tools and should be stored in racks or in cases with compartments and not left about on benches or machines.

Hand reamers

Reamers for hand operation are provided with square-ended shanks as seen in Fig. 233A, for holding in a tap wrench. To facilitate entry of a parallel reamer into the hole, the end is formed with a short bevel lead and, in addition, a short taper lead which extends over about a quarter of the flute length. This taper lead helps with the initial lining-up in the hole and gives a progressive cutting action. Bevel and taper leads are shown in Fig. 233B.

Taper lead reamers are satisfactory when the taper lead can pass clear through the work, but for deeper passes, reamers with bevel lead only are used. A hand socket-reamer for Morse tapers is illustrated in Fig. 235. Taper pin reamers are mentioned later.

Machine reamers

For adaption in lathe spindles, tailstocks and turrets, machine reamers are provided with taper shanks, but they are also made with parallel shanks for holding in chucks. All are normally made with bevel lead only, but they can be obtained with taper lead as well. For bottoming in blind holes, cutting edges are made with square corners. To prevent reamers from 'chattering' and producing poorly finished holes, the spacing of the cutting edges is varied slightly around the reamer during manufacture.

In Fig. 234 is shown a reamer with short, straight flutes with a

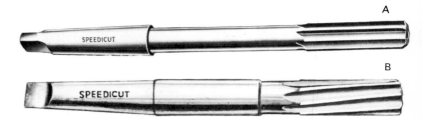

A

B

Figure 234 Machine reamers. A. Chucking reamer. B. Jig reamer.

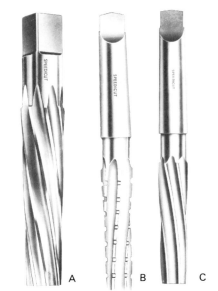

Figure 235 Socket reamers (for morse tapers).
*A. Hand reamer – finishing. Also
made as a roughing reamer.
B. Machine reamer. Roughing.
C. Machine reamer. Finishing.*

Figure 236 Adjustable reamer

bevel lead. The machine jig reamer has a parallel shank accurately ground to size and this part runs in a bush fitted in a jig which is designed to guide the reamer at work.

Reamers for making standard tapers are commonly used in pairs, the *roughing reamer* being used in opening out a parallel hole and this is followed by the *finishing reamer*. Note the notches cut in the roughing teeth which serve to break the chips and to help in rapid cutting. The right-hand spiral helps in feeding-in which is not an undesirable feature for course cutting in tapered holes. The finishing reamer has a left-hand spiral.

Drill sizes and reaming speeds

The following suggested allowances for machine reamers of standard design are reproduced by kind permission of Firth Brown Tools Ltd., Sheffield.

Reamer size range	Allowance for reaming
1·5 to 3·0 mm	0·13 to 0·20 mm
3·0 to 6·0 mm	0·15 to 0·28 mm
6·0 to 12·5 mm	0·25 to 0·38 mm
12·5 to 25 mm	0·25 to 0·50 mm
25·0 to 38·0 mm	0·38 to 0·65 mm

Material allowance left in the hole for hand reaming is usually 0·05 to 0·10 mm.

It must be remembered that faulty drill point grinding will affect the allowance left in the hole. The drill point grinding should be checked before use.

Feeds and speeds for reaming will be largely dependent on the material being machined, on the type of reamer and on the condition of the machine. As a guide for using standard reamers of high-speed steel, the *feed* can be taken as two to three times that for a drill of the same diameter and the *speed* as two thirds to three quarters of that for a drill of the same diameter. An appropriate coolant should always be used freely in reaming.

Adjustable reamers

An adjustable reamer is shown in Fig. 236. These tools are made with 4, 5 or 6 blades and they are very useful because it is possible to ream to *any* size within the range of adjustment of each reamer. This range is not large, and it is necessary to hold these reamers in sets, one or two on their own being of little use. The tapered blades slide in identically-tapered slots cut in the body of the tool and adjustment is effected by turning the two end nuts in unison, thus moving the blades in either direction along the slots. The nuts also serve to retain the blades in their slots, an internal bevel engaging over the bevelled ends of the blades.

Taper reamers and taper pins

The taper pin provides an excellent means of securing things like pulleys, gears and collars to shafts, as shown in Fig. 238. Taper pins are made to a standard taper of 1 in 48 and are bought ready-made, being specified by the larger diameter. Taper-reamers

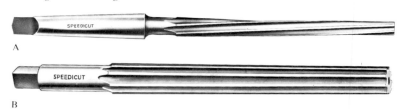

Figure 237   Taper-pin reamers.
A. Machine reamer.
B. Hand reamer.

Figure 238   The taper-pin used in fixing a collar on a shaft

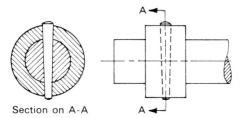

Section on A-A

are made specially for these pins. With the component on the shaft, the initial hole is drilled to the smaller diameter and the hole is then reamed out until the pin can be pressed home 'finger tight' after which it is tapped firmly into place.

Cutting fluids

Whilst it is possible to carry out some machining operations dry, wet machining with the appropriate cutting fluid (coolant) offers many advantages, giving extended tool life, a better finish and allowing higher cutting speeds. Today, even the traditional 'no coolant' cast iron can be machined wet and not only does this give better results, but it solves the problem of fine swarf penetration into bearings, slides and electric motors. The use of coolant in the *drilling* of cast iron is not recommended, however, as this tends to cause clogging in the drill flutes.

In the school workshop, it is often sufficient to feed cutting fluids on with a small brush, but this is better if done with a drip-can mounted above the machine. The ideal way is, of course, by means of a coolant pump circulating filtered fluid which can be directed in a continuous flow over the work and tool point.

Many kinds of cutting oil are available nowadays, covering the needs of every machining operation on different metals. Those cutting oils most likely to be found in the school workshop fall into two groups, viz: (1) the soluble oils, and (2) the neat oils.

Soluble oils

These are mineral oils containing emulsifying agents which enable them to be mixed with water and to remain stable. The oil is always added to the water and the ratio of the mix will depend on the work in hand. Soluble oils are inexpensive, they find many applications in the machining of metals and although often employed more for their coolant properties, they do provide some measure of lubrication. Heavy duty soluble oils, containing EP (extreme pressure) additives are available and with much-improved lubricant properties, the range of applications of these fluids is extended considerably.

Neat cutting oils

These are marketed in many forms and except for screw threading and tapping, they are not likely to be in general use in the school workshop.

Neat mineral oils   These low viscosity oils are suitable only for light machining, mainly in free-cutting steel and brass as the lubricant film will not stand up to any heavy tool loading. They are used more for their coolant properties and a good flow should be maintained.

Mineral and fatty oil mixtures   These mixtures of neat mineral oils and fatty oils (e.g. lard oil) have a wider range of applications than the neat oils. With better lubricant properties, they are used in medium–heavy machining in lathes, thread milling, screw-cutting and other such work in which heavier tool loading takes place.

Sulphurised oils   With the level of sulphur and its manner of incorporation arranged to suit any particular working conditions, these neat cutting oils form a very useful group of fluids. They are used mainly for their lubricant properties in heavy lathe work, gear cutting and screw-cutting and with pressurised coolant systems in deep drilling, boring and trepanning in nickel and copper alloys. Some of these oils cause staining of these two alloys, but this can be avoided by the proper selection of the cutting oil.

Sulphured oils   These are a variation of the sulphur-bearing neat oils and have similar applications. They cause staining of the high nickel and copper alloys.

Neat oils containing sulpho–chlorinated additives in the form of chemical compounds form another group and these have EP (extreme pressure) properties for severe working conditions in machining stainless steels and high duty nickel alloys.

Table 12   Cutting fluids for high-speed drills

Aluminium and its alloys	Soluble oil, paraffin.
Copper	Soluble oil; lard oil.
Brass	Dry, soluble oil.
Cast iron	Dry, soluble oil.
Chilled cast iron	Soluble oil.
Malleable iron	Soluble oil.
Mild steel	Soluble oil, sulphurised oil.
Alloy steels	Sulphurised oil.
Stainless steels	Sulphurised oil.

13

The lathe

Although the lathe is basically a machine for generating cylindrical forms, it is in fact much more than this, being a readily adaptable piece of mechanism which can be used to perform numerous other machining operations in addition to its basic functions.

The work, normally rotating towards the operator, can be set up between two centres which engage in countersunk holes at either end, or it can be gripped in a chuck or bolted to a face-plate. The cutting tool, mounted on top of the carriage, can be moved along the machine or square across it and these two motions perform the basic functions in the generation of a true cylinder. The lengthwise traverse of the tool is commonly referred to as 'sliding' which produces a round face and the cross-traverse as 'surfacing' (or 'facing') which produces a flat surface.

In addition to sliding and surfacing, the lathe can be used to produce tapered work, to cut screw threads, for boring and recessing, for profiling (shaping to contours), whilst the chucks and face-plates can be used in machining a variety of flat, cylindrical or irregular forms. A further range of operations can be undertaken by reversing the locations of tool and work, the tool rotating whilst the work is held on the carriage and brought up to the tool.

Many types of lathes are made, some being designed for repetition work, and these are the *automatic, capstan* and *turret* lathes. Some are designed for special purposes, for example, the *brass finishing* lathe—used exclusively for that one metal whilst the *spinning* lathe is used in producing bowl forms from sheet metal. The lathe which is of direct concern here is the *centre* lathe, designed primarily for turning work held between centres or when held in chuck or on the face-plate. The centre lathe appears in a great many forms and whilst generally made as a screw-cutting lathe, it is also made in a simple form, without lead-screw or automatic feeds for the very young pupil who naturally finds it easier to learn the basic principles on an uncomplicated machine. Such machines are known as *basic training* lathes, not to be confused with the *training* lathes used by engineering apprentices. These lathes often embody many of the features found in the production models.

The centre lathe

The main parts of the centre lathe are seen in Fig. 239.

The bed
This is the foundation of the lathe, and made in cast iron, it is usually of a very robust box-like form, ribbed on the inside and ported so that coolant and swarf can pass through easily. The top

Figure 239   A centre lathe
(The Colchester Lathe Co. Ltd.)

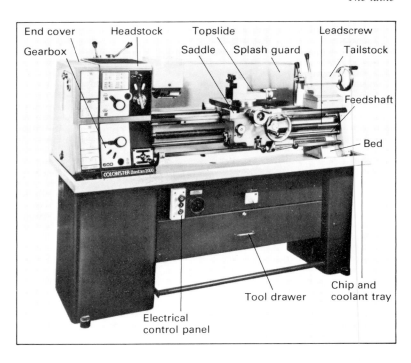

surfaces of the bed, known as the 'ways' are accurately machined
and often hardened, the satisfactory working of the lathe being very
largely dependent on the alignment of these surfaces which are
usually finished by precision grinding. A lathe bed is shown in
Fig. 240.

Figure 240   Lathe bed, with gap-piece.
(The Colchester Lathe Co. Ltd.)

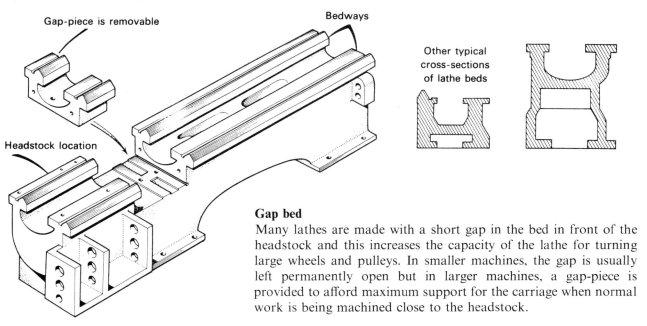

Gap bed

Many lathes are made with a short gap in the bed in front of the
headstock and this increases the capacity of the lathe for turning
large wheels and pulleys. In smaller machines, the gap is usually
left permanently open but in larger machines, a gap-piece is
provided to afford maximum support for the carriage when normal
work is being machined close to the headstock.

Headstock

At the left, and in the form of a stout box-casting, the headstock

Figure 241   Cut-away of the Colchester
'Bantam' headstock
(The Colchester Lathe Co. Ltd.)

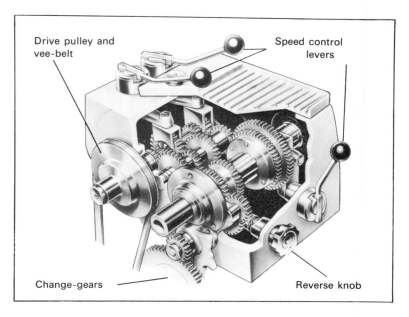

Drive pulley and
vee-belt

Speed control
levers

Change-gears

Reverse knob

is precisely located and bolted to the bed. It is occasionally cast in one piece with the lathe bed. The headstock carries the spindle in precision bearings which must take both radial and end loads. They are usually of the tapered-roller type and on assembly, are pre-loaded to eliminate end-float and side-play in the spindle.

The spindle is hollow, to accommodate long bars in the chuck and the inner end of the bore is machined to a standard taper to receive the live centre or other accessories as required. The Morse standard taper is used on English lathes. The 'live' centre is so called because it is the one which always rotates with the work and is associated with the driving. The hollow spindle facilitates the ejection of the live centre with a length of rod passed through the bore.

The traditional English spindle nose is threaded so that chucks, face- and catch-plates can be screwed on against a shoulder and over a plain portion (register) which aligns the component. See Fig. 249.

The driving mechanism is inside the headstock and in a basic training lathe for young pupils, this is often simply a four- or five-step cone pulley on the spindle, driven by an identical pulley mounted the opposite way round on a lay shaft which is driven by the motor. This range of four or five speeds is doubled in the screw cutting lathe by engaging a back gear mechanism which reduces all speeds in a set ratio. The back gear is used in screw cutting and the low speeds it gives are useful in turning large diameters and machining hard materials. A back gear mechanism is seen in Fig. 242.

The moving of the belt drive on stepped pulleys is not necessary in the all-geared headstock in which one belt drive brings power into the assembly, after which, speed changes are made through gears, operated from external hand controls. In conjunction with

Figure 242   Lathe headstock with back-gear engaged

Explanation: Belt driven pulley A and gear-wheel B are permanently connected and when back-gear is engaged, are disconnected from the spindle and are free to rotate thereon.

   The reduction drive is then from A to B to C to D and to E. Gear-wheel E is locked to the spindle.

   When back-gears C and D are disengaged (by sliding along), pulley A is re-locked to the spindle, giving a direct drive.

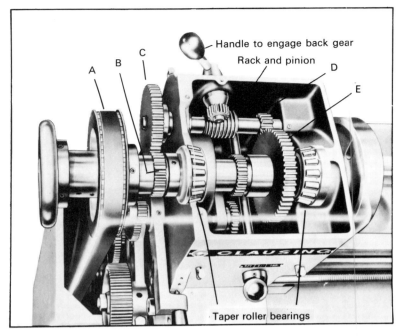

a foot operated spindle brake, the all-geared head makes speed changing a very fast operation, but brakes can only be fitted where chucks (etc.) are directly mounted on the spindle. See under 'Chuck mountings'.

   Another method of speed changing which avoids stopping to change a belt over employs two variable-width vee pulleys. Both split at the bottom of the vee and as one pulley opens out along the axis, the other closes, the vee belt sinking in one pulley as it opens, whilst rising in the other pulley as it closes. This gives an infinitely variable speed range which can be adjusted with the machine running.

Tailstock

The tailstock supports the 'free' end of the work and is used also in the drilling and reaming of work held in chuck or on face-plate. It slides on and is guided by the bed-ways and in most lathes is made in two parts which permit of a lateral adjustment. This is used in off-centre taper-turning. The casting is bored to receive the barrel (or 'sleeve') whose axis is precisely in line with that of the spindle. The inner end of the barrel is machined to receive the tapered centre which can be of the stationary or rotating kind. The taper-socket in the barrel is used for holding taper-shank drills, reamers or other accessories. At the outer end, the barrel is threaded to take the adjusting screw which is operated by a hand-wheel.

   Major adjustments to the location of the tailstock are made by sliding it along the bed and clamping it by operating a lever, after which, fine adjustments to bring the centre up to the work can be made with the hand-wheel. The barrel also, can be clamped after setting, so that it cannot slack off during working.

Figure 243   Centre lathe tailstock
(The Colchester Lathe Co. Ltd.)

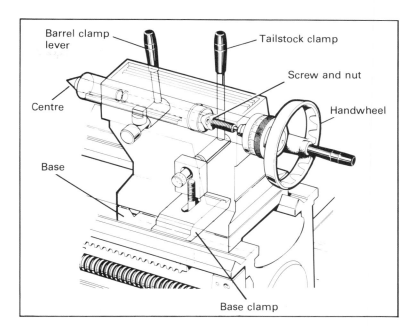

Carriage or saddle

This forms the base of the unit which supports the cutting tool
and it can be traversed along the whole length of the bed by hand
control or by power feed. It can be clamped at any point along the
bed. A cross slide is provided for cross traversing or 'surfacing'
and on this slide is mounted the compound slide (top slide) which
can be pivoted and locked at any angle for use in turning short
tapers.

   To the front of the carriage is fixed the apron which extends well

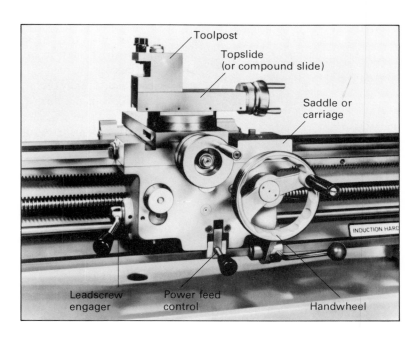

Figure 244   Lathe carriage
(The Colchester Lathe Co. Ltd.)

down over the front of the bed and here are found the controls for hand- or power-feeding when surfacing, sliding or screw-cutting. Hand-traversing of the carriage is by rack and pinion, the hand-wheel turning the pinion and the rack being fitted under the over-hang of the bed-way.

Lead-screw

The lead-screw, which transmits feed motion for screw-cutting, extends the whole length of the bed, passing behind the apron. It can be engaged with, or freed from the carriage by a clutch mech-anism which can be operated whilst the lead-screw is turning. This clutch is quite simple, consisting of a large split nut ('half nuts') which can be opened or closed over the lead-screw by the move-ment of the lever on the apron. This mechanism is only used when screw-cutting.

Feed shaft

In addition to the lead-screw, a feed shaft is employed in operating the carriage or the cross slide in automatic turning. The lead-screw is not used for this purpose to avoid wearing it on work for which it is not needed (it is a costly item) and also because the feed it gives would often be too fast.

The feed shaft, with a key-way (a lengthwise slot), runs alongside the lead-screw and passes behind the apron where a keyed worm wheel, mounted on the shaft, turns with it and is free to slide along it. The worm wheel drives a gear wheel and from this, the feed can be directed either to the cross slide or to the carriage by operating a control on the apron. On some lathes, the lead-screw itself is made with a key-way cut through the threads. The key-way drives the worm wheel and the screw is used for screw-cutting.

Automatic turning is very useful in long traverses, the steady movement of the carriage giving a superior finish to that usually obtained by hand feeding. One point to note is that in end facing with automatic feed it is impossible to maintain a constant cutting speed since the speed at the work periphery will be at its maximum and this will diminish towards the centre. A compromise must be sought in these situations.

The motion for the lead-screw and the feed shaft is taken from the spindle and because the revolutions of the lead-screw *must* be positively related to the spindle for screw-cutting, the drive is always taken through a gear train. This subject is dealt with more fully under 'Screw-cutting' and for the moment, it will be sufficient to know that the velocity ratio of spindle to lead-screw can be changed to cut various thread pitches, that the rotation of lead-screw and feed shaft can be reversed and that either or both can be taken out of drive when not required.

Most lathes are fitted with some kind of safety device which either prevents the accidental engagement of more than one feed at the same time, or in the event of two feeds being engaged toget-her, prevents damage being done, sometimes with a slipping clutch

Figure 245   Chucks
   A. Three-jaw self-centring chuck.
   B. Four-jaw independent chuck
(F. Pratt Engineering Corporation P.L.C.)

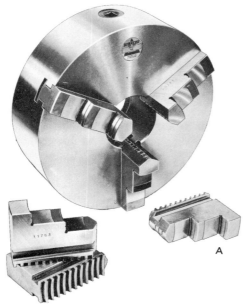

A

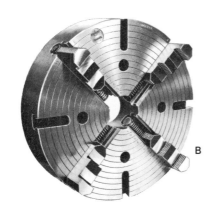

B

Figure 246   Cut-away showing scroll and gears in a self-centring chuck
(F. Pratt Engineering Corporation P.L.C.)

mechanism or with a shear pin which breaks under any abnormal load.

Lathe sizes

The size of a lathe is commonly expressed in the UK by the height of the centres over the lathe bed, indicating the radius of a cylinder which will clear the bed, but quite often the 'swing' of a lathe is quoted and this refers to the diameter of such a cylinder. Whichever way the size is expressed, it must be remembered that the work has to clear the lathe carriage when turning between centres. The bed length of a lathe does not indicate its capacity which is quoted as length between centres.

Work holding and driving

Chucks

Every lathe should be equipped with two chucks, one a self-centring (SC) 3-jaw chuck and the other a 4-jaw independent chuck, both of the size recommended by the lathe manufacturer. Both types are used in many different machining operations on short work pieces which can be held in the chuck, whilst longer items can be supported on the tailstock centre or a steady at the outer end. Long lengths of bar, can, of course, be passed right through the hollow spindle whilst gripped in the chuck.

Self-centring chucks   The 3-jaw SC chuck will automatically centre rounds or hexagons, all jaws opening or closing together as the scroll is turned with the key. The jaws are matched to the scroll during manufacture and each is numbered so that it can be returned to its correct slot after removal.

For holding large diameter work, scroll chucks are supplied with spare sets of jaws with reversed steps. The jaws themselves cannot be reversed. To remove the jaws, the chuck is opened out until all three jaws can be withdrawn as they disengage from the scroll. Re-assembly with either set of jaws is done in the following manner: the scroll is turned as for opening and when the scroll end has disappeared from No. 1 slot, No. 1 jaw is pressed home and engaged by closing the chuck. When the scroll end appears in No. 2 slot, it is wound back a little and No. 2 jaw is pressed home and engaged with the scroll. This is repeated for No. 3 jaw.

SC chucks are also made with two, four and six jaws, and of these, only the 4-jaw chuck is likely to find uses in the school workshop as it will centre square bar stock.

Jaws with external steps can be used to hold large rings or tubes by opening them on to the inside of the work.

Scroll (SC) chucks will centre work with reasonable accuracy, but unless great care is taken, they will quickly be thrown out of truth, mainly by wear or straining of the scroll from over-tightening or from digging-in which throws heavy loads on jaws and scroll, especially if short work pieces are wrenched from the chuck. Chuck

Figure 247   Draw-in collet chuck

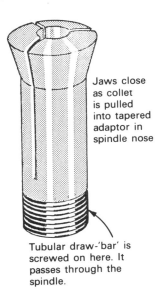

Jaws close
as collet
is pulled
into tapered
adaptor in
spindle nose

Tubular draw-'bar' is
screwed on here. It
passes through the
spindle.

jaws should be removed at regular intervals for the cleaning of the scroll, the jaw teeth and the slides. Over-lubrication is not a good thing, since excess oil will either be thrown out or will form a destructive grinding compound with any fine swarf.

The effect of inaccurate centring can be nullified by planning chuck jobs so that all of the important operations are carried out at one setting of the work. Once the job is removed, it is difficult to get it running true again.

Independent jaw chucks   Whilst the 4-jaw independent chuck is indispensable for holding work of irregular shape and for off-centre turning, it can also be used for holding squares or rounds. Centring takes a little longer but it can be done very accurately using each individual jaw adjustment. The procedure for centring in the 4-jaw chuck is described under 'Chuck-work'. Independent jaw chucks are supplied with only one set of jaws since these are reversible.

Draw-in collet chuck   The draw-in collet provides a quick and accurate means of holding small parts for models, instrument- and clock-making. Made of heat treated steel, the collet is in the form of a sleeve, bored to receive round, hexagon and square sections closely approximating to the bore size.

The collet, split into three or more segments, is drawn into the lathe spindle with a threaded tube (draw-bar), the tapered end bears against a matching taper inside an adaptor or 'closer' on the lathe spindle and the collet closes on to the work. Because of its restricted range of adjustment, it becomes necessary to hold one collet for each size and section of bar likely to be machined and this could mean a large number.

Figure 248   The parts of the Burnerd Multisize collet chuck
Key operated type is shown *(F. Pratt Engineering Corporation P.L.C.)*

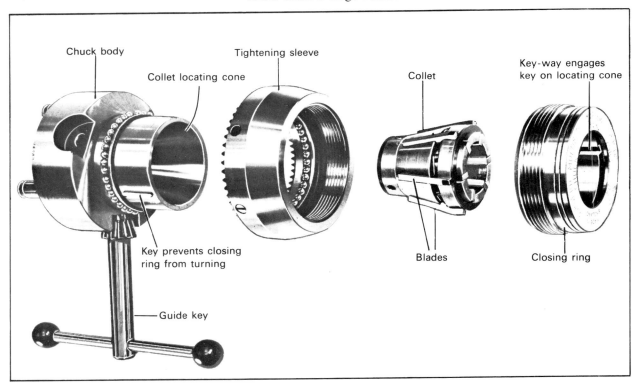

Chuck body

Collet locating cone

Tightening sleeve

Collet

Key-way engages
key on locating cone

Key prevents closing
ring from turning

Guide key

Blades

Closing ring

'Multiblade' collet chuck The 'Multiblade' collet, shown in Fig. 248, consists of a steel body carrying six spring loaded blades, arranged radially. When the collet is pushed into a conical housing, the blades move in with a parallel grip with a range of movement of more than 3 mm. On releasing the pressure, the springs retract the blades, allowing them to move forwards, releasing the work.

With this larger range of adjustment, fewer collets will be required and a total of twenty will hold any size of bar between 1·5 mm and 62 mm, round or hexagon. These collets are part of an integrated system of work holders in which any one collet can be used in a range of closing devices which include: (1) key operated chucks for lathe work, (2) lever or power operated chucks which can be opened or closed whilst the machine is running. There are also vertical mounting chucks for use in milling machines and drill or tool holders for use on capstan and automatic lathes.

A key-operated chuck is shown dismantled in Fig. 248. The key rotates the tightening sleeve on its ball-race. The thread on the inside of this ring draws back the closing ring which is prevented from turning by means of the guide key. This closing ring draws the collet back into the conical housing, closing the blades.

Chuck mountings

For many years, the normal method of mounting a chuck on the spindle-nose has been by means of a thread and register on the spindle, on to which screws a back-plate. The chuck, in its turn is bolted to the back-plate. In its initial assembly, the back-plate is screwed on to the spindle-nose and is then faced and finished dead to size to fit into a recess formed in the back of the chuck. The two are then screwed together and from then on, that chuck and back-plate 'belong' to that particular lathe. This method of mounting is shown in Fig. 249 and attention is drawn to the plain-shouldered portion (register) which centres the chuck. This mounting exhibits several undesirable features and there is an increasing trend for chucks to be mounted directly on to spindles made to various International Standards' Specifications, some of which are shown in Fig. 250. The advantages which these spindle-nose forms offer are: (1) the register is quite positive and is not subject to the wear which takes place when chucks are screwed on to the spindle, (2) the chuck is held very securely with no danger of its 'running off' when the lathe is stopped (even when the spindle is fitted with a brake), (3) the overhang is reduced and with the chuck much closer to the bearings, the whole assembly is much more rigid, making for better work, and (4) the chuck is quickly mounted and removed, except with the type A–1, where the chuck is bolted to a flange in a semi-permanent mounting.

Whatever form of mounting is used, it is very important that both spindle and chuck registers and threads are quite clean before assembly. When removing chucks, the operator should always be ready to take the weight which comes suddenly, to avoid damage to lathe bed or fingers. A softwood block, resting on the lathe bed is good 'accident prevention' here.

Figure 249 Threaded lathe spindle with chuck and backplate mounting

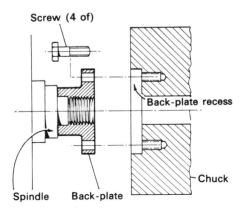

*Figure 250   American spindle noses with
appropriate direct mounting chucks shown below
(F. Pratt Engineering Corporation P.L.C.)*

Spindle type A1.   Spindle type D1.   Spindle type L.
Short taper.   Cam-lock.   Long taper key drive.

Figure 251   Face-plate and dogs
Work can be bolted direct on to the face-plate
(F. Pratt Engineering Corporation P.L.C.)

Face-plate

This accessory is used for mounting work of awkward shapes
which cannot readily be chucked. A face-plate is seen in Fig. 251.

Catch-plate

The catch-plate, mounted on the lathe spindle is commonly used
to drive work between centres, a driving pin engaging with a
'carrier' (or 'dog') which screws on to the end of the work. Catch-
plates are often made with a radial slot across the face so that the
driving pin can be located at any distance from the centre. With
the pin removed, a bent-tail carrier can then be used for driving,
the tail engaging in the slot.

*Figure 252   Work on centres, driven by straight-
tail carrier and catch-plate
(The Colchester Lathe Co. Ltd.)*

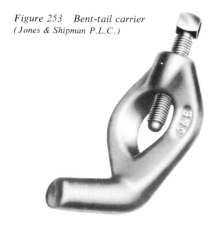

*Figure 253 Bent-tail carrier
(Jones & Shipman P.L.C.)*

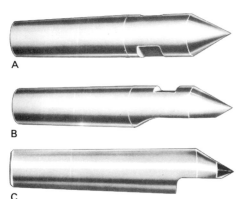

*Figure 254 Lathe centres, two shown with
spanner flats. A and B are of carbon or high-
speed steel and C is carbide tipped. B and C are
half-centres.*
(Jones & Shipman P.L.C.)

A

B

C

Figure 255 Live tailstock centre

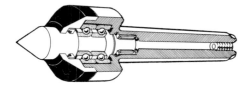

Lathe centres

These are commonly made from high-speed steel and are hardened, but in fact, it is not essential for the live centre (in the spindle) to be hardened as there is no rubbing. Tailstock centres are also made with cemented carbide tips which give long and arduous service. Centres are accurately ground to standard tapers with the points usually finished to an included angle of 60°. The live centre is adapted to the spindle socket by means of a taper sleeve.

It is of the utmost importance that the centres fit perfectly in the spindle and tailstock barrel and before insertion they should be wiped clean and inspected for damage, the slightest burring of the tapers causing them to run out of truth.

The spindle and tailstock tapers also require attention and cleaning should be done with a rag on a *stick* (not the finger) and *never* with the spindle revolving. The tailstock centre is removed by retracting the barrel and when it is almost home, the end of the screw will eject the centre. The tailstock centre-point will require lubrication because the work is turning and its adjustment up to the work must be made carefully so that all end-float is eliminated without any undue pressure which will quickly cause local heating. The work will heat and expand under heavy cutting and will bind on the centre and damage it if the pressure is not relieved by a re-adjustment. Long bars will almost certainly show enough expansion to cause binding with only a slight rise in temperature and the adjustment and lubrication of the centre must be watched carefully.

Live tailstock centre

The use of a live (revolving) tailstock centre eliminates friction (but not work expansion). One of these centres is shown in Fig. 255. Other kinds are made for different conditions of service and with various point forms, including conical adaptors for centring tubes. The centre rotates on precision bearings which take radial and thrust loads and elaborate precautions are taken to prevent the ingress of swarf or coolant. The bearings are lubricated for life and the unit should never require dismantling.

Half centre The use of a half centre facilitates the end-facing of work between centres by allowing the tool to be fed right in. For end-facing with a normal centre, the tool tip must be ground back at a little less than 60°.

The truing of centres At the first signs of wear, centre points must be re-trued and this can be done with a tool-post grinder (a small, self contained grinding machine), mounted on the top slide which is set over at 30°. With the centre rotating slowly in the headstock, the grindstone is traversed, slowly, back and forth along the cone, taking only the very lightest of cuts. When the best possible finish has been achieved with the grinder, the cone can be given a high finish by honing with a perfectly flat stone. Lathe bed and slides are kept covered during grinding to keep all abrasive grit away.

*Figure 256   A rotating tube centre, shown drawn
away from the work
(The Colchester Lathe Co. Ltd.)*

Carriage stop

This is a very useful device for halting the carriage at predetermined points along the bed and can be used for the repeated finishing of parts of identical lengths. Lathes are sometimes fitted with single stops, but the one shown in Fig. 257 has five stops which can be set to different lengths and then selected by rotating the turret mounting.

*Figure 257   A. Five position turret type bed
                    stop
             B. Standard bed stop
             C. Micrometer bed stop
(The Colchester Lathe Co. Ltd.)*

Graduated dials

The cross- and top-slide hand wheels are fitted with graduated dials giving accurate indications of slide movement in setting the depth of cuts. The dial is in the form of a collar which rotates with the hand wheel, usually through a friction drive which allows of its independent rotation. This enables one to set the depths of cuts from a zero reading by turning the dial and without altering the tool position. Dial graduations are read against a zero line scribed on the slide body.

It must always be remembered that any adjustment of the cross slide will be doubled off the work diameter unless the lathe is fitted with a *direct reading* dial which shows the amount taken off the diameter.

Because of market requirements, UK manufacturers now supply lathes which operate in (1) metric terms only, i.e. with metric pitch lead screw and with dials reading in millimetres (to 0·02 mm), (2) English terms only, i.e. with English pitch lead screw and dials reading to 0·001 ins, or (3) combinations of both, e.g. English pitch lead screw with dials reading in millimetres or with dual reading dials which give inch or metric readings as required.

Dual reading diais have been developed to cope with metrication in the UK and one of these dials is seen in Fig. 258. These dials can be fitted as standard equipment on new machines or can be fitted to machines already in use. They are designed for single reading, i.e. when set to read inches, only inch graduations are visible and when set to read metric, only metric graduations are visible. The conversion, which is instantaneous, is brought about by sliding the thimble in or out, a system of sun and planet wheels giving precise conversions from inches to millimetres.

Figure 258   The Colchester dual reading dial, English/Metric
(The Colchester Lathe Co. Ltd.)

Tool posts

Two commonly used tool posts are shown in Figs. 259 and 260. The American 'ring and rocker' post is shown holding a tipped tool but it can also be used for tool holders. Tools are quickly adjusted at centre height by moving the rocker which beds on the loose

Figure 259   The 'ring and rocker' toolpost
Note that the tool is set to centre-height

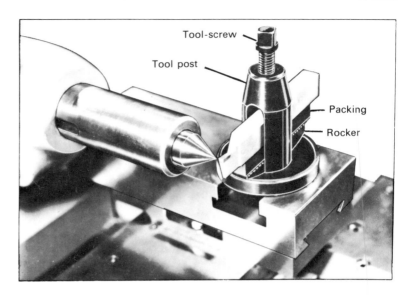

ring. The four-way post is more suited to repetition work where a cycle of operations is to be performed, but nevertheless, it will be of occasional use in the school workshop.

In Fig. 261 is shown a modern slotted-block tool post which dispenses with the need for packings to set the tool-height, this adjustment being made by means of a knurled screw. The tool, still in its holder, can be quickly removed for sharpening and no adjustment is needed when it is replaced in the post. See also Fig. 269 (page 171).

Figure 260   A four-way (turret) toolpost
(The Colchester Lathe Co. Ltd.)

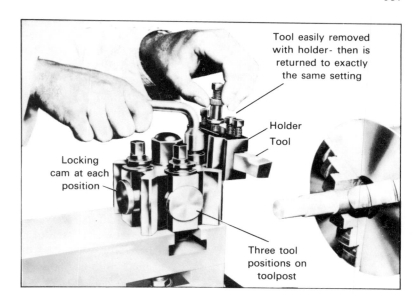

Figure 261   The 'Colchester' quick-change toolpost
(The Colchester Lathe Co. Ltd.)

Lathe tools

However good a lathe may be, its efficient operation and the quality of the finish on its products will be dependent on the tools used.

Figure 262   Lathe tools

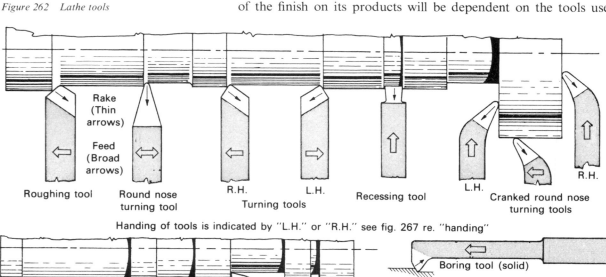

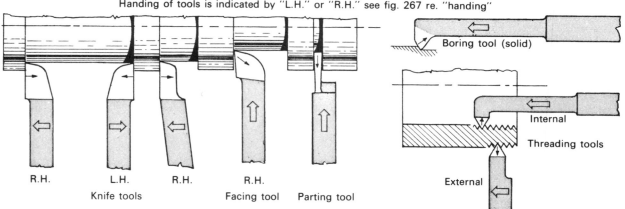

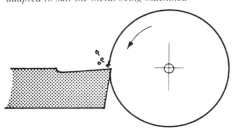

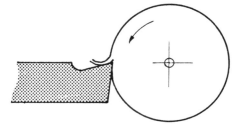

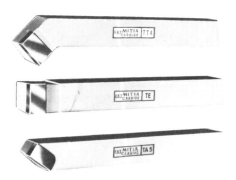

Brittle metals shear and break
up under pressure against
a near-flat face

Ductile and soft metals form a
flowing chip over a steeper face

Apart from the actual shape of the tool point, the material of which it is made is of prime importance, the essential qualities being *toughness* which enables it to withstand shock and heavy pressure, and *hardness* which enables it to hold a cutting-edge. Although carbon tool steel has these properties when properly heat-treated, its applications are limited and it has been largely replaced by the high-speed steels and other alloys which retain a cutting-edge for much longer periods and under much more rigorous conditions, viz.: heavy cuts at elevated temperatures without losing their hardness. The air hardening property of high-speed steel is improved further by the addition of cobalt in *super* high-speed steel which can be used on hard materials. The other alloys referred to are non-ferrous, they are extremely hard and brittle (and expensive) and are used in the form of tips which are brazed or butt welded on to shanks, often of high tensile steel. Tipped tools are also made with expendable tips which are held in place with a small clamp and when dull, the tip is discarded and replaced with a new one. Stellite (an alloy of cobalt, chromium and tungsten) is used in making tips and the hardest are made from the cemented carbides (for example, tungsten carbide). All permit of cutting-speeds well in excess of those possible with high-speed steels.

Lathe tools can be divided into four groups:
1. Solid (one-piece) tools of carbon—or high-speed steel, gripped directly in the tool post.
2. Tool holder bits of high speed steel and of square or round section. Held in tool holders.
3. Tipped tools of various kinds.
4. Special tools, e.g. boring tools, boring bars which hold tool bits, dee bits, form tools of various kinds and knurling tools.

In Fig. 262 is shown a selection of solid tools and in Fig. 263 are three tool holders, one straight and two cranked (to right and left) with tool bits. The advantages which these bits offer are that they are economical of high-speed steel which is expensive and they can be removed from the tool holder for sharpening and replaced with a minimum of adjustment. Knurling and thread form-tools are shown later.

Tool angles
The wedge form of the cutting part of a lathe tool involves two components, viz, *clearance* below the cutting edge, without which the tool could only rub on the work, and *rake* which is the slope on the face, away from the cutting edge. Whilst clearance varies only slightly for different purposes, rake shows marked variations, being adjusted to suit the metal being turned. The direction of rake is determined mainly by feed direction and the shape of the cutting edge.

Clearance
Clearance, formed on both the major and minor flanks of the tool is kept as small as possible, consistent with the proper working

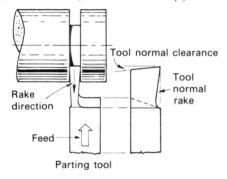

Figure 266   *Rake, feed direction and chip-flow*

Parting tool

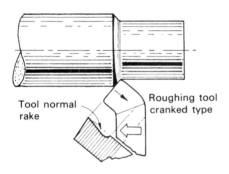

Roughing tool
cranked type

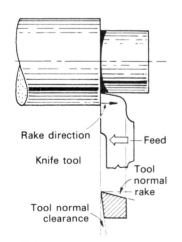

Knife tool

Note:
Direction of rake dictates the
line of chip-flow, which
should be directly away from
cutting edge and work face

of the tool. Excessive clearance reduces support for the cutting edge and increases the tendency to chatter. In addition to the slight variations in clearance for different metals, there are several cases where further adjustments are required, viz.: (1) because of the convex face of the work in turning, front-cutting tools will operate with slightly reduced clearances, but *not* for surfacing cuts, (2) for traversing cuts, the correct clearance is important and where the work is of small diameter, clearance may need to be increased slightly because the helical form of the transient surface becomes more pronounced, unless the feed speed is reduced, (3) boring tools will require increased clearance to avoid rubbing on the concave work surface. A second flank will provide relief at the heel and with very small bores, this secondary angle may have to be quite large.

Rake and cutting action

Tools for brittle metals like hard brass and cast iron, are formed with little or no rake, the near-flat face presented to the work causing the waste metal to shear and break away in small chips. Where the metal forms a flowing chip (and many metals do this), the tool must be given rake because the waste metal cannot be forced off by shearing, but must be lifted off by the wedge action of the tool. Chip pressure is very considerable when heavy cuts are taken and tool cutting parts weakened by excessive rake or clearance will be prone to chatter and to digging in caused by the 'feeding in' effect of pressure on a sloping face.

Rake should produce the smallest possible chip deflection whilst leaving the cutting part stiff enough to withstand the load without springing. For very hard metals rake is quite small, e.g., about 10° for tool steel, increasing to 30° or more for soft and ductile metals like copper and aluminium.

In Fig. 266 are seen examples showing how rake direction influences the line of chip flow from the transient surface. Whilst this is an important feature in tool designing, there are also other factors to be considered.

Tool geometry

The geometry of the parting off tool is probably the least complicated and though shown in Fig. 266 with the major cutting edge perpendicular to the tool axis, it is usually formed at a small angle to give a clean break through. For the tool shown in Fig. 266, the direction of feed motion aligns with the plane of normal rake and with the tool set horizontally in the lathe, there is a simple and obvious relationship between tool angles and surfaces both in its making and in its operation.

Tools, however, are produced with the cutting edges in a variety of orientations and when in use, the tool shank may be set at any angle in relation to the work surface. The angles thus formed by tool cutting edges, faces and flanks relative to the resultant cutting direction and to the work surfaces are known as 'working angles' which are not always readily orientated or measured in the

*Figure 267 Lathe and tool nomenclature and
            angles.*

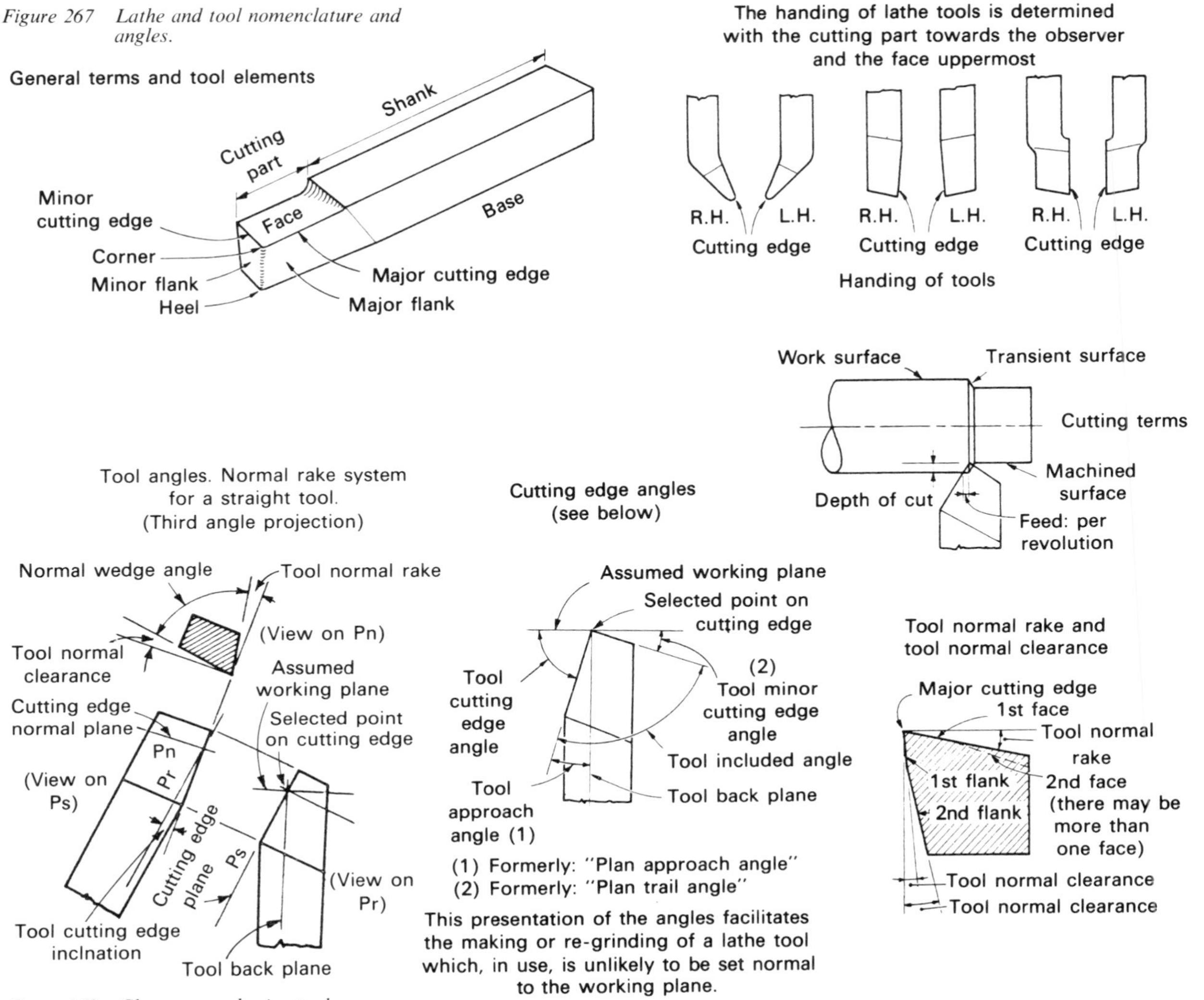

General terms and tool elements

The handing of lathe tools is determined
with the cutting part towards the observer
and the face uppermost

R.H.   L.H.   R.H.   L.H.   R.H.   L.H.
Cutting edge   Cutting edge   Cutting edge

Handing of tools

Shank

Cutting
part

Base

Face

Minor
cutting edge

Corner

Minor flank

Heel

Major cutting edge

Major flank

Work surface   Transient surface

Cutting terms

Depth of cut   Machined
                      surface

Feed: per
revolution

Tool angles. Normal rake system
for a straight tool.
(Third angle projection)

Cutting edge angles
(see below)

Normal wedge angle   Tool normal rake

(View on Pn)

Tool normal
clearance

Cutting edge
normal plane

Assumed
working plane

Selected point
on cutting edge

(View on
Ps)

Pn

Pr

Cutting edge plane

Ps

(View on
Pr)

Tool cutting edge
inclnation

Tool back plane

Assumed working plane

Selected point on
cutting edge

(2)
Tool minor
cutting edge
angle

Tool
cutting
edge
angle

Tool included angle

Tool
approach
angle (1)

Tool back plane

(1) Formerly: "Plan approach angle"
(2) Formerly: "Plan trail angle"

This presentation of the angles facilitates
the making or re-grinding of a lathe tool
which, in use, is unlikely to be set normal
to the working plane.

Tool normal rake and
tool normal clearance

Major cutting edge
                1st face
                    Tool normal
                    rake
1st flank   2nd face
2nd flank   (there may be
                more than
                one face)
            Tool normal clearance
            Tool normal clearance

Figure 268 Clearance on boring tools

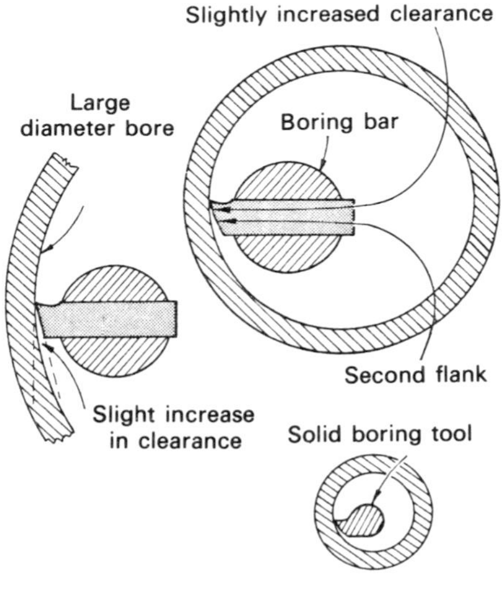

Slightly increased clearance

Large
diameter bore

Boring bar

Second flank

Slight increase
in clearance

Solid boring tool

making or the re-grinding of the tool.

The recommendations of the British Standards Institution in resolving these problems involve the use of two systems of reference planes through a 'selected point' on the cutting edge by means of which 'tool angles' and 'working angles' can be defined. The first, known as the 'tool-in-hand' system defines the geometry of a tool to facilitate its manufacture whilst the other, known as the 'tool-in-use' system, defines the effective tool geometry when it is performing a cutting operation.

The nomenclature for defining rake, clearance and other cutting tool angles is known as the 'normal rake system' and is the preferred system replacing the former 'maximum rake system'.

It is not possible to go further into this subject within the context of this book and the reader who seeks further information is advised to refer to the British Standards publication BS 1296 Part 2, 'Glossary of Terms for Single Point Tools'.

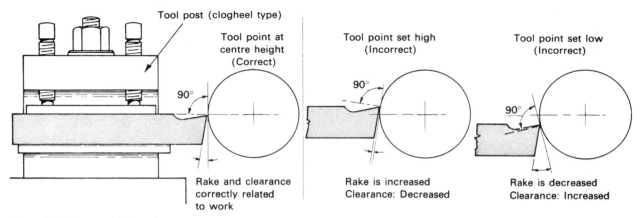

Tool post (clogheel type)

Tool point at centre height (Correct)	Tool point set high (Incorrect)	Tool point set low (Incorrect)
90°	90°	90°
Rake and clearance correctly related to work	Rake is increased Clearance: Decreased	Rake is decreased Clearance: Increased

Figure 269   Setting of lathe tools

Cutting speeds

Cutting speeds are usually expressed in terms of metres per minute and these are the speeds at which the tool should pass over the work to produce the best results at suitable speeds. Cutting speeds are governed by two factors: (1) the hardness of the metal being cut, and (2) the type of tool being used, HSS and tipped tools operating at much higher speeds than carbon steel tools.

To maintain these speeds, small diameter work will have to turn much faster than larger diameters. To convert the speeds given in Table 13 into lathe spindle speeds (rev./min.), the following formulae are applied:

$$\text{rev/min} = \frac{\text{Speed in m/min} \times 1\ 000}{\pi \times \text{work dia. in mm}}$$

Example: Cutting speed: 20 m/min. Diameter of bar: 50 mm.

$$\text{rev/min} = \frac{20 \times 1\ 000}{\pi \times \text{dia.}} = \frac{20\ 000}{3 \cdot 14 \times 50} = \frac{20\ 000}{157}$$
$$= 127 \text{ rev/min approximately.}$$

A number of cutting speeds are given in the table and these are assumed to be for moderate cuts. Rake and clearance angles are also given:

Table 13   Cutting speeds for turning (HSS tools)

	Cutting speed m/min	Rake angle	Clearance angle
Mild steel	24–30	20°	8°
Tool steel	12–18	10°	6°
Grey cast iron	18–24	0–5°	6°
Hard brass	45–120	3–8°	10°
Soft brass	60	8–12°	10°
Copper	60	20–30°	10°
Aluminium	300	30°	10°
Phosphor bronze rod	30	8–12°	8°
Phosphor bronze, cast	45–90	0°	6°
Gunmetal, cast	45–90	8–12°	8°

Steadies

Two kinds of steady are used for supporting long work against

Figure 270   Using a fixed steady for centre drilling when work cannot be passed through the lathe spindle
(The Colchester Lathe Co. Ltd.)

the pressure of the tool. The *fixed steady* is secured to the lathe bed whilst the *travelling steady* is mounted on the carriage and moves along the work behind the tool, as each cut is taken. The fixed steady can be used to support the end of a bar, gripped in the chuck, for end-facing, for centre drilling, for boring or for threading.

14

Lathework

Figure 271   The centre drill

Type A (double-ended)

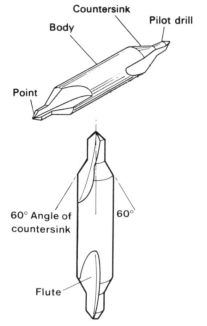

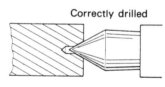

Correctly drilled

Too-deeply drilled

Method of finding
centre of bar stock

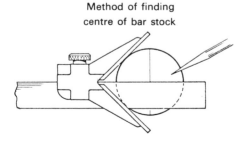

Turning on centres

The centre drill

The first operation in the turning of work between centres is the drilling of the holes for mounting the work and for this, the combined drill and countersink (centre drill) is used. Three types of drill are made (A, B and R), but only the double-ended type A is considered here.

Table 14   Centre drill sizes

Pilot drill diameter mm	Body drill diameter mm
1	3·15
1·6	4·0
2·0	5·0
2·5	6·3
3·15	8·0
4·0	10·0
6·3	16·0
10·0	25·0

These sizes are quoted from the B.S.328 (Part 2) 1972. Overall and pilot lengths are omitted. In ordering centre drills, quote only the type and diameters, e.g. A. 2·5/6·3. Details of types B and R can be found in the above B.S. specification. Type A drills with pilots of less than 1 mm are single ended.

The hole at the bottom of the countersinking leaves clearance for the lathe centre point and provides a reservoir for lubricant. When centre drilling in the lathe, the bar can be passed through the spindle if not too large and held in the 3-jaw chuck. The appropriate cutting fluid should be used and the drill must not be bumped against the work or forced as this might cause the point to split and break off in the work. If the bar is too large for the spindle bore, it can be gripped in a chuck with the free end supported in a fixed steady as seen in Fig. 270. Faulty centre drilling is illustrated in Fig. 271. When a bar has to be finished to length between centres, the allowance for machining should not be excessive, otherwise the bearing surfaces on the centres will become too slight when the facing is done.

Turning example

A piece of work for turning on centres is shown in Fig. 272 with suggestions for the operations involved. The bar should be cut off long enough to allow for a carrier and some clearance for the turning tool.
1. Both ends should be faced and centre drilled with a No. 3 or 4 centre drill. In the end facing, care should be taken to avoid

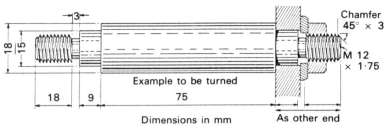

Figure 272   A turning example
(The Colchester Lathe Co. Ltd.)

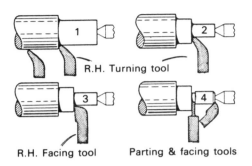

R.H. Turning tool

R.H. Facing tool   Parting & facing tools

Chamfer 45° × 3

M 12 × 1·75

Example to be turned

Dimensions in mm   As other end

18   9   75

leaving a centre 'pip' which may cause the centre drill to start off centre.

2. A work piece on centres is shown in Fig. 252 fitted with a straight carrier. In Fig. 290, a bent tail carrier is seen. The back centre adjustment must be made carefully to avoid undue pressure and friction. Many turners fill the centre hole with tallow initially and in any case, the centre must be lubricated during working, with oil. During working, slackness of the centres is often indicated by a rattling from the driving pin striking the carrier tail (or from the catch plate slot) as cuts are started. The back centre should be checked at intervals for heating.

3. If the end facing tool is left in the tool post, it can be used, with the work stationary, to scribe a short line as a guide for setting up the next tool accurately to centre height.

4. Alternative turning tools are shown in Fig. 262, but beginners will probably feel safer using a cranked tool, since they will be working towards a carrier.

5. The reduction of the bar to size is started off with hand traversing and when the work is approaching finished size, a fine automatic feed can be engaged, using a nicely honed finishing tool. The bar should be marked clearly to indicate a limit for turning to avoid striking the carrier. Cutting oil should be used freely to promote a good finish.

6. Note that the locating spigot does not pass right through the hole and this ensures that the nut grips tightly against the framework.

7. On reversing the work to repeat the operations, it may be more convenient to drive by the spigot, using a smaller carrier with a brass pad to prevent damage to the finished surfaces. Length can be checked over the shoulders with sliding calipers or a rule measurement may be considered satisfactory, in which case, a stop of some kind should be held against the left-hand shoulder from which the measurement is made.

8. Since this job is an exercise in turning, the threads should be cut in the lathe and this subject is dealt with under a separate heading.

Taper turning

There are several ways in which tapers can be turned: (1) the compound slide rest can be swivelled round for turning short internal or external tapers, (2) the tailstock can be offset for longer external tapering, (3) the taper turning attachment can be used

for external tapers and for boring short internal tapers, and (4) a straight edged turning tool can be used for very short tapers.

Tapers can be expressed in three ways: (1) as a given amount on the diameter per unit length, e.g. 10 mm per 250 mm, (2) as an incline, e.g. 1 in 20 on the diameter, and (3) as an included angle.

Where tapering is to be done with the tailstock offset, the amount of offset in each case is found as follows:

(1) Required taper: 10 mm per 250 mm. If the work is 250 mm in length, then the offset would be 5 mm, i.e. one half of the inclusive taper. The offset would be proportionately larger or smaller for other lengths. For example: for this taper on a length of 175 mm, the offset would be:

$$\text{one half of } \tfrac{175}{250} \text{ ths of 10 mm} = 3 \cdot 5 \text{ mm}$$

(2) The inclusive taper can be found by dividing the length of the work by the length quoted for the unit taper. Thus, for a taper of 1 in 20 on a bar 250 mm in length, the inclusive taper would be: $250 \text{ mm} \div 20 = 12 \cdot 5 \text{ mm}$. The tailstock would be offset a half of this, i.e. $6 \cdot 25$ mm.

(3) Where the taper is given as an included angle, the tailstock must be offset so that the work axis is inclined at a half of this angle. The offset is calculated by trigonometry. Let L be the length of the work, let A be one half of the included angle and let x be the amount of offset. Then, $x = L \times \tan A$. For example, if L is 250 mm and A is $4°$, then $x = 250 \times \tan 2° = 250 \times 0 \cdot 0349 = 8 \cdot 72$ mm.

Before adjusting the tailstock, it is first clamped lightly and after releasing one of the adjusting screws, both are used to move the tailstock towards the tool so that the small end of the taper is at the tailstock. The screws are finally tightened up against each other.

A rough measurement of the offset is found by reading the datum line against the scale on the tailstock base, but the offset can in fact, be measured quite accurately from a short piece of bar held in the tool post. The gap between the bar and tailstock

*Figure 274   Taper turning on centres with
tailstock offset*

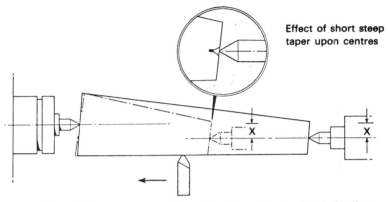

**Effect of short steep
taper upon centres**

Note: Different taper on different lengths with same tailstock offset

barrel is measured with the vernier calipers before the tailstock is
offset and from this measurement is deducted the required offset.
The tailstock can then be moved over this distance.

Measurement of the offset can also be done with the work set
up on centres and with a dial gauge held in the tool post, the offset
over a known distance along the work can be accurately measured.
The dial gauge plunger must, of course, be at centre height.

One very important point which must never be overlooked
in taper turning is that the tool point *must* be set exactly at centre
height otherwise an incorrect taper will be generated.

One effect of taper turning on centres which should be considered is that whilst the work axis is aslant to the lathe axis, the
centres remain parallel to it. This uneven bearing on the centres is
probably of little consequence in slight tapers but with steep
tapers this is not a good thing. The use of a live tailstock centre
gets over the problem of the uneven rubbing, to a limited extent.

*Figure 275   Taper turning with offset tailstock.
Observe the scale and zero line on tailstock base
(The Colchester Lathe Co. Ltd.)*

Test turning

The tailstock must be re-aligned after being offset and the re-alignment can be checked by turning a test bar. The bar, of 250 to 300 mm in length and around 25 mm diameter, is mounted on centres and is 'waisted' to leave a collar at each end. A light finishing cut is taken from both collars at the same cross slide setting and their diameters are compared. The tailstock is adjusted so that both collars finish at identical sizes.

Taper-turning attachment

A taper-turning attachment is shown in Fig. 276, and this device eliminates the need to set the tailstock over. It locks on the rear of the lathe bed and has an adjustable slide which, linked to the top slide of the lathe, moves it across as the carriage is traversed. The graduations on the taper slide adjustment indicate the total of 'inclusive' taper, i.e. it is not necessary to halve it, as in off-setting the tailstock. It is well nigh impossible to get the correct setting of the slide from the scale, however carefully the witness mark is read against the graduations, and it is necessary to get the taper started and then to check it by measuring the offset. Modern taper attachments are made with micrometer adjustments for fine settings.

Figure 276   Taper turning attachment in use (The Colchester Lathe Co. Ltd.)

Chuck-work

4-jaw independent chuck

The independent-jaw chuck is apt to be put aside in favour of the self-centring chuck in which work is quickly set up, but the independent chuck offers two big advantages, (1) it is possible to centre a job very accurately by manipulation of each jaw, and (2) the extra jaw gives a much firmer hold on the work. In centring

Figure 277   Facing work in a 4-jaw independent chuck
(The Colchester Lathe Co. Ltd.)

Figure 278   Dial test indicator in use, mounted on a magnetic base
(Hydro Machine Tools Ltd.)

Figure 279   Drilling work in the chuck (collet type chuck)
(The Colchester Lathe Co. Ltd.)

work, the concentric circles scribed on the face serve as a guide for an approximate setting and then with the lathe running, a piece of chalk may be used to mark high-spots on round work. With lathe stopped, the jaw or jaws opposite the high side are eased off a fraction and the jaw or jaws opposite are tightened to move the work over. The chalk mark is rubbed off and the process repeated until a full circle is marked. Precise centring will require the use of the dial indicator and this is shown in use in Fig. 278 checking concentricity in a 3-jaw chuck.

Drilling in the chuck

Before attempting any drilling, the work should be faced, as an uneven surface will cause the drill to start off-centre. The work should first be centre drilled and for large drills, pilot holes will reduce the feed pressure required. Where the hole is deep, the drill should be withdrawn to clear the swarf at intervals, there being a tendency to clogging with horizontal drilling. Flooding with coolant will also assist with swarf removal.

Holes of any appreciable size in castings are made by coring and this leaves a rough hole which requires opening out to size. After facing up the casting, the hole is opened out with a core drill which is made specially for this work. The core drill is described in Chapter 12. To facilitate an accurate start, the hole should first be chamfered with a lathe tool.

Reaming

Reaming has been discussed in Chapter 12 and this process is used extensively in lathework where satisfactory results are always assured because it is possible to bore out a hole before reaming. This assures positive axial alignment and the reamer, adapted in the tailstock, will follow the hole readily. A copious supply of cutting fluid should be used when reaming and, if the hole is deep,

Figure 280   Reaming in the lathe
(The Colchester Lathe Co. Ltd.)

the reamer should be withdrawn for clearing the flutes. When bottom reaming a blind hole, a taper-lead reamer can be entered first if depth permits, to give the bottom reamer a start.

Boring in the chuck

Boring is done by passing a single-point tool through a hole previously made by drilling or by coring. Even though the original hole may be off-centre, the boring tool will bring it into line as it is traversed parallel to the work axis. The hole can be bored right out to its finished size but this takes time and, wherever possible, the boring should be taken to a few thousandths under size and finished by reaming.

When machining castings, an attempt should be made to get the point of the tool right under the skin with a heavy first cut otherwise the cutting-edge will be quickly rubbed off by the glass-hard skin. This may not be possible if the surface is too irregular, of course.

A solid boring tool and a boring bar for use with tool bits in boring deeper holes are shown in Fig. 281. Boring tools for small-diameter holes will require increased clearance and with support for the cutting-edge thus reduced, there will be a tendency to chatter if heavy cuts are taken. A very good tool for finishing deep, small diameter bores out to size is the 'D' bit which is shown in Fig. 282. When a hole is finished out to size with a boring tool, the final cuts should be quite light ones so that the tool does not spring and it is a good plan to traverse the tool at least twice at the same setting to ensure parallelism.

Figure 281   Solid boring tool and double ended boring bar (American type)

Figure 282   'D' bit
Cutting fluid is fed from end of the shank through a small bore

Escape channel for cutting fluid when boring blind holes

Half-round 'D'-section

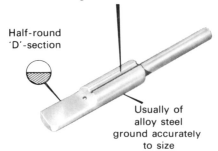

Usually of alloy steel ground accurately to size

Figure 283   Boring a component in 4-jaw independent chuck   *(The Colchester Lathe Co. Ltd.)*

Parting off

The operation of parting off requires a narrow tool and although its depth can be increased up to a point to compensate for this, there is an inherent tendency to springing. It is necessary to pay careful attention to the grinding of the point, the setting and the feed-rate. To part off cleanly without chatter, the lathe must be in good condition, that is without slackness in the slides or wear in the spindle bearings which will allow the work to ride up on the tool, causing chatter and digging in. By keeping the tool clearance as small as possible and with a reduced top rake, the tool point is given maximum support. A slight taper on the tool width from front to back prevents rubbing on the sides of the cut. The cutting-edge can be ground very slightly askew and this gives an easier break through, especially when parting off tubes.

Figure 284   Parting off
(The Colchester Lathe Co. Ltd.)

Figure 285   Parting off tool and holder
(Jones and Shipman P.L.C.)

The carriage should be locked in position and the tool, set exactly at centre height and with a minimum of overhang, is fed slowly and evenly into the work. Plenty of the appropriate cutting fluid should be applied. Tool breakages sometimes occur when swarf packs between the tool and the sides of the recess and to avoid this, the recess can be widened by taking a second cut before finally parting the work off. Proceeding in this way, parting off should not be a difficult task and is always better for being carried out as near as possible to the chuck.

Turning and boring a bush
In Fig. 286 the steps in making a mild steel bush are shown. Note that all operations except the last are done at one setting of the work. This item is selected to show the procedure for boring, but the bush could, in fact, be finished to size equally well by reaming. In using the boring tool, it must be remembered that it will spring if heavy cuts are taken and will produce a tapered bore. When the boring is approaching finished size the tool should be honed and when only a few hundredths mm remain on, more than one pass at each setting on automatic feed will ensure parallelism. Taking a

Figure 286   Turning and boring a bush
(*The Colchester Lathe Co. Ltd.*)

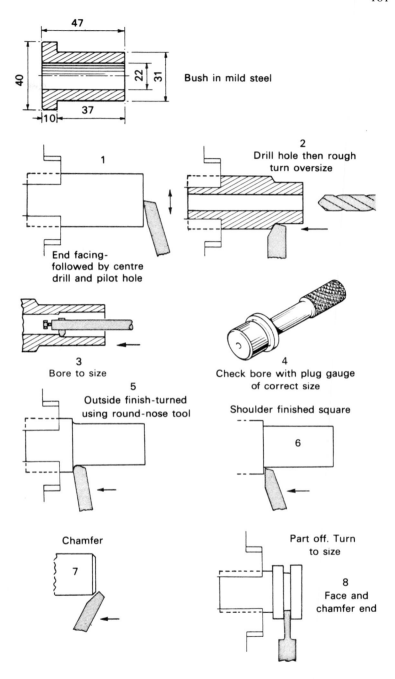

very careful measurement with Vernier calipers and then checking it, the bare estimated cut is put on to bring the bore out to size. The tool is fed in for about 2 mm and is then withdrawn. The plug gauge is then offered up to the hole and if it will not enter under *very gentle* pressure, a 'shade' more cut is put on and another cut taken. If the gauge now enters, the cut can be taken a little further and the hole again checked with the gauge and if still satisfactory, the cut can be completed under automatic feed. If the

Finished component-ring casting

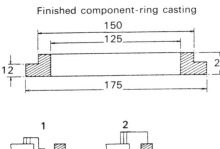

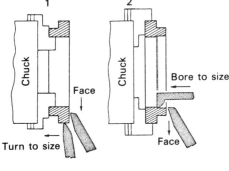

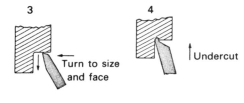

gauge will not enter to its full depth after this, a second traverse at the same setting should be tried before any more cut is put on.

In finishing the outsides of the bush, an alternative method would be to mount the bush on a mandrel between centres, after boring is complete. This avoids re-chucking the work, which, although satisfactory in this case, is not always to be recommended. See under the heading 'Mandrels'.

Other uses of the chuck

Chucks can be used in a number of ways and one of these is illustrated in Fig. 287, in which the sequence of operations in turning a ring casting is shown. Off-centre turning or boring can be done by setting the work over in a 4-jaw independent chuck. Where the work is of a light or delicate ring-form which cannot readily be gripped in a chuck, it can sometimes be mounted on an arbor after boring out to size. The arbor would be made to suit the job by centring a short piece of bar in the chuck and turning it to a tight fit in the work which is then pressed on to the arbor and turned to size. Since there is only a friction grip, only very slight cuts can be taken. The arbor could, of course, be given a slight taper. It should be left in the chuck after turning to size and whilst the work is pressed home. The chuck can often be used in conjunction with the tailstock centre instead of turning on both centres. When held like this, slender work will be more rigid because of the grip from the jaws and will be less likely to spring under pressure from the tool.

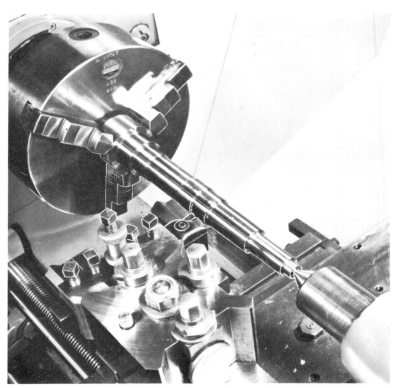

Other operations

Face-plate work

The face-plate is used for operations which cannot conveniently be performed in the chuck and for work of unusual shape, often in the form of castings. Work is held on the face-plate by bolting through any convenient holes or by using clamps. When a heavy piece of work is mounted off-centre, a counterweight should be added to maintain the balance, otherwise the lathe will vibrate. Care should be taken not to distort the work or the face-plate when tightening bolts or clamps, packings being inserted where necessary to obtain an even bearing against the plate.

The face-plate can be used effectively in turning large wheel castings in which there are suitable openings through which holding bolts can be passed. One side of the wheel is faced and the hole bored or reamed to size with the wheel on the face-plate. Next, a short piece of bar is taper turned to adapt in the lathe spindle and the protruding portion is reduced to form an arbor to receive the wheel which is then re-mounted with the machined face against the face-plate. In this way, a truly concentric wheel, free from wobble can be turned.

Figure 289   Work mounted off-centre on the face-plate
Note the counter-balance weights
(*The Colchester Lathe Co. Ltd.*)

Mandrels

A mandrel is a slightly tapered spindle or other device rotating between centres, on which previously-bored and part-machined work can be mounted for further turning operations. The simplest and most commonly-used form of mandrel (or mandril) is a round bar of carbon steel, hardened and ground with a very slight taper so that it can be entered in a finished bore and pressed home tightly. The centres are formed in recessed ends so that they are not damaged when arbor and work are assembled. Small flats are provided for the driving dog. Although mandrels can be driven

Figure 290   Turning with work mounted on a mandrel between centres
(*The Colchester Lathe Co. Ltd.*)

Figure 291   Knurling
(The Colchester Lathe Co. Ltd.)

home with a soft hammer, assembly is best done in a press.

Other types of mandrel include the *stepped* mandrel which offers a selection of sizes, the *screwed* mandrel for the mounting of threaded bores and the *expanding* mandrel.

Knurling

Round handles and tools are often impressed with a pattern to form a hand-grip and this is done with a knurling tool, one of which is shown in Fig. 291. The knurling tool is held in the tool post and with the lathe at slow speed, it is fed into the work at the right-hand end until the pattern is clearly impressed by the wheels. The tool is traversed slowly (with plenty of oil if the job is of steel) to the other end and without disengaging the wheels, is returned to the starting point when more cut is put on and the traversing repeated if the impression is not deep enough.

Boring on the lathe

Accurate boring can be done with the work mounted on a boring-table on the lathe cross slide, with a stout boring bar mounted between centres. The bar is pierced at the middle to receive a small tool bit—round- or square-section—and this is held by a grub-screw. The work is traversed on automatic feed whilst the boring bar is turning and provided that a stiff bar is used (to allow for the weakening caused by piercing) good results can be obtained, the only snags being that it is difficult to measure the amount of cut put on at each adjustment and unless some sort of gauge is made, there is no way of measuring the bore without some dismantling.

Milling in the lathe

Many lathe manufacturers produce milling attachments which enable small work to be handled. The attachment usually consists of a vertical slide with vice which replaces the compound slide rest, and work held in the vice can be manoeuvred vertically, longitudinally or across the cutter which is held in the chuck or adapted in the spindle-nose. The design of a lathe does not lend itself to milling operations beyond small and light work and its application is restricted to the small workshop.

Threading in the lathe

Screw-threading with taps and dies can be done quite easily and accurately in the lathe. No power feeds are used, the chuck and tailstock being used to ensure accurate work by keeping the taps and dies in line or square to the work.

Work which has been drilled out to a tapping size in the chuck is left there and the drill changed for the appropriate tap in the tailstock drill-chuck. The lathe chuck is turned by hand whilst the whole tailstock is brought up to feed in the tap. Some care must be taken when feeding and withdrawing small taps, otherwise the thread may be stripped because it is not strong enough to move such a weight. The tailstock should be pushed gently to avoid such damage. With small sizes it is probably safer to use the tailstock chuck only for lining-up and starting the tap, afterwards finishing it with the tap wrench in the usual way. Large taps can be lined up by using the tailstock-centre in the centre-hole on the tap-end, turning the tap with a wrench.

When making external threads, the end of the bar should be faced and chamfered in the chuck. The tailstock-centre is removed and with the tailstock locked at a convenient point, the barrel is brought to bear on the stock and die, holding them quite square to the work. The chuck is turned with the left hand and the right hand is used to feed the barrel forward. The stock-handle bears on the top slide and is prevented from turning. Once the die has made a good start, all can be removed from the lathe and threading continued in the vice if it is of a large size and is not easy to complete in the lathe.

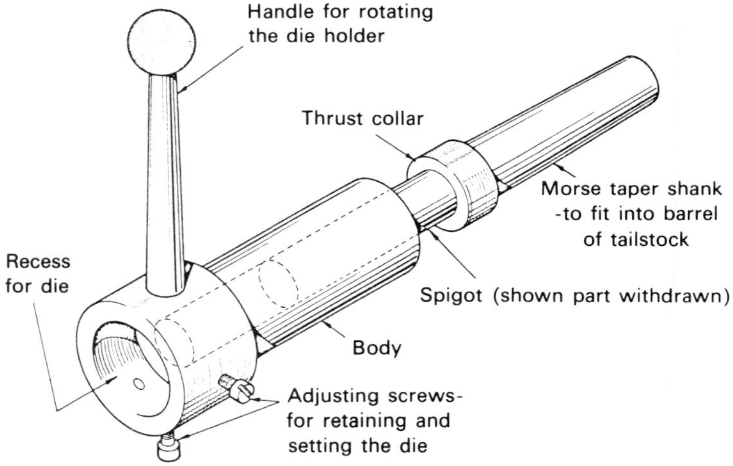

*Figure 292   Tailstock die-holder
(The Colchester Lathe Co. Ltd.)*

Handle for rotating
the die holder

Thrust collar

Morse taper shank
-to fit into barrel
of tailstock

Recess
for die

Spigot (shown part withdrawn)

Body

Adjusting screws-
for retaining and
setting the die

The tailstock die-holder is a useful appliance which can be used for threads of a moderate size and this is shown in Fig. 292. The taper shank adapts with the tailstock barrel and pressure to start the thread is applied through the hand-wheel, the die being turned by means of the handle of the die-holder. In screwing the die off, care must be taken not to let the barrel obstruct its movement or the thread may be damaged.

Screw-cutting in the lathe

The means by which the lathe carriage is traversed in screw-cutting has already been touched on briefly and this is amplified in the diagram in Fig. 293 which shows how the motion is taken from spindle to lead screw and carriage in the 'traditional' lathe. In a geared headstock, the drive from spindle to first driver, with reverse mechanism, is enclosed.

To cut a thread of any particular pitch, it is necessary to relate the carriage-traverse precisely to the rotation of the work and this is done by relating the sizes of the change wheels in the gear-train. In all cases, the pitch of the lead-screw must be taken into account

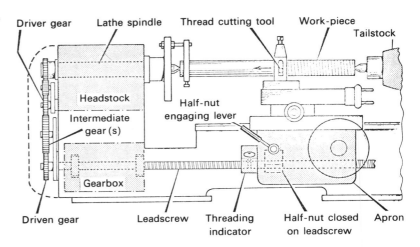

Figure 293   Diagram showing how movement of carriage is related to the rotation of work

The driver (stud) gear is reversed by means of a tumbler mechanism. See Fig. 294. The gears in the train are shown of different thicknesses for clarity

since this will affect the ratio when rotation is converted into lateral movement.

The lead-screw drive

In Fig. 294 is shown a 'standard' drive mechanism but before studying this further, two simple facts concerning speed ratios must be understood, viz.: (1) a small wheel driving a larger one will bring about a speed reduction and vice versa, and the ratio of the speeds will vary inversely as the ratio of the wheel sizes, or, with gear wheels, as the ratio between the number of teeth on each wheel. Thus, a 20-tooth wheel driving a 60-tooth wheel will effect a speed reduction of 3:1 and so on, (2) a third wheel

Figure 294   A 'standard' change gear mechanism with tumbler reverse gear

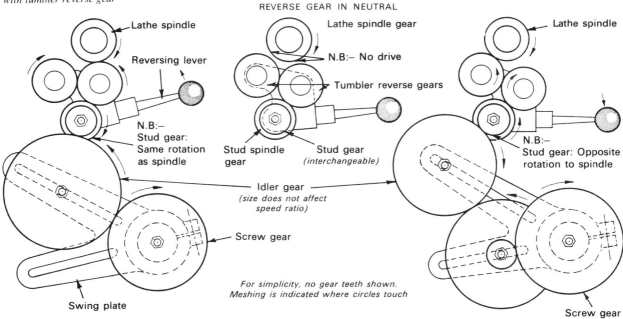

(or 'idler') meshing in between two others will not affect the ratio, but will cause the 'driven' wheel to turn in the same direction as the 'driver'.

From Fig. 294 it will be seen that the drive from the spindle gear is taken to a driver or stud gear which turns at the same speed. The drive is taken through a 'tumbler' gear mechanism which is used to reverse the rotation so that the carriage can be traversed in either direction. Placed in the neutral position, the tumbler disconnects the gear-train altogether when the feed-motion is not required. From the stud gear, either a *simple* or a *compound* gear-train can be taken to the lead-screw.

Simple train

Where the speed change can be brought about with one pair of change wheels, a simple train is used, the two wheels connect stud to lead screw through an 'idler' whose size is immaterial and determined mainly by the size of the gap between driver and driven wheels.

Compound train

Where the speed change requires two pairs of change wheels a compound train is used and this must occupy the same space. The first pair of wheels connects stud to intermediate pin and the first wheel of the second pair, also mounted on the intermediate pin and keyed to the other wheel, drives the lead-screw wheel. The wheels on the intermediate pin are not idlers, one is a driven wheel and the other a driving wheel.

For each different pitch required, the gear train must be dismantled and re-assembled with other wheels and all brought into mesh by adjusting the swing plate. However well practised one may be, this takes time which can be saved if a quick-change gear box is fitted as indicated in Fig. 293. These gear boxes, often of the Norton type, are driven from a simple train which, with one wheel change, provides a wide range of drive speeds.

Setting up a gear train

Before opening the end cover to expose the tumbler reverse and the gear train, the lathe must be isolated by turning off its main switch; simply pressing the stop button on the machine does not provide sufficient safeguard.

All screw cutting lathes are supplied with screw cutting charts showing the selection and arrangement of the gears for any desired thread and where a metric thread is to be cut from an English lead screw, this can be done by the inclusion of a transposing gear with 127 teeth in the gear train.

The facility for cutting metric threads is now an important design feature in modern, geared head lathes, the cutting of English or metric threads being quickly arranged by selecting the required pitch at the gear box, regardless of whether the lead screw is in English or metric pitch.

Geared head lathes

In this kind of lathe, the 'all geared head' allows of quick spindle speed changes by the operation of selector levers. Such a lathe is shown diagrammatically in Fig. 295 and when fitted with a two-speed motor, a maximum of sixteen spindle speeds are available. From the spindle, a gear train takes the drive to a gear box which enables a comprehensive range of lead screw speeds to be obtained. Automatic feeds are taken to the carriage through a separate feed shaft, also driven through the gear box.

Figure 295   The Bantam lathe
Drive is taken from spindle through reversing mechanism and end train to the gearbox. Thence to the carriage via the lead screw or the feed shaft. Lathe controls are shown 'ghosted'.
(The Colchester Lathe Co. Ltd.)

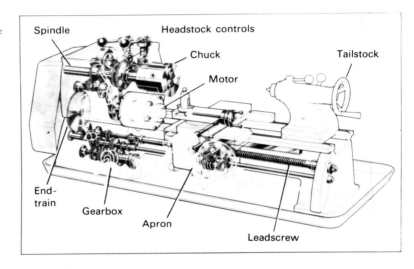

Threading tools

In Fig. 296 is shown a tool ground for cutting a 'vee' thread, the front angles being formed accurately with the aid of a screw-cutting gauge, also shown. For threading in brass or cast iron, little or no rake is given and for steel, the rake can be reduced a little to avoid weakening the tool point which is honed to form a root radius. The crest radius is formed later by chasing, which see.

Figure 296   Vee threading tools

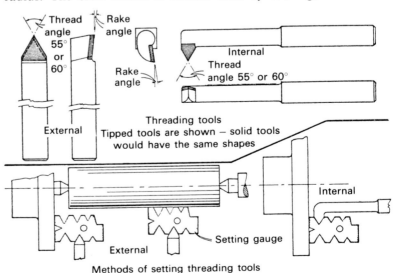

Figure 297 Gauges used in screw cutting
(Moore & Wright (Sheffield) Ltd.)

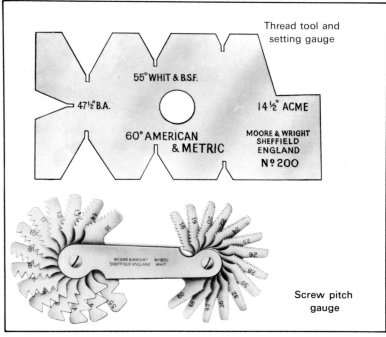

Figure 298 Form thread-cutting tools

Clearance angles should not be excessive or the tool point will be weakened, but it must be remembered that the helical form of the thread will necessitate a larger clearance on the feed side.

Form threading tools are easily adjusted for centre height and need grinding only on the top face. Tools for cutting square threads should be given a slight side clearance, just as on a parting-off tool.

There are two ways in which the tool can be fed into the work when cutting vee threads: (1) by radial feeding with the cross slide which causes the tool to cut with both edges, and (2) by tangential feeding as in Fig. 299B. The objection to feeding with the cross slide is that two lines of chip-flow converge at the tool point, this causes a restriction in the flow and a poor finish on the thread flank. In tangential feeding, the compound slide is swivelled round with its axis at one-half of the thread angle and feed is put on with the compound slide-screw. The cross slide-screw is used only to withdraw the tool at the end of each cut before returning the carriage in readiness for the next. In this way the cutting is done with only one side of the tool and with rake adjusted to suit this side cutting, the chip flow is much more satisfactory.

Thread dial indicator (English pitches)

Lathes with English pitch lead screws are almost invariably fitted with this attachment which permits of the disengagement of lead screw and carriage at the end of a pass and their correct re-engagement so that the tool picks up in the partly cut thread. Through the indicator body passes a spindle with a worm wheel drive from the lead screw. A dial at the other end shows four main divisions, each of which is again divided, making eight in all. A zero line is scribed on the body which is usually secured with one screw only

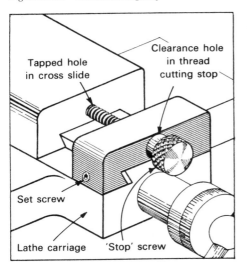

Figure 299A   Thread cutting stop

Tapped hole
in cross slide

Clearance hole
in thread
cutting stop

Set screw

Lathe carriage   'Stop' screw

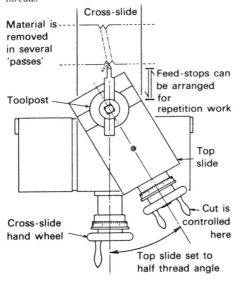

Figure 299B   Top slide setting for cutting vee threads

Cross-slide

Material is
removed
in several
'passes'

Toolpost

Feed-stops can
be arranged
for
repetition work

Top
slide

Cut is
controlled
here

Cross-slide
hand wheel

Top slide set to
half thread angle

Figure 300   Thread dial indicator
(The Colchester Lathe Co. Ltd.)

so that it can pivot to disengage the worm drive when not required.

The calibration is so arranged that when any of the lines is opposite the zero, the half nuts can be engaged with the lead screw. The number of teeth on the worm wheel is a multiple of the tpi of the lead screw, e.g. with an 8 tpi lead screw, the worm wheel usually has 16 teeth. With the lead screw turning and the carriage stationary (half nuts disengaged), the dial will be turning and for cutting an *even* number of tpi, the half nuts are engaged by operating the lever at the moment that any of the eight divisions coincides with zero. For cutting *odd* numbers of tpi, the half nuts are engaged when any of the numbered divisions is opposite zero. For *fractional* tpi, the engagement is made only when the original starting division is opposite zero.

The lever which engages the half nuts is usually interlocked with the automatic feed making it impossible to engage both at the same time. Even so, it is good practice to check that no other feed is engaged before starting screw cutting.

Cutting a vee thread (English pitches)

With the lathe set up and the work piece chamfered or domed to produce a clean start to the thread, a light trial cut can be taken and checked to see that the lathe is cutting the desired pitch. Where a thread is required to stop part way along the work, a recess should be provided to accommodate the tool point. Not only does this make a neat job, but it gives the operator a little space and time for safely disengaging the half nuts. For this reason above all others, screw cutting calls for the operator's undivided attention.

At the completion of each cut, the tool is withdrawn with the cross slide from the work and the carriage is traversed back so that the tool is just past the end of the work piece, in readiness for the next pass. Assuming that tangential cutting is being employed, then the next cut is put on with the compound slide hand wheel and the cross slide is returned to its original setting. In returning the cross slide to the same position each time, some kind of stop is desirable. Such a device is often in the form of a knurled head screw protruding from the front of the cross slide and passing through a clearance hole in a block fixed to the carriage. The screw head, previously adjusted, stops the cross slide at the same point each time it is fed in. Alternatively, the cross slide dial can be set at zero with the tool point touching the work face before any cuts are taken. The slide is then returned to this zero reading when setting the tool for each pass.

Cutting a vee thread (Metric pitches)

In cutting Metric threads from an English lead screw, the thread dial indicator cannot be used and once the half nuts have been engaged for taking the first cut, they must remain engaged during the entire operation. The carriage is returned for each new cut, after withdrawing the tool from the work, by reversing the whole

Figure 301 Screw cutting with work on centres
(The Colchester Lathe Co. Ltd.)

Figure 303 Internal threading of a blind hole
(The Colchester Lathe Co. Ltd.)

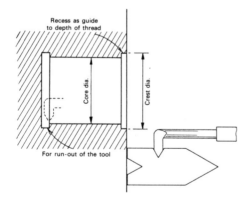

machine, i.e. reversing it from the motor. Only in this way can the correct pick up be assured at each pass.

This procedure is often necessary even on lathes with Metric lead screws as they are not always fitted with thread dial indicators, and although correct pick up is ensured at each pass, it does slow the work down since the carriage must travel back at the same speed as in taking a cut.

Finishing of vee threads

Internal and external threads which have been partly cut in the lathe can be finished to size and form with taps and dies or by *chasing*. Hand chasers for internal and external threads are shown in Fig. 302 and in using these, a stout bar for a tool rest is clamped in the tool post so that the top edge of the chaser is at centre height. Held very firmly with both hands, the chaser is pressed into the thread as the work is turning and the tool is picked up in the thread, travelling along with it and cleaning it up in passing. It also forms the crest radius at the same time. The thread can be tested for size with a screw ring-gauge and in the absence of this tool, the mating component or a new nut can be used.

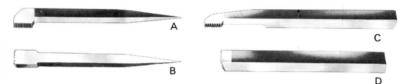

Figure 302 Chasers. A and B. Hand chasers,
internal and external. Handles not shown
C and D. Chasers for use in the tool post.

Internal threading

Although the same routine applies for internal threading, it is a little more difficult as the tool point cannot be seen. Tangential cutting is not attempted and the feed is put on with the cross slide. If the hole is blind, a recess is necessary to accommodate the tool point at the end of the cut and this should be wide enough to allow a small margin of error in disengaging at the exact moment. If the tool shank is marked with chalk, paint or sticky tape, there is no great difficulty about stopping the feed at the same place any number of times provided one's full attention is devoted to the job. A short recess at the outside end, bored to the crest diameter of the thread is a great help in threading to the right depth and this point is illustrated in Fig. 303.

Multiple threads

Where it is desired that a thread shall impart rapid movement to a component, a coarser thread with a greater than normal pitch can be used, but because this involves cutting a larger thread form, the component itself would be weakened and so an increased lead is always obtained by employing multiple start threads in which two, three and four separate threads are cut side by side. If one of these threads is traced from the start, it will be found that in one revolu-

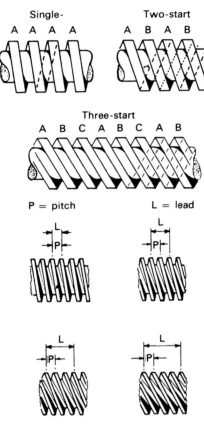

Effect of number of
starts upon the screw 'lead'

tion the distance travelled axially (i.e. the lead) is equal not to the pitch of the thread, but to two, three or four times the pitch according to the number of threads or 'starts' employed. From Fig. 304, it will be seen that although the lead is increased, the size of the thread is unaltered.

In setting up for cutting multiple-start threads, the *lead* of the desired thread is used, *not* the pitch. A single thread is first cut to its full depth and if the compound slide-rest has previously been set parallel to the lathe axis, all that is required to cut further threads is to feed the tool along for a distance equal to the pitch of the thread, no alteration being made to gear-train or work setting. This setting of the compound slide, however, prevents tangential feeding being employed. As an alternative to this method, the work can be rotated through 180° for a two-start and through 120° for a three-start thread when the first thread is completed. This indexing can be accomplished in two ways: (1) by fitting extra, equally-spaced driving studs on the catch-plate so that the work can be taken off the centres and rotated to engage the carrier with another stud or the work can be driven with the face-plate, a bent-tail carrier engaging in the slots. The carrier should not be removed for adjusting on the work, or (2) by gear indexing which entails the rotation of lathe spindle and work. In gear index-ing, the train is disengaged by withdrawing the first driven wheel, the spindle and work are then rotated the required amount and the gears re-engaged. It is necessary to mark the gears in some way (chalk or paint dab) so that they can be re-engaged correctly and, of course, the first driver wheel must contain a number of teeth divisible by the number of starts required.

Left-handed threads
There is little more involved here than running the lead-screw in reverse so that the carriage traverses from left to right. It is neces-sary to form a recess in which the tool can be started unless the work has previously been shouldered. Left-hand threads can also be cut with the tool turned upside down in the post and with the work turning in reverse. The feed will then be from right to left.

15

Milling and shaping

Milling

In milling, a multi-toothed cutter, rotating at a fixed position on the machine, shapes the work as it is traversed across the cutter. The work is firmly secured on the machine table which can be adjusted to set the depth of cut and can be traversed in at least two directions in the horizontal plane. In some machines, a vertical traverse also is possible.

Milling machines

The milling machine is made in different forms and in many sizes and these can be grouped under three headings: (1) the *plain* or *horizontal* milling machine, (2) the *vertical* milling machine, and (3) the *universal* milling machine. Within the scope of this work, it is possible to enlarge only on the applications of the horizontal and vertical machines, these being the kinds most likely to be found in school workshops. The universal miller is so called because it can be used in a very wide range of operations. With a swivelling table and a dividing head, it can be used for work mounted between centres and for gear-cutting in addition to the normal run of work. It can also be used for vertical milling by fitting a vertical head attachment.

The horizontal (or plain) milling machine

From Fig. 305, it will be seen that the main part (or column) is in the form of a heavy box-casting. The motor and driving mechanism are housed here and the drive is taken to the spindle which runs in precision bearings at the top of the column. The spindle is hollow and the nose is made with a standard taper socket (Morse, Brown and Sharpe, or Jarno) and into this fits the arbor, tapered likewise. It is held firmly by a draw bolt passing through the spindle and in large machines, power is transmitted through driving dogs and slots on spindle and arbor respectively and sometimes the arbor is bolted to the spindle-nose. The outer end of the arbor is supported by the over arm which carries one (and sometimes two) bracket bearings. The over arm, in the form of a stiff bar or casting, is adjustable for reach and on large machines is braced by a frame bolted to the knee of the machine.

A very robust casting forms the knee and is mounted on slides on the front of the column. It is adjustable for height through a hand-wheel, gearing and a screwed shaft. When adjusted, it can be locked and is given extra support by means of an adjustable leg which bears on the machine base. On the knee is mounted the

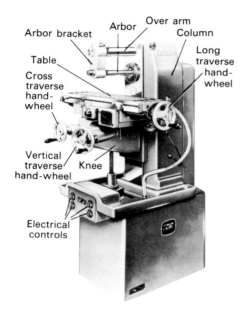

Arbor bracket · Arbor · Over arm · Column · Table · Long traverse hand-wheel · Cross traverse hand-wheel · Vertical traverse hand-wheel · Knee · Electrical controls

Figure 305   Horizontal (plain) milling machine (above)
Vertical milling machine (below)
(Gate Machinery Co. Ltd.)

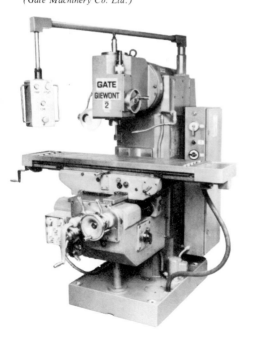

Figure 306   Universal milling machine (Gate Machinery Co. Ltd.)

saddle which can be traversed in line with the spindle by hand-feed, and on the saddle is mounted the machine table with hand- or power-feeds in a longitudinal traverse at right-angles to the spindle. Thus, the work can be manoeuvred in three directions and by means of micrometer dials on the hand-wheels, accurate adjustments can be made in relation to the cutter. The table is provided with tee-slots for clamping work or machine vice.

Cutters are positioned on the arbor by means of spacing collars, all being held firmly together by tightening down a nut on the end of the arbor. The nut should not be tightened until the arbor is supported at its outer end in the bracket. For most work, the friction grip from the collars is sufficient to drive the cutter and this friction drive provides a measure of protection from damage, if the cutter and work jam up for any reason. Keyways in cutter and arbor are provided if required. A great variety of cutters is available and of these, a number are made for direct mounting in the spindle nose, for mounting on stub arbors or for holding in special chucks.

The vertical milling machine

From Fig. 305 it will be seen that whilst the vertical machine resembles the horizontal one in other respects, the spindle itself is upright. Cutters adapt to the spindle with taper shanks and drawbars hold them tightly, or they can be held in chucks. The machine head can be swivelled to either side up to an angle of 45°, making it possible to take angular cuts without disturbing the work from its setting. Vertical milling is generally employed in lighter work of a more diverse nature and includes the machining of dies, jigs, recesses, keyways, tee and dovetail slots and slides. Knee, saddle and table are similar to those on the horizontal machine.

Figure 307   A. Cylindrical cutter with spiral teeth. High power type
B. Cylindrical cutter Helical type

Milling cutters

A great range of cutters is available and they can be grouped under the following headings: (1) *plain* or *cylindrical cutters,* used in machining flat surfaces and cutting only with their sides. These are all arbor-mounting cutters, (2) *face cutters* which do their main work with teeth formed on the ends, (3) *side and face cutters* which cut on both periphery and face, (4) *saws* and *slotting cutters* which produce plain, tee and dovetail slots, (5) *form cutters* which produce rounded corners, hollows, gear-teeth, etc., and (6) *inserted-tooth cutters,* usually made in the larger sizes of face and cylindrical mills.

Cylindrical cutters

Several kinds of cylindrical cutters are made for the machining of flat surfaces, the larger ones being known also as slab cutters. Up to 175 mm in length, the largest are 130 mm in diameter. Above this size, the body is often made from high tensile steel with inserted blades. The spiral form of tooth gives a better cutting

Figure 308   Facing cutter. Inserted teeth

action than that obtained with straight-cut teeth because a shearing action is introduced and the 'overlapping' of the cutting-edges when at work gives a continuous action with less tendency to vibration and chatter.

In Fig. 307 are shown two cylindrical cutters, designed primarily for use as surfacing cutters, with teeth on the periphery only. The helical cutter is used for heavy cuts and leaves a good finish. Cylindrical cutters are often made with nicked ('gashed') edges and these are effective in breaking up the chips so that they are more easily flushed away. The nicks are staggered so that the work face is unmarked.

Face cutters

Also known as 'face mills', these cut with teeth formed on the end face but some are made with teeth on the periphery. An inserted tooth face-cutter is shown in Fig. 308 and this is for mounting on a stub arbor, one of which is shown in Fig. 309. The slots at the rear of the cutter engage with driving dogs on the arbor. Larger face mills, from 100 to 300 mm in diameter, are of the inserted-tooth type, with high-speed or tipped teeth mounted in a body made from high tensile steel.

Figure 309   A. Facing chuck for holding screw-bore cutters
*   B. Stub arbor*
(Aurora P.L.C.)

Shell end-mills

These are really facing-cutters with peripheral teeth and they are so called to distinguish them from the solid type of end mill. They are usually bored for stub-arbor mounting, the cutting-face is recessed for a securing screw whilst the rear is slotted to mate with driving dogs on the arbor. Shell end-mills are also made with an internal thread for mounting on a threaded arbor or chuck, one of which is seen in Fig. 309.

Figure 310   Shell end mill

End mills

This type of cutter is designed to do most of the cutting with its end face, the end teeth continuing along the side for an average distance of about twice the diameter. End mills are made from 2·5 to 50 mm in diameter and with various types of shank and the side teeth are cut in a spiral form, for right- or left-hand rotation in cutting. The manner in which the mill is held in the machine determines the direction of the spiral, tanged taper-shank mills having a slow spiral *opposite* to the direction of rotation which gives a negative rake to the end cutting-edges. This avoids

Figure 311   End mills
A. With screw shank
B. Chuck for holding screw-shank
cutters
C. With taper shank
D. With taper shank and tang
E. With parallel shank

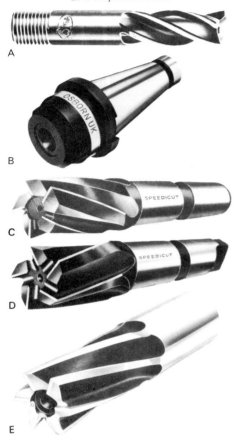

any tendency to feed into the work and keeps the end mill pressed firmly into the taper socket. It is more satisfactory to use *tapped* taper-shank end-mills which can be held with a draw bolt, and these are made with the spiral in the direction of rotation, giving them a positive rake.

End-mills are also made with parallel shanks for chucking and with screw shanks for holding in special chucks as seen in Fig. 311.

Side and face cutters

These cutters are made with teeth on both faces and on the periphery and are frequently used in gang and straddle milling as shown in Fig. 313. They are not used in the accurate milling of slots at one pass because a tolerance must be allowed on the cutter width due to re-grinding. They can, of course, be used in slotting in excess of their width by moving the machine table over.

Figure 312   A. Side and face cutter.
B. Side and face cutter with staggered teeth

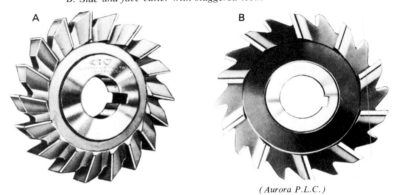

(Aurora P.L.C.)

Side and face cutters, in addition to being made with straight teeth cutting on both sides, are also made with skew-cut teeth which are staggered, i.e. alternate side teeth are omitted.

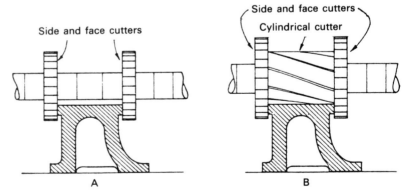

Figure 313   A. Straddle milling example
B. Gang milling example

Slitting saws

Made from 63 to 315 mm in diameter, the slitting saw is used in many jobs from parting off and slitting of thin sections to the cutting of deep and narrow slots. For work in thin materials, small toothed saws with a fine pitch are used, just as in hack

Figure 314 A. Metal slitting saw
B. Slotting cutter

sawing. Each diameter is made in a small range of thicknesses, the overall range being from 0·25 to 6 mm. The thinner saws must be used with extreme care and should not be used when a thicker one would be suitable. Saws are slightly hollow ground to give clearance and can also be obtained with side teeth (side chip-clearance) in sizes above 1·6 mm.

Slotting cutter

Shown in Fig. 314, the slotting cutter is made with teeth on the periphery only, and the sides are gound slightly hollow for clearance when cutting. It is used for the accurate milling of slots and is usually made with straight-cut teeth in small widths and with spiral-cut teeth on wide cutters.

Slot drills

From Fig. 315 it is seen that the slot drill is made with only two teeth on the end and side. With this cutter it is possible to feed straight into the work and then to traverse the work across the rotating drill which will produce an accurate slot to its own width.

Tee-slot cutter

With the characteristics of a side and face cutter and made integral with a screw shank, the tee-slot cutter is used in the under cutting of slots previously made with slotting cutter or slotting drill.

Woodruff keyseat cutter

This cutter is, in effect, a small slotting cutter, but is made in one piece with taper or parallel shank. It is used in cutting seatings in shafts for keys made to British Standards specifications.

Figure 315 Milling cutters
A. Slot drill with screw shank
B. Tee slot cutter
C. Woodruff cutter with staggered teeth
D. Woodruff cutter
(Aurora P.L.C.)

Figure 316 Dovetail slot cutter

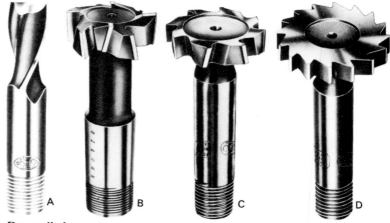

Dovetail slot cutter

Shown in Fig. 316, this cutter is used in the forming of machine slides and is made with included angles of 45, 60 or 90°. With sharp and fragile teeth points, it should not be used with excessive feed-rates.

Figure 317   *Angle cutters*
          A. Single angle cutter
          B. Equal angle cutter
          C. Double unequal angle cutter

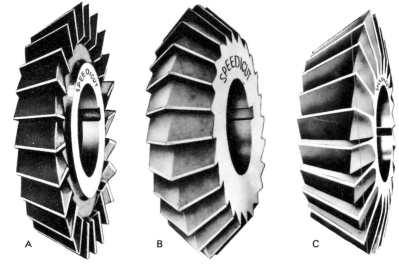

Figure 318   *Cutter with form-relieved teeth*

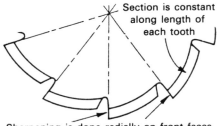

Section is constant
along length of
each tooth

Sharpening is done radially on front faces
only, so that cutter always produces
the same section

Figure 319   *Form cutters*
          A. Corner rounding cutter
          B. Concave cutter
          C. Convex cutter
          D. Involute gear cutter

(Aurora P.L.C.)

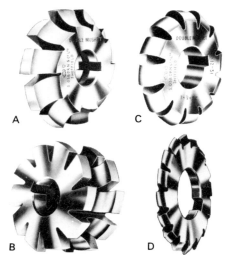

Angle cutters

These offer a quick and convenient way of milling small angular surfaces and vee grooves without tilting the work. A *single angle* cutter is shown in Fig. 317, and these are made in common angles from 60° by fives, up to 85°, the angle being measured between the flat cutting-face and the conical face in a radial plane. An *equal angle* cutter is shown and the angle is the *included angle* between the conical faces, measured radially. Also shown is a *double-unequal angle* cutter, the angles of which are measured separately in a radial plane between the sides of the cones and their plane of intersection.

Form cutters

A variety of form cutters is made for producing hollows, rounded edges and corners; fluting in drills, reamers and taps; and for gear-teeth. Clearance behind the cutting-edge is provided by *relieving,* as seen in Fig. 318, and these cutters are sharpened on the front face only of each tooth. In this way they will reproduce identical profiles after repeated sharpenings and this is important with gear cutters, for example, which are given top relief only, other forms often being given side relief as well.

Fly cutter

This is a single-point cutter which can often be made in the workshop for jobs which do not justify the expense of large milling cutters or for which there is no suitably sized cutter. Fly cutters are designed on similar lines to a boring bar or boring head, the cutter being mounted in an arbor or carrier of some kind, such as that shown in Fig. 320. With these cutters it is possible to machine quite large radius sweeps, taking light cuts with a very slow feed.

Cutting action

The cutting action in milling is unlike the continuous cutting in turning or in drilling. With the cutter rotating against the feed, as

Figure 320   An example showing use of a fly cutter (right)

Figure 321   Chip formation in milling

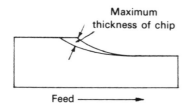

Figure 322   Milling cutter angles
Negative rake is employed with tungsten-carbide tipped tools.

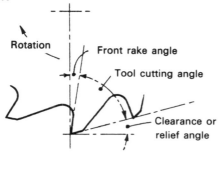

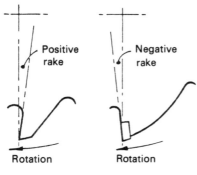

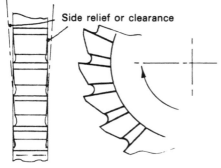

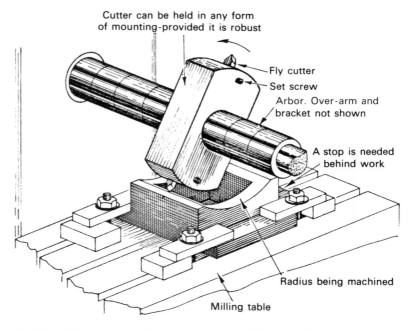

Cutter can be held in any form of mounting-provided it is robust

Fly cutter

Set screw

Arbor. Over-arm and bracket not shown

A stop is needed behind work

Radius being machined

Milling table

in Fig. 321, each tooth takes a cut building up from zero to a maximum thickness, when quite suddenly, the pressure against the feed is released. This 'interrupted' cutting action tends to cause chatter, accentuated when straight toothed cutters are operated with excessive feed.

Angled (skew cut) teeth promote smoother cutting and a better finish because of their slicing action and because the pressure is not released suddenly, eliminating shock. The only cutters commonly made with straight teeth are slitting saws and the narrower slotting cutters.

As with all cutting tools, milling cutter teeth are formed with rake and clearance angles. Each tooth is formed with a double relief (or clearance) the small primary clearance affording maximum support for the cutting-edge and ensuring a reasonable working life for the cutter before regrinds approach the second relief angle.

Handing of cutters
A few points on the handing of cutters should be understood. Cylindrical and helical cutters are obtainable with right- or left-hand spirals, but this is not the *handing* of the cutters. They can be used to cut in either direction because they are reversible on the arbor. Care must be taken when ordering shell end-mills as they are not reversible. Viewing the spindle from the nose end, a right-hand shell mill will cut in a counter-clockwise direction and should have right-handed helical cutting-edges and vice versa. Single-angle cutters are specified as right- or left-hand cutting, viewing the spindle as before, with the flat side of the cutter outwards. Double-angle cutters are specified in the same way, with the more obtuse (or flatter) side outwards.

Figure 323   Up-cut milling with side and face cutter
(Gate Machinery Co. Ltd.)

Milling operations

The work in Fig. 323 is shown being fed against the cutter rotation and this is known as up-cut milling—the method commonly used in school workshops and in general milling practice. There is always a tendency in up-cut milling for the cutter to lift the work. In down-cut (or 'climb') milling, the cutter turns in the opposite direction and presses the work firmly down on to the table. Because

Figure 324   A selection of milling operations

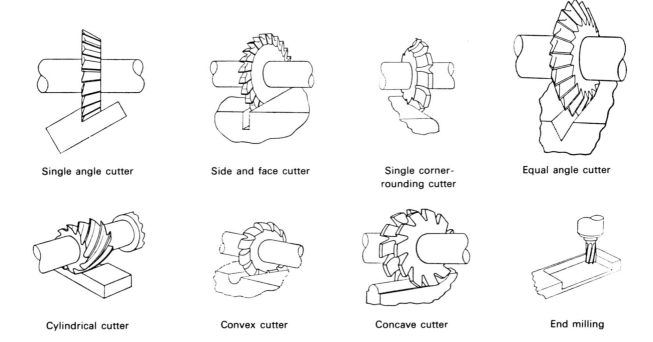

Single angle cutter

Side and face cutter

Single corner-rounding cutter

Equal angle cutter

Cylindrical cutter

Convex cutter

Concave cutter

End milling

Figure 325   Shell end milling

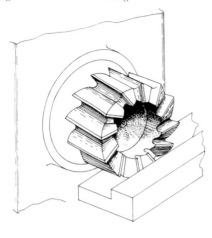

of the tendency of the cutter to ride or 'climb', this method can be used only on robust machines in which all back-lash in the feed mechanism is eliminated, the slightest amount of play here allowing the cutter to snatch when feed is put on, with resulting damage to work and cutter. The work must be held very securely and should be provided with some kind of stop on the table to make certain it does not move.

The liberal use of cutting fluid in milling is very important, not only because of cooling and lubrication, but as a means of washing away chips from the cutter edges. In industrial processes, coolant is usually flooded into the cutting area through large hoses and whilst this cannot be done in the school workshop, the principle at least, can be borne in mind.

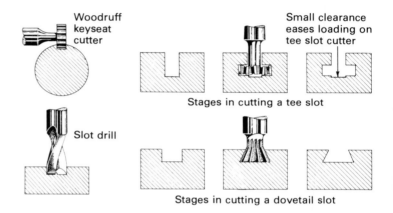

Figure 326   Milling slots

The utmost care should be taken to prolong the life of cutters by avoiding heavy cuts and over-fast feeds. Where castings are to be milled, the hard skin should be removed by some other means, if possible, as this skin will quickly dull the cutting-edges. If the skin cannot be removed before milling, then an endeavour must be made to get the first cut to lift it off cleanly, avoiding rubbing at all costs.

*Figure 327   Milling with a helical cutter
(Gate Machinery Co. Ltd.)*

Cutter and feed speeds

Before thinking of cutter speeds in terms of rev/min, the peripheral speed must be considered in terms of *metres per minute* and related to the particular metal being machined. Assuming good machining conditions, i.e. work securely held, machine not worn and sharp cutters of HSS the following peripheral speeds can be taken as a guide:

	m/min
Mild steel	24–30
Straight carbon steel	18–24
Nickel steels	12–18
Medium cast iron	15–18
Phosphor bronze	12–18
Brass	30–46
Leaded brass	40–58

Saws should be run at 25 to 30 per cent lower speeds.

From the peripheral speed and from the diameter of the cutter, the rev/min can be calculated by applying the formula:

$$\text{rev/min of cutter} = \frac{\text{Peripheral speed (m/min)}}{\text{Circumference of cutter (in metres)}}$$

Example

Peripheral speed: 18 m/min. Diameter of cutter: 125 mm.

$$\text{rev/min} = \frac{18}{3 \cdot 14 \times 0 \cdot 125} = \frac{18}{0 \cdot 39} = 46$$

It is necessary also, to relate the table feed-rate to each particular cutter and to the metal being machined. Feed-rate is sometimes quoted as mm *per revolution*, but it is better to work on a basis of mm *per tooth per revolution*, since all cutters do not have the same number of teeth and will accept higher or lower feed-rates in consequence.

The following recommendations can be taken as a guide:

Feed per tooth for cast iron

Face mill	0·25 to 0·50 mm
Shell end-mill	0·18 to 0·28 mm
Spiral end-mill	0·08 to 0·20 mm
Slotting cutter	0·15 to 0·30 mm
Saw	0·03 to 0·08 mm
Spiral plain mill	0·25 to 0·38 mm
Form mill (Form relieved cutter)	0·10 to 0·15 mm

From the feed-rate per tooth, as given above, the feed-rate per minute is calculated as follows:

Feed per tooth per revolution × number of teeth × rev/min = feed-rate per minute.

Holding the work

Before mounting the work on the machine, the operations should be planned so that they are carried out in a sequence which will avoid unnecessary re-setting. Where possible, any large surface which might be used as a datum from the table in subsequent operations, should be machined first. The table should be set as

Figure 328   Machine vices
   A. Swivel base machine vice
   B. Universal swivel machine vice
   C. Milling machine vice suitable for
      narrow table
Charles Taylor (Birminghan) Ltd.)

close as possible to the column and the work mounted so that the cutter is near the spindle nose. In this way, the work is done under the most rigid conditions obtainable. Work can be bolted direct to the table, or mounted on an angle plate or other fixture and if small, can probably be held satisfactorily in a robust machine vice. Properly made tee-bolts should always be used for holding work or vice on the table.

It must always be remembered that the work is to be held against the thrust of the cutter and that in up milling there is a tendency for the work to lift.

Aligning the work

On many occasions, precise alignment of the work is not essential and a strip of metal, dropped into the table slot provides a ready means of lining up. The square can be used from the table edge or from table top to the arbor when crosswise alignment is needed.

When accurate setting is required, the dial indicator is employed with a magnetic base and planted, probably on the machine column. With the plunger depressed against a machined face of the work and the dial adjusted to a zero reading, mis-alignment will be revealed when the work is traversed past the instrument.

Setting up the cutter

Before touching the spindle, arbor or any other moving part, the machine should be isolated so that there is no risk of its being started from the starter button. It is generally better if the work is set up before the cutter is mounted on the arbor or in the spindle nose, this leaves more room for working and there is no danger of cutting one's fingers on sharp edges.

Taper shanks of tool or arbor and the spindle taper bore must be wiped clean before assembly. Spacing collars and cutters must also be cleaned and care taken to offer them up square to the arbor before pressing them home, otherwise they may become jammed.

One obvious point must be considered at the moment of mounting the cutter and this concerns the direction of rotation— if the cutter is fitted the wrong way round all will need dismantling again. It is a good thing to watch the cutter as it starts for the first time to see that it *is* turning the right way, otherwise it could be damaged if fed whilst turning the wrong way.

The dividing head

The dividing head or indexing head is an accessory used on the milling machine in the accurate division of parts for the cutting of flutes, splines, slots, keyways, squares, hexagons, etc., and in gear-cutting. The head is mounted on the table and can be used for work between centres in conjunction with a tailstock, or it can be fitted with a chuck for the direct mounting of work.

Two kinds of dividing head are used, viz., the *plain* head, used in *simple* indexing and operated by hand, and the *universal* head, which in addition to hand operation in simple indexing, can be

Figure 329 Plain dividing head for direct indexing, with tailstock (Gate Machinery Co. Ltd.)

Figure 330 Plain dividing head for direct and indirect indexing, with tailstock (Gate Machinery Co. Ltd.)

Figure 331 Universal dividing head with tailstock and work-supporting jack, on a milling table (Gate Machinery Co. Ltd.)

used in work such as spiral milling. In its simpler form, the plain dividing head is fitted with a reversible indexing disc as seen in Fig. 329 carrying different numbers of slots on the two sides. This disc is mounted on the spindle, giving direct indexing, it is turned by hand after each setting and is locked by a spring-loaded plunger which engages in any chosen slot. The dividing is restricted to fractions in which the denominator is a factor of the number of divisions in the disc. The range of dividing is considerably extended when a reduction gear is employed in rotating the spindle, giving indirect indexing. This is done by means of a worm-drive, usually with a ratio of 40:1, the work being turned by a crank handle, 40 turns of which will give one whole turn of the spindle, 10 turns giving a quarter turn and so on. The crank is used in conjunction with a circular index plate. This is fitted behind the crank and is drilled with concentric circles of holes, each circle containing a different number, whilst the crank is fitted with a spring-loaded plunger which can be adjusted to pass over any of the circles. To avoid the continual counting of holes, a sector is provided and this has two arms which can be adjusted radially and locked, in any setting, to enclose the number of holes to be passed. The sector turns on the crank spindle in front of the plate.

A simple calculation is required to decide which circle of holes is to be used and to decide on the setting of the sector arms.

Example 1. The gear ratio must be considered when making calculations for dividing and to obtain, for example, 12 divisions on the work, the fraction $\frac{40}{12}$ will indicate that 3 full turns plus $\frac{1}{3}$rd of a turn are required for each division. The crank can be set to pass over any circle of holes divisible by 3 and the sector arms are set at 120°. It must be remembered that the sector arms will enclose

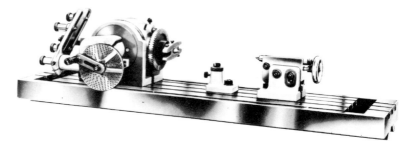

$\frac{1}{3}$rd of the total number of holes *plus* one; for example, if a 30-hole circle is used, 11 holes will be enclosed, the distance between them being $\frac{1}{3}$rd of the complete circle. At the start of the work, the trailing sector arm will be against the 'rear' of the plunger. When the first division is made, 3 whole turns will be made with the crank which will then be taken on to the leading sector arm and locked with the plunger. The sector is then immediately turned on in the same direction, the trailing arm again touching the 'rear' of the plunger in readiness for the next division.

Example 2. To obtain, say 44 divisions, the fraction $\frac{40}{44}$ indicates that no full turns are required and each crank movement will *pass* 40 holes on a 44-hole circle or 20 on one with 22 holes. With the sector set accordingly (to enclose either 41 or 21 holes) the divisions are easily made by first moving the crank from one arm to the next, immediately turning the sector on, in readiness for the next division, and so on.

Spiral milling

In spiral milling, the dividing head is geared to the table-feed screw through a simple or compound train, in order that the rotation of the work can be related to the feed. The gear-train is set up in much the same way as on a lathe, a set of change wheels being provided, and these are mounted on studs on a gear-fork.

Shaping

The shaping machine is used in machining surfaces and sections of all kinds, including curves, vee slides, keyways and so on. The machine is notable for the simplicity of its mechanism and the low cost of tools and because of these things and the variety of work it can produce, it is a very useful investment in any machine shop.

A general purpose shaper is shown in Fig. 332 the main parts being: (1) the *pedestal*, a very strong iron casting of box form with a sturdy base (the shaper is made also as a bench model), (2) the *ram*,

Figure 332 Shaping machiner (Gate Machinery Co. Ltd.)

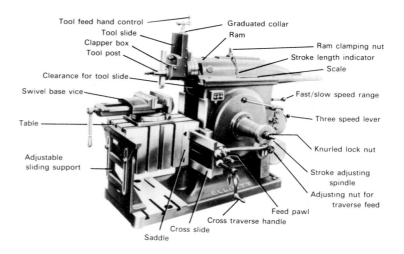

Figure 333   Bull gear for shaping machines

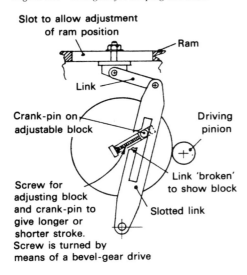

Slot to allow adjustment
of ram position

Ram

Link

Crank-pin on
adjustable block

Driving
pinion

Screw for
adjusting block
and crank-pin to
give longer or
shorter stroke.
Screw is turned by
means of a bevel-gear drive

Link 'broken'
to show block

Slotted link

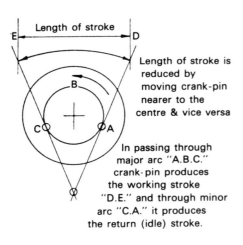

Length of stroke

E ◄─────────────► D

Length of stroke is
reduced by
moving crank-pin
nearer to the
centre & vice versa

B

C A

In passing through
major arc "A.B.C."
crank-pin produces
the working stroke
"D.E." and through minor
arc "C.A." it produces
the return (idle) stroke.

also an iron casting, which works in slides on top of the pedestal, carrying at its front end the tool-holding mechanism, (3) the *saddle* which is mounted on vertical slides on the front face of the pedestal, and (4) the *table,* made in several forms and mounted on cross slides on the saddle and which can be traversed by hand- or by power-feed. The capacity of a shaper is gauged by the length of its stroke. Bench models are often made with a 178 mm stroke, whilst those standing on the floor vary between 254 and 760 mm.

Driving mechanism

The drive for the ram provides for a return stroke which is faster than the cutting stroke and this is done through a slotted link mechanism as in Fig. 333. The location of the crank pin on the slotted driving wheel can be varied, and as the pin is moved nearer to the centre, the stroke becomes shorter, the maximum stroke being obtained with the pin furthest away from the centre. The manner in which the quick return stroke is obtained is also shown. Not only can the *length* of the stroke be adjusted in the manner described, but also its *location* over the table by adjusting the link connection to the ram as shown in the drawing.

The drive from the motor is taken through a lever-operated clutch and a gearbox which provides a selection of speeds. On the question of speed of stroke, it must be remembered that lengthening the stroke will increase the speed of the ram (which will have further to travel in the same time), unless, of course, a lower gear-ratio is selected at the same time. It is better to set the length of stroke first and then to select a gear-ratio to give the correct cutting speed.

The table can be traversed across the path of the tool by hand or power. The automatic feed to the traverse screw is shown in Fig. 332. A reversible pawl and ratchet-wheel mechanism turns the screw in either direction, the pawl being operated by a connecting rod which receives its motion from a pin working in a slotted disc. By varying the position of the pin in its slot, the movement of the rod can be varied to give coarser or finer feeds. If hand traversing is used, it is important to remember to put on the feed at the end of the return stroke. This is done automatically under power-feed.

The saddle and table

These can be raised or lowered on the vertical slides by a hand-operated screw and where an automatic down-feed is available, it is used in the machining of the side faces of work. The table, in the form of a box-casting, is tee-slotted on top and sides for holding the work direct or in a machine vice. The swivel-base type is generally used on the shaper. The outer end of the table is supported on an adjustable leg or frame, bearing on the machine base and often bolted to it. This support must always be slackened off before any adjustment is made to the table height, otherwise the screw and bevel gears may be damaged. Once the table height is set, the support should be adjusted carefully with the table in the mid position on the cross slide. Half-tables, with reduced depth, are used to give greater clearance under the ram for machining large work. Swivel and tilting tables are useful refinements which enable angular surfaces to be machined and are seen in Figs. 334, 335 and 336. Where both swivel and tilting tables are combined, the table is known as 'universal'.

Figure 334 Shaping machine with swivel table in use
This machine has an automatic tool lift which raises the tool clear of the work on the return stroke *(Gate Machinery Co. Ltd.)*

Figure 336 Shaping machine with universal table　　*(Gate Machinery Co. Ltd.)*

Tool holding

The front end of the ram is flanged and on the machined surface is mounted a swivelling head which can pivot up to 45° to either side. Locking bolts, passing through slots are tightened down when the head is set at the required angle, graduations being marked on the flange for this purpose. The tool is held in the clapper-box and this is mounted on a slide which gives a downward feed, the depth of each cut being set by means of a calibrated dial. The whole assembly is shown in the figures and it will be seen that the clapper-box pivots at the top so that on the return stroke it rides forward and the tool is drawn lightly over the surface on its heel. On clearing the work, it drops back in readiness for the next cut.

Figure 335 Shaping machine with tilting table
(Gate Machinery Co. Ltd.)

Shaping tools

The tools used in shaping are similar to lathe tools, but are usually a little deeper and can be made as solid tools or in the form of tool bits mounted in turret tool-holders. The load during actual cutting is probably no heavier than in turning, but there is an initial shock at the commencement of each cut and the tool point must not be weakened by excessive rake or clearance or it will not last very long.

Figure 337 Shaper tool with super H.S.S. cutter
The grooved seats enable the cutter to be held firmly to right or left *(Jones and Shipman P.L.C.)*

Holding the work

The methods of holding are often much the same as in milling, but the swivel machine vice is frequently used on the shaper. A heavy duty vice should always be used and with a swivel base, its useful applications are greatly increased. It is of the utmost importance that the work is held very securely against the thrust from the cutting-edge and it must be remembered that whilst this will tend to make long, flat objects *slide* along the table, there is also a *lifting* effect which will be more evident as the height to length ratio of the work increases. These points must be considered, especially with iron castings and where there is the slightest question as to the rigidity of the work or the clamping, extra support must be provided with angle plates or packings. Any movement of the work whilst machining could be disastrous for work and machine. Where necessary, small work in the vice should be bedded on parallel packings and it is a good plan, after a 'first pinch' has been taken, to tap the work down to ensure it is bedded, and then to tighten the vice very firmly. If unfinished cast surfaces must be held, they should be checked for high-spots first, and gripped with soft metal packings placed between jaws and work. Extra care must be taken in holding iron castings on the table because of the ease with which they are fractured. They must be bedded properly, especially at the clamping points, using metal packings where necessary to avoid distortion or fracture.

Work should always be set well back on the table and high enough to avoid having to reach down with extended slide or excessive tool length. Beneath the ram slides, an opening is provided to give clearance for the tool slide.

One very important point to check is that the head and clapper-box will clear all obstructions on the table. Where the machine is equipped with a hand-wheel, the machine can be 'turned over' by hand to check this clearance. Clearance must also be checked when working on a vertical face with the clapper-box tilted. If any part of the head or clapper-box should strike any fixed obstructions, serious damage would result, with a considerable element of personal risk into the bargain.

Setting the stroke

In deciding on the length of stroke, enough movement must be allowed to cover the surface comfortably, plus an allowance for the clapper-box to drop back before each stroke begins. Adjustments to the stroke length are made by turning the stroke-adjusting spindle after first slackening the knurled lock-nut. The spindle is usually turned clockwise to lengthen and anti-clockwise to shorten the stroke. With the length adjusted, the position of the stroke now requires setting so that the tool just clears at the outer end whilst leaving sufficient space at the rear for the tool to drop back ready for the next stroke. With the tool at the outer end of the desired stroke position, the ram clamping-nut is slackened and the machine is turned until the stroke-length indicator reaches the end of its forward travel. The clamping-nut is then tightened down and the stroke adjustments are complete.

16

Standard tables and other data

Table 15 Peripheral speeds for high speed steel drills

Material to be drilled	Speed (m/min)	Speed (ft/min)
Aluminium and aluminium alloys	60 to 90	200 to 300
Bakelite—Vulcanite	30 to 45	100 to 150
Brass	45 to 75	150 to 250
Brass—Leaded	60 to 90	200 to 300
Bronze—Ordinary	30 to 60	100 to 200
Bronze—High Tensile	21 to 30	70 to 100
Cast Iron—Soft	30 to 45	100 to 150
Cast Iron—Medium	24 to 27	80 to 90
Cast Iron—Hard	15 to 21	50 to 70
Cast Iron—Chilled	7 to 10	25 to 35
Copper	30 to 60	100 to 200
Duralumin	30 to 60	100 to 200
Magnesium and magnesium alloys	75 to 120	250 to 400
Malleable Iron	21 to 24	70 to 80
Mazak	60 to 90	200 to 300
Monel Metal	12 to 15	40 to 50
Steel—Free-cutting Mild	30 to 45	100 to 150
Steel—Up to 40 Tons Tensile	24 to 33	80 to 110
Steel—40 to 60 Tons Tensile	14 to 21	45 to 70
Steel—60 to 80 Tons Tensile	9 to 14	30 to 45
Steel—Over 80 Tons Tensile	4 to 7	15 to 25
Steel—Manganese	4 to 6	15 to 20
Stainless Steels—Group 'A'—Martensitic and Ferritic	9 to 15	30 to 50
Stainless Steels—Group 'B'—Austenitic and Heat Resisting	6 to 14	20 to 45
Stainless Steels—Group 'A'—Free-cutting (Ferritic)	15 to 18	50 to 60
Stainless Steels—Group 'B'—Free-cutting (Austenitic)	12 to 15	40 to 50
Wood	90 to 120	300 to 400

Speeds in the region of 50 per cent of the above are recommended for carbon steel drills.
The speeds quoted are only a basic guide. If conditions permit it may be found possible to increase the above values.
By permission of Firth Brown Tools Ltd.
The metre/minute speeds have been appended by the author.

Table 16   Conversion of cutting speed in feet per minute to revolutions per minute (fraction size drills)

Drill diameter in inches	Cutting speeds in ft/min 30	40	50	60	70	80	90	100	110	120	130	140	150
	Revolutions per minute												
$\frac{1}{64}$	7 334	9 779	12 223	14 668	17 112	19 557	22 001	24 446	26 891	29 336	31 780	34 225	36 669
$\frac{1}{32}$	3 667	4 889	6 112	7 334	8 556	9 779	11 001	12 223	13 445	14 668	15 890	17 112	18 335
$\frac{3}{64}$	2 445	3 259	4 064	4 889	5 704	6 519	7 334	8 149	8 963	9 778	10 593	11 408	12 223
$\frac{1}{16}$	1 833	2 445	3 056	3 667	4 278	4 889	5 500	6 112	6 723	7 334	7 945	8 556	9 167
$\frac{5}{64}$	1 467	1 956	2 445	2 934	3 422	3 911	4 400	4 889	5 378	5 867	6 356	6 845	7 334
$\frac{3}{32}$	1 222	1 630	2 037	2 445	2 852	3 260	3 667	4 074	4 482	4 889	5 297	5 704	6 112
$\frac{1}{8}$	917	1 222	1 528	1 833	2 139	2 445	2 750	3 056	3 361	3 667	3 972	4 278	4 584
$\frac{5}{32}$	733	978	1 222	1 467	1 711	1 956	2 200	2 445	2 689	2 934	3 178	3 422	3 667
$\frac{3}{16}$	611	815	1 019	1 222	1 426	1 630	1 833	2 037	2 241	2 445	2 648	2 852	3 056
$\frac{7}{32}$	524	698	873	1 048	1 222	1 397	1 571	1 746	1 921	2 095	2 270	2 444	2 619
$\frac{1}{4}$	458	611	764	917	1 070	1 222	1 375	1 528	1 681	1 833	1 986	2 139	2 292
$\frac{5}{16}$	367	489	611	733	856	978	1 100	1 222	1 345	1 467	1 589	1 711	1 833
$\frac{3}{8}$	306	407	509	611	713	815	917	1 019	1 120	1 222	1 324	1 426	1 528
$\frac{7}{16}$	262	349	437	524	611	698	786	873	960	1 048	1 135	1 222	1 310
$\frac{1}{2}$	229	306	382	458	535	611	688	764	840	917	993	1070	1 146
$\frac{9}{16}$	204	272	340	407	475	543	611	679	747	815	883	951	1 019
$\frac{5}{8}$	183	244	306	367	428	489	550	611	672	733	794	856	917
$\frac{11}{16}$	167	222	278	333	389	445	500	556	611	667	722	778	834
$\frac{3}{4}$	153	204	255	306	357	407	458	509	560	611	662	713	764
$\frac{13}{16}$	141	188	235	282	329	376	423	470	517	564	611	658	705
$\frac{7}{8}$	131	175	218	262	306	349	393	437	480	524	567	611	655
$\frac{15}{16}$	122	163	204	245	285	326	367	408	448	489	530	571	611
1	115	153	191	229	267	306	344	382	420	458	497	535	573

By permission of Firth Brown Tools Ltd.

Table 17 Conversion of cutting speeds from metres per minute to revolutions per minute

Drill diameter in mm	Cutting speeds in m/min								
	10	15	20	25	30	35	40	45	50
	Revolutions per minute								
1	3 183	4 774	6 366	7 957	9 549	11 140	12 732	14 323	15 915
2	1 591	2 387	3 183	3 978	4 774	5 570	6 366	7 161	7 957
3	1 061	1 591	2 122	2 652	3 183	3 713	4 244	4 774	5 305
4	795	1 193	1 591	1 989	2 387	2 785	2 546	3 580	3 978
5	636	954	1 273	1 591	1 909	2 228	3 183	2 864	3 183
6	530	795	1 061	1 326	1 591	1 856	2 122	2 387	2 654
7	454	682	909	1 136	1 364	1 591	1 818	2 046	2 273
8	397	596	795	994	1 193	1 392	1 591	1 790	1 989
9	353	530	707	884	1 061	1 237	1 414	1 591	1 768
10	318	477	636	795	954	1 114	1 273	1 432	1 591
11	289	434	578	723	868	1 012	1 157	1 302	1 446
12	265	397	530	663	795	928	1 061	1 193	1 326
13	244	367	489	612	734	856	979	1 101	1 224
14	227	341	454	568	682	795	909	1 023	1 136
15	212	318	424	530	636	742	848	954	1 061
16	198	298	397	497	596	696	795	895	994
17	187	280	374	468	561	655	748	842	936
18	176	265	353	442	530	618	707	795	884
19	167	251	335	418	502	586	670	753	837
20	159	238	318	397	477	557	636	716	795
21	151	227	303	378	454	530	606	682	757
22	144	217	289	361	434	506	578	651	723
23	138	207	276	345	415	484	553	622	691
24	132	198	265	331	397	464	530	596	663
25	127	190	254	318	381	445	509	572	636

Table 18   Decimal and metric equivalents of fractions

Note: 1 inch = 25·4 millimetres

Inches	Decimal equivalent to four places	Millimetre equivalent	Inches	Decimal equivalent to four places	Millimetre equivalent
$\frac{1}{64}$	0·0156	0·3962	$\frac{33}{64}$	0·5156	13·0962
$\frac{1}{32}$	0·0312	0·7925	$\frac{17}{32}$	0·5312	13·4925
$\frac{3}{64}$	0·0469	1·1913	$\frac{35}{64}$	0·5469	13·8913
$\frac{1}{16}$	0·0625	1·5875	$\frac{9}{16}$	0·5625	14·2875
$\frac{5}{64}$	0·0781	1·9837	$\frac{37}{64}$	0·5781	14·6837
$\frac{3}{32}$	0·0938	2·3825	$\frac{19}{32}$	0·5938	15·0825
$\frac{7}{64}$	0·1094	2·7788	$\frac{39}{64}$	0·6094	15·4788
$\frac{1}{8}$	0·1250	3·1750	$\frac{5}{8}$	0·6250	15·8750
$\frac{9}{64}$	0·1406	3·5712	$\frac{41}{64}$	0·6406	16·2712
$\frac{5}{32}$	0·1562	3·9675	$\frac{21}{32}$	0·6562	16·6675
$\frac{11}{64}$	0·1719	4·3663	$\frac{43}{64}$	0·6719	17·0663
$\frac{3}{16}$	0·1875	4·7625	$\frac{11}{16}$	0·6875	17·4625
$\frac{13}{64}$	0·2031	5·1587	$\frac{45}{64}$	0·7031	17·8587
$\frac{7}{32}$	0·2188	5·5575	$\frac{23}{32}$	0·7188	18·2575
$\frac{15}{64}$	0·2344	5·9538	$\frac{47}{64}$	0·7344	18·6538
$\frac{1}{4}$	0·2500	6·3500	$\frac{3}{4}$	0·7500	19·0500
$\frac{17}{64}$	0·2656	6·7462	$\frac{49}{64}$	0·7656	19·4462
$\frac{9}{32}$	0·2812	7·1425	$\frac{25}{32}$	0·7812	19·8425
$\frac{19}{64}$·	0·2969	7·5413	$\frac{51}{64}$	0·7969	20·2413
$\frac{5}{16}$	0·3125	7·9375	$\frac{13}{16}$	0·8125	20·6375
$\frac{21}{64}$	0·3281	8·3337	$\frac{53}{64}$	0·8281	21·0337
$\frac{11}{32}$	0·3438	8·7325	$\frac{27}{32}$	0·8438	21·4325
$\frac{23}{64}$	0·3594	9·1288	$\frac{55}{64}$	0·8594	21·8288
$\frac{3}{8}$	0·3750	9·5250	$\frac{7}{8}$	0·8750	22·2250
$\frac{25}{64}$	0·3906	9·9212	$\frac{57}{64}$	0·8906	22·6212
$\frac{13}{32}$	0·4062	10·3175	$\frac{29}{32}$	0·9062	23·0175
$\frac{27}{64}$	0·4219	10·7163	$\frac{59}{64}$	0·9219	23·4163
$\frac{7}{16}$	0·4375	11·1125	$\frac{15}{16}$	0·9375	23·8125
$\frac{29}{64}$	0·4531	11·5087	$\frac{61}{64}$	0·9531	24·2087
$\frac{15}{32}$	0·4688	11·9075	$\frac{31}{32}$	0·9688	24·6075
$\frac{31}{64}$	0·4844	12·3038	$\frac{63}{64}$	0·9844	25·0038
$\frac{1}{2}$	0·5000	12·7000	1	1·0000	25·4000

By permission of Firth Brown Tools Ltd.

Table 19 Tapping drills ISO metric thread (coarse pitch series)

All sizes are in millimetres

Nominal diameter of thread	Tapping drill sizes Recommended	Alternative	Nominal diameter of thread	Tapping drill sizes Recommended	Alternative
M2.0 × 0.40	1.60	1.65	M 8.0 × 1.25	6.80	6.90
M2.2 × 0.45	1.75	1.80	M 9.0 × 1.25	7.80	7.90
M2.5 × 0.45	2.05	2.10	M10.0 × 1.50	8.50	8.60
M3.0 × 0.50	2.50	2.55	M11.0 × 1.50	9.50	9.60
M3.5 × 0.60	2.90	2.95	M12.0 × 1.75	10.20	10.40
M4.0 × 0.70	3.30	3.40	M14.0 × 2.00	12.00	—
M4.5 × 0.75	3.70	3.80	M16.0 × 2.00	14.00	—
M5.0 × 0.80	4.20	4.30	M18.0 × 2.50	15.50	—
M6.0 × 1.00	5.00	5.10	M20.0 × 2.50	17.50	—
M7.0 × 1.00	6.00	6.10			

Recommended drills give engagements in excess of 80 per cent. Alternative drills give engagements of around 70 per cent, which is adequate for general use and results in fewer tap breakages, especially in the small sizes. This table has been compiled from B.S. 1157: 1975.

Table 20 Metric wire sizes

All sizes are in millimetres

Standard metric sizes R40	Nearest former SWG size, with its exact metric equivalent		Standard metric sizes R40	Nearest former SWG size, with its exact metric equivalent		Standard metric sizes R40	Nearest former SWG size, with its exact metric equivalent	
12.50	7/0	12.70	2.36	13	2.34	0.475	—	—
11.80	6/0	11.79	2.24	—	—	0.450	26	0.457
11.20	5/0	10.97	2.12	—	—	0.425	27	0.417
10.60	—	—	2.00	14	2.03	0.400	—	—
10.00	4/0	10.16	1.90	—	—	0.375	28	0.376
9.50	3/0	9.45	1.80	15	1.83	0.355	—	—
9.00	2/0	8.84	1.70	—	—	0.335	29	0.345
8.50	0	8.23	1.60	16	1.63	0.315	30	0.315
8.00	—	—	1.50	—	—	0.300	31	0.295
7.50	1	7.62	1.40	17	1.42	0.280	—	—
7.10	2	7.01	1.32	—	—	0.265	32	0.274
6.70	—	—	1.25	18	1.22	0.250	33	0.254
6.30	3	6.40	1.18	—	—	0.236	34	0.234
6.00	4	5.89	1.12	—	—	0.224	—	—
5.60	—	—	1.06	—	—	0.212	35	0.213
5.30	5	5.38	1.00	19	1.02	0.200	—	—
5.00	6	4.88	0.95	—	—	0.190	36	0.193
4.75	6	4.88	0.90	20	0.91	0.180	—	—
4.50	7	4.47	0.85	—	—	0.170	37	0.173
4.25	—	—	0.80	21	0.81	0.160	—	—
4.00	8	4.06	0.75	—	—	0.150	38	0.152
3.75	9	3.66	0.71	22	0.71	0.140	—	—
3.55	—	—	0.67	—	—	0.132	39	0.132
3.35	10	3.25	0.63	—	—	0.125	—	—
3.15	—	—	0.60	23	0.61	0.118	40	0.122
3.00	11	2.95	0.56	24	0.56	0.112	41	0.112
2.80	—	—	0.53	—	—	0.106	—	—
2.65	12	2.64	0.50	25	0.508	0.100	42	0.102
2.50	—	—						

The standard metric sizes are those given in B.S. 4391:1972. The SWG figures have been appended by the author for comparison. They have been aligned as nearly as possible but in most cases they are not equivalents.

Bibliography

Books

D. J. O. BRANDT, *The manufacture of iron and steel,* English Universities Press

P. A. CARTWRIGHT, *Metal finishing handbook,* Blackie

JOHN DEARDEN, *Iron and steel today,* Oxford University Press

R. A. HIGGINS, *Engineering metallurgy Parts 1 and 2,* The Higher Technical Series

W. R. LEWIS, *Notes on soldering,* The Tin Research Institute

R. T. Z. SERVICES, *The Consolidated Zinc Corporation Ltd.,* Rio Tinto Zinc

Useful addresses

The Aluminium Federation, Broadway House, 60 Calthorpe Road, Edgbaston, Birmingham B15 1TN

British Steel Corporation, 12 Addiscombe Road, Croydon CR9 3JH

Burmah–Castrol Industrial Ltd., Industrial Lubricants Divison, Burmah House, Pipers Way, Swindon SN3 1RE (Handbook, *Talking about cutting fluids*)

W. Canning and Co. Ltd., Greenhill Crescent, Holywell Industrial Estate, Watford, Herts (Handbooks on Bronzing, Metal colouring and lacquering, and Electroplating)

Copper Development Association, Orchard House, Mutton Lane, Potters Bar, Herts, EN6 3AP

Index